megafraud in the misapplication
of the income/excise tax

C. Fenner Goldsborough

Copyright © 2010 by C. Fenner Goldsborough

ISBN 978-1-4507-1049-7
Second Edition 2012

DEDICATION

    To my close friend and fellow Constitutionist, John L. Sasscer, whose guidance, vast knowledge and advice in writing this book was invaluable. And also to my long-suffering wife, Joann, without whose tireless energy in typing and retyping of the text, including Internal Revenue Code sections and court decisions would have been totally impossible. Finally, thanks, to my grandsons Jeremy and Wesley Goldsborough for their graphic design expertise in production of the book and audio CD.

DISCLAIMER

    To the best of his knowledge and belief, the author attests to the accuracy of both the statutory and court quotations contained in this book. However, the opinions and commentary on these statutes (Code sections) and court decisions are those of the author alone and are not to be considered to be legal advice. The reader is advised to consult a licensed attorney for verification and/or interpretation of the opinions expressed herein.

Super Scam
480 Nottingham Rd. W.
Gaylord, MI 49735
(989)448-8592
www.super-scam.com

TABLE OF CONTENTS

Prologue 4

Preface 10

Chapter I: Constitutional Taxing Authority and Restrictions 16

Chapter II: The Sixteenth Amendment-The Myth and the Reality 38

Chapter III: Whose Receipts Are "Income"? 50

Chapter IV: The Internal Revenue Code-A Masterpiece of Trickery and Deception 62

Chapter V: Social Security-A Flat-Rate Income Tax And Voluntary Withholding 76

Chapter VI: IRS' Illegal Collection Activities 100

Chapter VII: Limitations of the I.R. Code 136

Chapter VIII: Affidavit of Revocation and Recission-An Essential Document 153

Chapter IX: Frequently Asked Questions and Answers 173

Epilogue 189

PROLOGUE

I am a former Federal political prisoner. There are more political prisoners like me in these United States, some also having served jail terms for government-fabricated <u>non</u>-crimes. Webster's *Third New International Unabridged Dictionary* (1981) defines a "political prisoner" as "a person imprisoned for a political offense". In the same dictionary "political" is defined as "of, or relating to matters of government <u>policy as distinguished from</u> matters of <u>law.</u>" (emphasis added). Therefore, the political prisoner is punished for violating government <u>policy</u>-not <u>law</u>. But in their wisdom, the founding fathers decreed in our national Constitution that our people shall retain their sovereignty, unlike the parliamentary system of England and further established our nation as one of <u>law</u> with, the Constitution as the <u>supreme</u> law. <u>All statutory</u> law enacted by the national or state legislatures is, by reason of the basic provisions of the Constitution, and subsequently the Fourteenth Amendment, subservient to, and therefore <u>required to be in conformity</u> with the Constitution. Any vocal dissent or disagreement with government <u>policy </u>(not law) is clearly protected by the second clause of the First Amendment which guarantees our inalienable right to freedom of speech. However, such policy dissent, when directed at <u>government's</u> violation of law by their unlawful misapplication of the income/excise tax to the earnings of U.S. citizens, which is the subject of this book, is vigorously attacked by our government despite the First Amendment.

An understanding of the distinction between government <u>policy</u> and <u>law</u> is important. Under our constitutional <u>law</u> system, our government, should they wish to punish <u>policy</u> dissent, must attempt to fabricate a legal or <u>lawful</u> basis to do so. As respects personal income taxes, they are required to devise some scheme to convert the <u>policy </u>dissent to a violation of <u>law</u>. They attempt to accomplish this by writing that portion of the Internal Revenue Code which applies to income taxes in such a manner, as this book will show, that it only <u>appears </u>to legally impose taxes on the earnings of U.S. citizens. In fact, this book's analysis of the wording in the Internal Revenue Code shows that the Internal Revenue Code <u>is</u> in conformity with the Constitutional prohibitions against taxation of U.S. citizens' earnings or other receipts.

Examples of United States political persecution of various forms of government <u>policy</u> protest by individuals and groups are revealing. The

Congressional House Committee on Un-American Activities of Senator Joseph McCarthy's 1950's era is well known for its attacks on Communist groups. Political activist groups, both militant and passive, such as the N.A.A.C.P., Southern Christian Leadership Conference, the Black Panthers, the Ku Klux Klan, to name a few organizations of both the political right and left, all have leaders who have felt the heavy hand of our government's political wrath. Some, like Martin Luther King of the S.C.L.C., met death by assassination for their political activism.

In sharp contrast to my book, the dissent voiced by these groups all took the form of a violation of recognized and <u>acknowledged law</u> with which they disagreed. Black activist Rosa Parks admitted that she was in violation of the local statute which required blacks to sit in the back of the bus. She was protesting the <u>inequity, as she saw it, of law</u>. She never questioned its <u>applicability</u> or <u>jurisdiction</u> over her. Although this writer happens to agree with Ms. Parks' <u>opinion</u>-one which later cost Martin Luther King his life-there was no jurisdictional dispute as to the <u>applicability</u> of the law to her. In that sense, her action was pure protest of existing <u>law</u>. My fight, however, differs in that it is a jurisdictional protest against government <u>misapplication</u> of the income tax <u>law</u> to the millions of U.S. citizens who don't owe the tax because our Constitution forbids any direct taxation on U.S. citizens' earnings or other receipts.

The noteworthy distinction between the civil revolutionary groups and some religious fundamentalists is that the former are challenging existing statutory law only on grounds of its' <u>unjustness</u> as they perceive it; the latter challenge its' <u>applicability</u> to them, or, otherwise stated, its <u>jurisdiction</u> over them. These religious groups reason that the various state statutes which require registration or licenses with Federal or state education departments are in clear non-conformity with the religious freedom clause of the First Amendment. Such licensure, their argument states, grants sovereignty and, consequently, control to the state, rather than to God, over their children's education. They see this unacceptable deviation from the necessary nexus between the Bible and their academic goals-as an usurpation of authority which, they say, is guaranteed to the people by the First Amendment.

A third and perhaps unique group of legal activists to which this writer belongs has become increasingly vocal in recent years. We call ourselves "Constitutionists" because of our dedication to the Constitution and its' mandates. Because our focus is on constitutional limitations applicable to the taxing authority of Congress, we are also called "tax patriots". I was a leader in one such group of many throughout the country. Our particular brand of education was highly vocal. I engaged in extensive writing on the subject, spoke publicly at seminars and educational meetings and had media exposure. Before I learned how to defend myself through diligent study of the law, my early activity earned me only near bankruptcy and a short, one-year jail term, which did not change the truth of my beliefs or create remorse for my actions. To the contrary, I am even more dedicated today than ever before to spread the truth. Government's ridicule of us does nothing to change the <u>truth</u> of our position. Interestingly, our dissent differs from the civil revolutionaries, such as Dr. King. Unlike their revolutionary dissent, we have no argument with existing law-we don't question its wisdom or justice. Our argument is <u>purely jurisdictional</u>, in both a statutory <u>and</u> a constitutional sense. We agree that the statutory law, the Internal Revenue Code, and the Constitution are in conformity with one another, as government states. However, we charge that the Internal Revenue Code has been intentionally written in a deceptive, confusing and difficult-to-understand manner, and that the IRS, acting in their capacity as the collection and enforcement agency for government, has <u>knowingly</u> alleged an <u>inapplicable</u> and <u>unlawful</u> misapplication of the Internal Revenue Code to many millions of American wage and salary earners who have <u>no</u> obligation, <u>either under statutory law or the Constitution</u>, to pay the government <u>any</u> portion of their earnings or other receipts.

Although the IRS sometimes suggests correctly, but weakly, in <u>some</u> of their literature, that the filing of income tax returns by most Americans who are engaged in no unlawful or government-privileged activities <u>is voluntary</u>, the IRS' <u>policy</u> (not law) calls for the <u>mandatory</u> filing of tax returns by <u>all</u> working citizens and the payment of income taxes on their earnings! The extremely clever, insidious and even criminal propaganda which has been spoon-fed to the public for many years, along with the fear and intimidation tactics for which the IRS is so well known, has persuaded all but a very few, such as these Constitutionist groups, that this government <u>policy</u> is, in fact, law, and the statistics showing the effectiveness of this deceit speaks for itself. The success of <u>voluntary</u> (by law) "withholding" as a collection method for income taxes which, <u>by law, are not owed</u>, best illustrates this. Almost every employer in the nation has been duped into incorrectly believing that they are <u>required by law</u> to withhold income taxes from their employee's paychecks. But if, in fact, the <u>law required</u> them to do so, why are they also simultaneously <u>required</u> to obtain authorization;

i.e., permission from every employee to withhold via a signed (by the employee) Form W-4 Withholding Allowance Certificate? Since when is permission from the employee required for his boss (meaning his employer) to obey Federal law? There can be only one answer: no such requirement by law exists. However, the deception is now so complete, through decades of custom, that some employers have gone so far as to enter into conspiracy with the Internal Revenue Service to deny employment to those prospective employees who, through their own independent research, have the gumption to demand, through refusal to permit the withholding, that they be allowed, in accord with statutory law, (and also the Fifth Amendment) to keep all the full fruits of their labor! Such action can only be called, properly, conspiracy to commit theft by the employer and the Internal Revenue Service, to the end that government policy (not law) be enforced! Who, indeed, now becomes the lawbreaker?

Unfortunately, the Constitutionist is at a disadvantage, both in the courtroom, when improperly charged by government, as well as on the lectern as an educator. A closed mind is almost impossible to penetrate, and that closed mind is more the norm than otherwise, due not just to the propaganda skills of the IRS, but also to the support government has from prestigious professionals. Judges, lawyers and particularly tax lawyers, accountants, bankers, insurance companies and most of their agents and financial planners-all of whom have a huge financial interest in maintaining the scam-often conspire effectively with the IRS against the Constitutionist. Huge quantities of tax forms of all kinds, deceptively suggesting false legal requirements, are indiscriminately offered in prominent places readily accessible to public traffic in banks, post offices, libraries and thousands of government buildings for months before the mythical "filing" date of April 15th each year. Radio and TV stations all across the land air more thousands of "taxpayer awareness" or "tax tip" programs, all totally but incorrectly presumptive of a valid and lawful jurisdiction of the Internal Revenue Code to tax the earnings of working Americans!

Compliance with statutory law-that is, law enacted by Congress, this writer believes, is always mandatory; it cannot be voluntary, for if it were, the "law" would not be "law", but rather mere "suggestion". Otherwise stated, "law", by its very nature, is mandatory-that is to say, it requires performance (or, more frequently, in a criminal context, non-performance) of a specified act or acts. Setting aside, for purposes of this discussion, the applicability or jurisdiction of any statute (law), and assuming that such jurisdiction exists, the word "compliance" is harmonious with the word "law", in that "compliance" with the commands of the law, <u>for those to whom the law applies</u>, is <u>required</u> under penalty of punishment as set forth in the statute (law). So we can conclude logically that the word "voluntary", being the opposite of "compulsory", is contradictory when used with the "compulsory" word "compliance". Yet these two words-"voluntary compliance" are used repeatedly in the IRS propaganda-instruction booklets and educational materials. If the law <u>applies</u> to us to start with, is it not true that we had <u>better</u> comply-that is, if we don't want to pay the fine or go to jail (or both) for <u>non-compliance</u>? So, how can there be such a thing as "voluntary" compliance? Do they mean to tell us, in all truth, that it is <u>voluntary</u> to comply? Who is kidding who here? For the Constitutionist the answer is clear-the IRS is trying to fool the reader into <u>volunteering</u> to file and pay because the IRS knows very well that the Internal Revenue Code contains <u>no</u> statute requiring U.S. citizens to file or to pay income taxes on their wages, salaries or other receipts. Indeed, it cannot, for to do so would bring such law into losing conflict with the supreme law-the Constitution. Although aware of this statutory subservience and the Constitutional restriction against any direct taxation of the people, our government, through the IRS, has nonetheless intentionally misled the public to believe, through such double-speak as "voluntary compliance", that they are required by law to file and pay income taxes on their earnings and other receipts. "Voluntary compliance" is only one example of the deception and trickery the IRS employs throughout their literature and educational materials which will be discussed in this book.

Finally, this writer charges that the majority of our Federal judiciary is in complicity with the executive branch of government in foisting this jurisdictional deception <u>un</u>lawfully on a bamboozled citizenry. And of the three branches, the judiciary is the most culpable for this legal travesty, in that they have the professional legal training, as well as the opportunity and the duty, to support the Constitution if they would but have the political courage to do so.

This writer acknowledges the consummate skills employed by government to sell the personal income tax scam to the American public as though it were law. The noted author Carl Sagan, in the February, 1987 issue of *Parade Magazine*, in an article entitled *The Fine Art of Baloney Detection,* wrote about this skill as follows:

...Credulous acceptance of baloney can lose you money; that's what P.T. Barnum meant when he said, 'There's a sucker born every minute.' But it can be much more dangerous than that, and when governments and societies lose the capacity for critical thinking, the results can be catastrophic...

...One of the saddest lessons of history is this: If we've been bamboozled long enough, we tend to reject any evidence of the bamboozle. We're no longer interested in finding out the truth.
<u>*The bamboozle has captured us*</u>*. It is simply too painful to acknowledge-even to ourselves-that we've been so credulous...*(emphasis added)

...Finding the occasional straw of truth awash in a great ocean of confusion and bamboozle requires intelligence, vigilance, dedication and courage. But if we don't practice these tough habits of thought, we cannot hope to solve the truly serious problems that face us-and we risk becoming a nation of suckers, up for grabs by the next charlatan who comes along.

As the <u>supreme law of the</u> land, our Constitution means what it says and it says what it means. The continued violation of its mandates and restrictions by government must cease, lest our people lose the last vestige of their sovereignty which was so eloquently embodied in the Declaration of Independence. Concern over the will of the people to protect that precious sovereignty was perhaps prophetically expressed by Benjamin Franklin who was asked by a European constitutional convention observer following the drafting of the Constitution in 1787: "Well, Dr. Franklin, what does your nation have here?" To which the eminent chairman of the convention replied: "A republic, sir...a republic, if we have but the will to keep it!" This writer prays that our people find the courage, perhaps in part through knowledge gleaned from this book, to invoke that will through the veil of fear of the IRS that now permeates our nation, lest our republic, indeed, be forever bamboozled on this vital issue.

PREFACE

Most working Americans today have either read or heard that there is something terribly wrong with our personal income tax system-that maybe there is truth in what they have been hearing more frequently each year-that working Americans, for the most part, don't even owe Big Brother an income tax. This book is primarily a textbook. It will prove why so many Americans who suspect that they have been scammed are correct. It will also explain how cleverly our Federal government, through the IRS, has deceived most of the public for decades into believing a monstrous lie-one that has sold working Americans into falsely believing that the law requires them to pay a substantial portion of their earnings to the government as "income" tax. In truth, however, the fact is that our Constitution itself forbids any direct tax on U.S. citizens. This book will also show how the Internal Revenue Code itself, which, as Federal law, must be written in conformity with the Constitution, does, in fact, comply with these constitutional prohibitions and restrictions even though the Code is cleverly disguised to make us think otherwise. Key sections of the Constitution, some U.S. Supreme Court decisions and the Internal Revenue Code, which <u>IS</u> written in conformity with the Constitution, are repeated many times throughout this book for emphasis because their importance must be imbedded in the readers' mind for a proper understanding of this subject.

Fortunately, public awareness of the income tax scam has been growing steadily over the past thirty years, during which time this writer and others have been researching and educating others on this subject. At the same time, because the deception has been so cleverly concealed by the IRS through the use of misleading words and defined "terms" in the Internal Revenue Code, finding and proving the truth has been a difficult task. The research that has been done over the years could be compared to finding many needles in MANY haystacks. After exposing the truth, some dedicated researchers who have had the courage to spread their knowledge to the public have been falsely prosecuted and otherwise illegally punished by government. We Americans don't like to believe that we have been deceived by our own government. To acknowledge that we have been conned is an insult to our intelligence and our sensitive egos. Consequently, we whistle-blowers have sometimes lost the respect of some family and friends who have refused to admit that their own government could be so outrageously corrupt. The life of a whistle-blower is never easy. Many have paid a dear price for waving the red flag at the biggest bully on the block!

Government's knowledge of the growing public awareness about the massive <u>mis</u>application of the income tax has created fear among politicians of a huge public outrage when the truth becomes widely known. This has led to proposals by government of alternatives to the income tax such as the FAIR TAX which is a proposed consumption tax on most retail sales of about 20%. Another is the so-called VAT, or value added tax that is used in western Europe. Although well-meaning, such plans, being proposed as alternatives suggest an undeserved legitimacy to the present corrupt system. The better solution, in this writer's opinion, is to force obedience by government to the present law by public outrage and demand, born of education, which is what this book is all about.

A former Commissioner of the Internal Revenue Service stated in an IRS instruction booklet: "Each year American taxpayers VOLUNTARILY file their tax returns…" (emphasis added). The U.S. Supreme Court also confirmed the <u>voluntary</u> nature of the income tax for citizens in the decision of **<u>U.S. v. Flora</u>, 362 U.S. 145** when it stated: "Our system of taxation is based upon <u>voluntary</u> assessment and payment, not upon distraint (force)." (emphasis added) As this book shows, the United States Constitution contains limitations on federal taxing powers which prohibit taxation of citizens or their earnings. For U.S. citizens, payment of income tax on their earnings is voluntary, not mandatory, because the law does not apply to them. The obvious question arises: why would the IRS Commissioner describe the agency's function as trying to achieve VOLUNTARY compliance if the law <u>required</u> citizens to file and pay-that is, if it were COMPULSORY? The answer is apparent-the Commissioner so described his agency's purpose because he was well aware that for citizens, who are merely exercising their God-given inalienable right to earn a living, the income tax laws do not apply to them in the first place. Those citizens who have unnecessarily filed income tax returns and paid income tax on their earnings have done so VOLUNTARILY through fear from a lack of understanding of the law and the deceptions practiced by the IRS.

Note how regularly the IRS publications which pile up in our post offices, libraries and other public places each year in mid-winter encourage us to file tax returns and VOLUNTARILY "pay our fair share". If, by law, we were all <u>required</u> to file and pay a substantial percentage of our wages, salaries or other receipts to Big Brother, would they not say that the law REQUIRES us to file and pay under threat of punishment? Yes, of course they would so threaten us, but, because they know that there is no statute that requires us to file <u>on our own behalf as individual citizens,</u> their use of the words "voluntary compliance" tells us that most of us have no obligation at law, and that they are merely asking for a donation!

Former IRS Publication 21, which has been widely distributed in high schools and colleges, also acknowledges that compliance with the filing requirement is <u>voluntary</u> for individual citizens and <u>at the same time</u> suggests that the filing of a return is <u>mandatory</u> when it states: "Two aspects of the Federal income tax system-<u>voluntary compliance</u> with law and <u>self-assessment</u> of tax-make it important for you to understand your rights and responsibilities as a taxpayer. 'Voluntary compliance' places on the taxpayer the responsibility for filing an income tax return. <u>You must decide whether the law requires you to file a return.</u> IF IT DOES, you must file your return by the date it is due." (emphasis added) Now wait just a minute! Here is our own government actually telling us that we should check out the law-that <u>maybe</u> we don't have to file and pay! Haven't we always known that <u>compliance</u> with <u>law</u> is mandatory?...that there are <u>consequences</u> in the form of penalties-either <u>civil</u> monetary penalties or even jail time for failure to obey (comply with) the law? Common sense tells us that compliance with law can't be <u>both</u> mandatory <u>and</u> voluntary. It must be one or the other. But here is the IRS <u>suggesting</u> that we research it ourselves-they aren't going to tell us whether or not we are <u>required</u> to file and pay! That determination is up to us! This book will tell you <u>why</u>, in all likelihood by law, you <u>don't</u> have to file or pay-unless you are one of a very, very few people! So now we know why the IRS asks us to "volunteer" to file and pay.

In the past, America prospered and became the greatest and richest, <u>debt-free</u> country in the world when individuals <u>paid no income tax</u> and government's revenues were raised by tariffs on imports and other constitutionally-authorized excise taxes on certain goods and on government-privileged activities such as those enjoyed by corporations. But now money is extorted by the IRS' deception and trickery about the income tax law from millions of U.S. citizens who don't owe it in order to support the non-productive sector, endless pork-barrel give-away's and bloated, needless bureaucracy which has now put our nation trillions of dollars in debt. Congress' projected spending for fiscal 2007 was 2.7 <u>trillion</u> dollars-an increase over 2006 by almost 13% increase! A billion dollars is 1,000 times a million; a trillion dollars is 1,000 billion; hence, Congress' 2007 budget of 2.7 trillion dollars was 2,700 billion dollars. Dividing this annual budget by 365 days in a year means our government spent 7.397

billion dollars every day of the fiscal year 2007! To raise this money in order to pay this inconceivable budget, our government must constantly sell bonds, both domestically to banks and individuals and in the world market and print huge amounts of unbacked currency for the Federal Reserve Bank <u>to use in buying up unsold amounts of newly- issued government bonds</u>.

Based upon the very reasonable presumption that our Congress will continue to spend far more than it takes in, the value of the dollar will continue to erode and interest rates must rise as our government is forced to pay higher and higher interest rates on its harder to sell bonds. Our nation's 2007 bonded national debt of roughly seven trillion dollars required payment of huge amounts of interest each year. Although interest rates vary from year to year, we can conservatively estimate an average interest rate on this bonded indebtedness of about 4 percent. Applying this percentage to this seven trillion dollar debt figure means an <u>annual </u>interest obligation of 280 billion dollars (this is .767 billion dollars a day!), and this is money that must be paid by our government each year-<u>not </u>on goods or services but on <u>interest alone</u>! As our country's debt grows ever larger each year, this monstrous interest figure grows with it, diminishing the purchasing power of all our dollars at an ever increasing rate! It is reasonable to assume that these 2007 debt and interest figures can have only increased since 2007. Income taxes paid by citizens because of fear and intimidation sharply reduce their earnings; they then buy less causing business to decline even more, leading to unemployment and depression, lowering the standard of living for all Americans. This misapplication of the income tax laws through trickery and deceit has created havoc in America's economy in addition to the harassment of our people by IRS' oppressive and unlawful collection tactics.

The unlawful collection of this tax enforced by fear and intimidation is as un-American as the origin of the income tax itself. A graduated income tax is the second plank of Karl Marx's Communist Manifesto.

Deceiving our citizens through deceptions and fear into voluntarily subjecting themselves to a tax they do not owe is **fraud**. *Black's Law Dictionary, 5th Edition*, defines "fraud" as follows: "An intentional perversion of truth for the purpose of inducing another, in reliance upon it, to part with some valuable thing belonging to him or to surrender a legal right."

Finally, after reading this book and learning the truth about this fleecing of the American public, the knowledge acquired will give our citizens the option to take the necessary steps to stop being a voluntary victim and start keeping ALL the fruits of their labor, to which they are constitutionally entitled! No refund should be expected for the many thousands that may have already been stolen by deception. From a practical standpoint this is virtually impossible. However, the future theft CAN be ended, and this book will give the reader the knowledge of how to do it for both the employed and the self-employed. Knowledge creates courage. David slew Goliath by gaining the knowledge and skill to kill him with his sling. By using the knowledge obtained through study of this subject, citizens will be better equipped to free themselves from the oppression caused by IRS' misapplication of the income tax law.

As this book will show, ALL the law is on our side-the Constitution, the statutory law in the Internal Revenue Code <u>and many</u> court decisions by our courts, including the U.S. Supreme Court. We need only the knowledge and the courage to <u>demand</u> that it be applied in such a way that its truth cannot be denied. Government officials, both Federal and state, including all judges, <u>are sworn by oath</u> to support and uphold the United States Constitution. Those, including Federal judges, who deny our position, violate this sacred oath and are subject to dismissal and other penalties for such violation of their oath.

A renowned aphorism about <u>truth</u> should be recalled by every judge, Congress member, accountant, IRS bureaucrat, tax preparer and lawyer who practices or condones the misapplication of the income tax law against many millions of U.S. citizens:

> *In these days of fear and confusion, let us remember that the endless repetition of a lie or the multiplication of an empty promise does not make a truth. Truth is something more than the greatest common denominator of mass ignorance and greed. It is never determined or demonstrated by majorities or pluralities of popular error and appetite. Ultimately, with God's aid, it always emerges and finally prevails, supreme in its power over the destiny of mankind and terrible in its retribution for those who deny, defy or betray it.*

As for truth, our Lord said it best in the gospel of John, chapter 8, verse 32:

"And ye shall know the truth, and the truth shall make you free."

CHAPTER I

CONSTITUTIONAL TAXING AUTHORITY & RESTRICTIONS

In order to understand how the citizens of this nation have been deceived into believing that they are subject to a tax on their earnings or other receipts, they need to become aware of the taxing limitations which are contained in the United States Constitution. The Constitution requires that all laws must be in conformity with the limitations contained in the Constitution itself. Any law which is in conflict with any provisions in the Constitution is <u>un</u>constitutional and has no force of law and is invalid. Let's examine the basic taxing provisions contained in the Constitution and the two classes of taxes authorized therein which are direct and indirect taxes.

The Federal taxing authority contained in Article 1, Section 8, Clause 1 of the Constitution states as follows: *"The Congress shall have the power to lay and collect Taxes, Duties, Imposts and Excises, to pay the Debts and provide for the common Defense and general Welfare of the United States; but all Duties, Imposts and Excises shall be uniform throughout the United States."* The U.S. Supreme Court has ruled that all Federal taxes are in one of the two classes-direct taxes or indirect taxes. As used in Article 1, Section 8, Clause 1 quoted above, the Supreme Court has identified the word "taxes" to mean <u>direct</u> taxes and "Duties, Imposts and Excises" to mean <u>indirect</u> taxes. The Supreme Court has often established what they call these two "great" classes of taxing authorities; namely "direct" and "indirect"; "indirect" meaning <u>Duties; Imposts and Excises</u>.

A <u>direct</u> tax is one whose payment or burden upon the person taxed must be borne or paid by that person directly, and cannot be transferred to another by some means such as a price increase. A direct tax is, therefore, unavoidable, in that it taxes the person or his property <u>directly</u> in contrast to an indirect tax such as a duty, impost, or excise, the payment of which <u>can</u> be avoided or transferred by such a price increase. Therefore, a tax on a citizen's wage or salary, being unavoidable, is a direct tax.

There are two provisions of the Constitution which restrict the imposition of direct taxes authorized in Article 1, Section 8, Clause 1 quoted above. The first of these restrictions on taxation is contained in Article 1, Section 2, Clause 3 which states: *"Representatives and direct taxes shall be apportioned <u>among the several states</u>...according to their respective* *numbers…"*. This means that any direct tax levied by Congress must be billed to each state in the union, each state's share being determined as that state's population relates to the population of the whole nation. Whenever, in our nation's history, a direct tax has been imposed, it should have been a set amount in millions of dollars, the total of which would be apportioned (divided) among the states of the union in proportion to the population of each state as it relates to the population of the whole country. For instance, let's assume that New York State's population, as determined by the last constitutionally-required census, is 10% of the entire nation's population. If the direct tax imposed by Congress was $10,000,000, then New York State's share of the tax would be 10% of the $10,000,000 or $1,000,000. New York State's government would be obligated to raise this amount from their citizens by whatever means their state constitution authorized. Historically, this has usually been by assessing all real estate in the state.

The second Constitutional restriction on the imposition of direct taxes is found in Article 1, Section 9, Clause 4 which states: *"No capitation or other direct tax shall be laid, unless in Proportion to the Census or Enumeration hereinbefore directed to be taken."* *Black's Law Dictionary, Fifth Edition,* defines a capitation tax as *"a tax or imposition upon the person."* As we will soon see in this chapter, the U.S. Supreme Court has interpreted this prohibition against any tax *"upon the person"* to include the person's labor in the form of his earnings from wages, salaries or other profits or gains. By prohibiting capitation taxes, the framers of the Constitution wisely prohibited the Federal government from having the power to impose any tax on the individual citizens of the nation. The phrase *"…unless in proportion to the Census or Enumeration herein before directed to be taken…"* is another reference to the limitation of the Federal authority to impose direct taxes on citizens, but rather only on the state governments as set forth in the apportionment requirement contained in Article 1, Section 2, Clause 3. Any Federal capitation taxes, being taxes on individuals on their earnings or other receipts, would be unconstitutional. Federal direct taxes on the states have been imposed only five times in United States history. The last direct tax was imposed in 1861 soon after the start of the War Between the States as an emergency measure to help the union pay for the war. This tax was probably unconstitutional but was never challenged.

There is also a restriction in the Constitution on the imposition of indirect taxes which is stated in Article 1, Section 8, Clause 1 quoted previously. This states: *"…but all Duties, Imposts and Excises shall be uniform throughout the United States."* This uniformity requirement for indirect taxes means that Duties, Imposts and Excises be levied in the same amount, form and substance in each of the states of the union. As an example, if a Federal excise tax of, say, eighteen cents is enacted by Congress on a gallon of gasoline, the Federal tax in all states of the union must also be eighteen cents. *Black's Law Dictionary, Fifth Edition*, defines "uniform" as "confirming to one rule, mode, pattern or unvarying standard." Also "equable" and "applying alike to all within a class". *Black's* defines "Duties" as a "tax on imports" and as a synonym for Imposts or customs, and defines "Imposts" as a synonym for "Duties". "Duties" and "Imposts" means the tariffs or charges applied to imports into the country. The constitutional uniformity requirement quoted in Article 1, Section 8, Clause 1 above means, as an example, that the same "Duty" or "Impost" charge on foreign goods coming into New York City must be the same as the charges for goods entering Philadelphia, Baltimore or any other U.S. city. Article 1, Section 8, Clause 1 also requires that "Excise" taxes be the same in all states. The Supreme Court in the case of Flint v. Stone Tracy Co., 220 U.S. 107, defines an excise tax as a "...*tax laid on the manufacture, sale or consumption of commodities, or upon licenses to pursue certain occupations, or upon corporate privileges.*" It is important that we understand from this definition that the thing being taxed as an "excise" is an "activity" that is not one of common or natural right, such as working for a living in a job that doesn't require a government-granted privilege or license.

The phrase "licenses to pursue certain occupations" in the Flint decision apparently refers to the small (about $10.00) license fee which was imposed on lawyers who exercised the privilege of practicing law in the Federal courts during the War Between the States. This license fee was repealed soon after the tax was imposed based upon the contention that the tax was discriminatory. An attorney by the name of William Springer had charged in his lawsuit that the excessive license fee charged was, in fact, a direct tax and, since it lacked apportionment, Mr. Springer contended that it was unconstitutional. The Supreme Court in 1867 in the decision of Springer v. U.S., 102, U.S. 586 disagreed with Mr. Springer holding that the tax was, in fact, in the nature of an excise and hence constitutional because it met the requirement of uniformity required of indirect excise taxes. To the best of this writer's knowledge, no other Federal license fee has ever been imposed on any occupation since the Springer case. The "income" derived from the activity of practicing lawyers is merely used to measure the amount of the tax. The "income" was not the subject of the tax.

It now becomes necessary to understand the difference between an "activity" that is of a revenue-taxable nature whereby a Federal indirect excise tax may be imposed and an activity that is a natural or "inalienable" right and, hence, a <u>non</u>-taxable activity. In order to first show that the simple right to earn a living is a <u>non</u>-taxable activity, let's first look at the Declaration of Independence:

> *We hold these truths to be self-evident, that all men are created equal, that they are endowed by their Creator with <u>certain inalienable rights,</u> that among these are <u>life, liberty and the pursuit of happiness</u>.*

Declaration of Independence, July 4, 1776

The U.S. Supreme Court in the case of **Butchers Union Co. v. Crescent City Co., 111 U.S. 746, at 756-757 (1883)** agreed with the Declaration, saying":

> *As in our intercourse with our fellow-men, certain principles of morality are assumed to exist without which society would be impossible, so certain inherent rights lie at the foundation of all action, and that upon the recognition of them alone can free institutions be maintained. These <u>inherent rights</u> have never been more happily expressed than in the Declaration of Independence, that new evangel of liberty to the people: 'We hold these truths to be self-evident'-that is <u>so plain</u> that their truth is recognized upon their mere statement-'that all men are endowed'-not by edicts of Emperors, or decrees of Parliament, or <u>acts of Congress</u>, but 'by their Creator with certain <u>inalienable</u> rights'-that is, <u>rights</u> which cannot be bartered away, or given away, or taken away except in punishment of crime-'and that among these are life, liberty and the pursuit of happiness, and to secure them...' governments are instituted among men, deriving their <u>just</u> powers from the consent of the governed.*
>
> *Among these inalienable rights, as proclaimed in that great document, is the right of men to pursue their happiness, by which is meant the <u>right to pursue any lawful business or</u>*

vocation, in any manner not inconsistent with the equal rights of others, which may increase their prosperity or develop their faculties, so as to give them their highest enjoyment.

The <u>common business and callings of life, the ordinary trades and pursuits</u>, which are <u>innocuous</u> in themselves, and have been followed in all communities from time immemorial, <u>must, therefore, be free in this country</u> to all alike upon the same conditions. The right to pursue them, without let or hindrance, except that which is applied to all persons of the same age, sex, and condition, is a distinguishing privilege of citizens of the United States, and an essential element of that freedom which they claim as their birthright. It has been well said that, '<u>The property which every man has is his own labor, as it is the original foundation of all other property, so it is the most sacred and inviolable.</u> The patrimony of the poor man lies in the strength and dexterity of his own hands, and to hinder his employing this strength and dexterity in whatever manner he thinks proper, without injury to his neighbor, is a plain violation of the most sacred property. (emphasis added)

Therefore, as we can see from this case, the Supreme Court has identified our labor-our ability to work for a living, as the most valuable and inalienable of all our property <u>rights</u>, and therefore, a fundamental right that is not taxable by the Federal taxing authority. Remembering that the Supreme Court is the highest authority in the land as to the meaning of both statutory law and the Constitution, let's take a look at a few other cases that identify our labor as our most valuable and non-taxable right. In the case of **<u>Allgeyer v. Louisiana,</u> 165 U.S. 578 (1897)**, the U.S. Supreme Court explained that our <u>right</u> to earn a living by any calling is a constitutional right and that we are all entitled to the <u>full fruits</u> of our own labor under the liberty clause of the Fourteenth Amendment to the Constitution. We find the following from the Supreme Court in reference to the Fourteenth Amendment:

<u>Allgeyer v. Louisiana</u>, 165 U.S. 578 (1897)

The liberty mentioned in that Amendment means not only

> *the right of the citizen to be free from mere physical restraint of his person, as by incarceration, but the term is deemed to embrace the <u>right of the citizen to be free</u> in the enjoyment of <u>all</u> his faculties: to be free to use them in all lawful ways; to live and work where he will; to earn his living <u>by any lawful calling</u>; <u>to pursue any livelihood or avocation</u> and for that purpose to enter into all contracts which may be proper, necessary, and essential to his carrying out to a successful conclusion the purposes above mentioned.* (emphasis added)

Thus, the Allgeyer Supreme Court said that our right to the use of ALL of our property, which includes our labor, is a constitutionally-guaranteed right as fundamental as our right to liberty and any other form of property. The reason why Congress could not have contemplated a tax on our citizen's labor becomes obvious when we see that the right to one's labor, as to one's liberty and property, is a right guaranteed by the Constitution and may not be tampered with. This point is clearly made in **Miranda v. Arizona, 380 U.S. 436 (1966)** where the Supreme Court said:

> *Where fundamental rights under the Constitution are involved there can be no rule-making or legislation which can abrogate them.*

And in **Murdock v. Pennsylvania, 319 U.S. 150 (1943)**, the Supreme Court said:

> *A state may not impose a charge for the enjoyment of a <u>right</u> granted by the Federal Constitution.*

A better understanding of the Murdock quotation above would be to substitute the word "protected" for the word "granted" because our right to our own labor which was referred to in the quotation is an inalienable right that was given to us by God and identified in the Declaration of Independence as such.

A state appellate court in the case of **Sims v. Ahrens, 271 SW 720 (1925)** stated:

> *An <u>income tax</u> is neither a property tax, <u>nor a tax on</u>*

occupations of common right but is an excise tax; legislatures may declare as privilege and tax as such for state revenue those pursuits and occupations that are not matters of common right but has no power to declare as privilege and tax for revenue purposes occupations that are of common right. (emphasis added)

So we have seen that a citizen's property in the form of labor is a matter of the most fundamental common right. The reason that taxation of such rights is prohibited was articulated early in this nation's history by Chief Justice Marshall when he said in:

McCulloch v. Maryland, 17, v.s. 316 (1819):

The power to tax involves the power to destroy.

Therefore, if a common and constitutionally-guaranteed right could, in principle, be taxed, then it would be possible to increase the tax rate to 100% of the value of that right and by so doing legislate that right out of existence and thus subvert the Constitution. And the Constitution is the only thing that ultimately stands between the individual citizen and tyranny. This point was again emphasized by the Supreme Court in the decision of:

Knowlton v. Moore, 178 U.S. 41 (1900) as follows:

The power to destroy which may be the consequence of taxation is a reason why the right to tax should be confined to subjects which may be lawfully embraced therein (emphasis added)

When we speak of income, the question immediately arises: "Are wages income?" Again we must look to the courts to find who has the authority to define the term "income" and what is the precise constitutional meaning of the term "income". Also, what is the meaning of the term "wages" and does the term "wages" mean the same as the term "income"? In answer to these questions, we again turn to the U.S. Supreme Court where the Court in the decision of **Eisner v. Macomber, 252 U.S. 189 (1919)** stated:

Eisner v. Macomber, 252 U.S. 189 (1919)

> *It becomes essential to distinguish between what is and what is not "income"…Congress may not, by any definition it may adopt, conclude the matter, since it cannot by legislation alter the Constitution from which alone it derives its power to legislate, and within whose limitations, that power can lawfully be exercised.*

So the Eisner court reserved to itself the prerogative of defining the constitutional meaning of the word "income" when they said:

> *Income may be defined as <u>gain derived from capital, from Labor or from both combined</u>, provided it be understood to include profit gained through a sale or conversion of capital assets.* (emphasis added)

"Gain" <u>derived from</u> the use of capital and labor restricted the Eisner definition of gain to <u>corporate</u> activity, as will be seen. In **Conner v. United States, 303 FSupp 1187 (1969)** the District Court stated:

> *Whatever may constitute income, therefore, must have the essential feature of <u>gain</u> to the recipient. This was true when the 16th Amendment became effective, it was true at the time of the decision in <u>Eisner v. Macomber</u>, it was true under Section 22(a) of the Internal Revenue Code of 1939, and it is likewise true under Section 61(a) of the 1939 Code, and it is likewise true under Section 61(a) of the Internal Revenue Code of 1954. <u>If there is no gain there is no income…</u>"* (emphasis added)

Note the emphasis on the element of "gain". The court recognized the necessity of a "gain" to properly define the term "income". This leads us to determine the meaning of the term "wages" to see whether or not "wages" includes within its meaning the essential feature of "gain".

The Supreme Court stated in **Coppage v. Kansas, 236 U.S. 1 at page 14 (1915):**

> *Included in the right of <u>personal liberty</u> and the right of private <u>property-partaking of the nature of each-is the right to make contracts for the acquisition of property. Chief</u>*

> *among such contracts is that of personal employment by which labor and other services are exchanged for money and other forms of property.* (emphasis added)

Having determined that "wages" are the result of an exchange of money or property for labor and/or service, let's look at what another court has to say about the nature of this exchange. The Supreme Court points out one aspect of the nature of this exchange by saying in the decision of:

Adkins v. Children's Hospital, 261 U.S. 521 (1923)

> *...there is a moral requirement implicit in every contract of employment, that the amount to be paid and the service to be rendered shall bear to each some measure of just equivalence...In principle, there can be no difference between the case of selling labor and the case of selling goods (property).* (emphasis added)

So the Adkins court again agrees that our labor is our property which we are morally bound to sell for wages according to "some measure of just equivalence". The equivalence requirement is obvious when we consider that an employer will not pay more than our labor is worth. Clearly there is no profit or "gain" in wages, but merely an equal exchange of the employee's property in labor and services for the employer's property in wages. This is an equal exchange of value for value and no "gain" is involved.

Congress could not have contemplated a tax on labor because the right to work is a fundamental non-taxable right protected by the Constitution. If Congress had the power to tax the exercise of a fundamental right it would be able to abolish that right by taxing it out of existence and thereby the Congress would have the power to subvert the Constitution's prohibition in Article 1, Section 9, Clause 4 against any capitation tax.

It seems obvious to this writer that this right we all have to make a contract for our labor or any other form of property tax-free would also include the right of citizens to contract with others for investment purposes in any and all forms of property, also tax-free. All of the court cases already quoted put us back to square one-that is that the income tax cannot possibly be applicable to the profit on investments or property dealings or exchanges of our unincorporated or unprivileged citizens, which is no doubt why the original income tax law was called the Corporation Excise Tax Act of

1909. This will be addressed in depth in Chapters II and III. A "taxpayer", then, is a corporate "person" or one (such as a non-resident alien as we will see in Chapter 3) who enjoys some privilege granted by government to pursue a government-privileged activity for which an indirect or excise tax may be charged, measured by the income the activity produces. The word "taxpayer" is defined in the Internal Revenue Code under Section 7701(a)(14) as follows: "The term 'taxpayer' means any person 'subject to' any internal revenue tax." An appellate court in the decision of **Houston Street Corp. v. Commissioner**, 84 F2d 821 (5th Circuit 1936) ruled that the words "subject to" and "liable for" a tax are interchangeable. And, as we will show in Facts #13 and 14 of this chapter following, two appellate court decisions of **Botta v. Scanlon**, 288 F2d 509 (1961) and **Higley v. Commissioner of Internal Revenue**, 69 F2d 160 (1934) tell us that for a person to be subject to a tax, there must be a statute (code section) stating clearly that his privileged activity makes him "liable for" the tax. Simply paying a tax such as a sales tax, real estate tax or other license tax does not place one in the legal status of "taxpayer" as that term is used and defined in the Internal Revenue Code. Such taxes are always imposed by states or sub-divisions of states-not by the Federal government. Therefore, in any event, such taxes could not qualify the payer of such license taxes to be in the category of "taxpayer" as that term is used in the Internal Revenue Code.

Explaining the status of a "non-taxpayer", a Federal Appellate Court stated in the decision of **Long v. Rasmussen, 281 F.236 at 238 (1922)**:

> *The revenue laws are a code or system in regulation of tax assessments and collection. **THEY RELATE TO TAXPAYERS AND NOT TO NON-TAXPAYERS**. The latter are without their scope. No procedure is proscribed for NON-TAXPAYERS and no attempt is made to annul any of their rights and remedies in due course of law. With them Congress does not assume to deal, and they are neither the subject nor **the object of the revenue laws**.* (emphasis added)

This same view was expressed by other courts in the following decisions:

Economy Plumbing and Heating v. U.S., 470 F2d. 585 at 589 (1972):

> *Persons who are not taxpayers are not within the system*

and can obtain no benefit by following the procedures prescribed for taxpayers such as the filing of claims for refunds…neither did the mere filing of claims for refunds make plaintiffs taxpayers when none of the requisites of the <u>status</u> of taxpayers were present. (emphasis added)

Stuart v. Chinese Chamber of Commerce of Phoenix, 168 F2d. 712 (1948):

Under the circumstances here recited, it is obvious the appellees are <u>not taxpayers</u> in the strict sense of the word, and therefore they do not come within the orbit of the income tax laws here involved. (emphasis added)

Also, **First National Bank of Emlenton Pa. v. U.S.**, 161 F2d Supp. 847 (1958):

The revenue laws are a code or system in regulation of tax assessment and collection. They <u>relate to taxpayers</u> and <u>not to non-taxpayers</u>. With them Congress does not assume to deal, and they are neither of the subject nor of the object of the revenue laws. (emphasis added)

    The fact is that the acquisition by U.S. citizens of money <u>as property</u> from labor, investment or any other endeavor, is a <u>natural right</u> for a natural person. However, it is not a natural right for an artificial person such as a corporation, its officers or stockholders acting for the corporation or for non-resident aliens or foreign partnerships who are not protected by our Constitutional restrictions against direct taxes. The corporation enjoys government-granted privilege of limited liability and perpetual life for which a <u>"return"</u> (an income tax) must be given back to government for the privileges which the corporation enjoys. By acquiring from the state the privileges from incorporation of perpetual life and limited liability inherent therein, the corporation must pay a tax which is <u>measured by the income or profits</u> which the corporation produces. As we can also see through examination of Sub-Title E of Title 26 of the Internal Revenue Code, other privileged activities such as the manufacture or distribution of alcohol, tobacco or firearms are also proper subjects of indirect taxation in the form of excises which can be used and are also measured by the income these privileged activities produce.

The Internal Revenue Code itself acknowledges the "non-taxpayer" status of U.S. citizens employed in unprivileged activities by specifically taxing the receipts of non-resident aliens or foreign partnerships ONLY from the sources in the United States under Section 1441(a) of the Internal Revenue Code. Such application of the taxing authority makes sense when we consider that, unlike citizens, non-resident aliens or foreign partnerships have no protection under the Constitution from taxation of their earnings or gains from property dealings in the U.S. The 30% tax rate identified in Section 1441(a) of the Code on such "items of income" as listed in Section 1441(b) is imposed in Section 871 of the Code, and liability for the deduction and withholding of this tax is set forth in Section 1461 on "every person required to deduct and withhold every tax". Usually this "person required" is the officer or other person acting on behalf of the corporation or non-resident alien who has the control of the "items of income" set forth in Section 1441(b). Of vital importance is the fact that Section 1461 which names the withholding agent ONLY as the person liable to withhold income tax is also the ONLY section in the I.R. Code making ANYONE liable for income tax!

The following FACTS are numbered for purposes of future study and as referenced elsewhere in this book:

FACT #1-U.S. CITIZENS ARE NOT REQURIERD BY LAW TO FILE FORMS 1040, AND THEY ARE NOT LIABLE FOR THE PAYMENT OF A TAX ON "INCOME" UNLESS THEY ARE WITHHOLDING AGENTS OR FIDUCIARIES FOR CORPORATIONS OR FOREIGN ENTITIES AS SHOWN BELOW.

There is no provision in the Internal Revenue Code imposing an "income" tax on monies received or earned by citizens residing within the states of the union, regardless of the amount, unless the money is received on behalf of, or payable to a corporation, a non-resident alien, foreign partnership or foreign corporation.

FACT #2-AMERICANS ARE MISLED AND DECEIVED INTO BELIEVING THAT THE "INCOME" TAX APPLIES TO THE GENERAL PUBLIC.

For years, the Internal Revenue Service has deceived the American people in a manner not equaled even by the Nazi Gestapo. Fear and bluff have been the IRS' major weapons. Americans have been falsely led to believe that they owe a tax on their earnings, that it is their "patriotic duty" to pay it and that there is no alternative to the IRS' abuse. These beliefs are simply untrue. Because accountants, tax preparers, tax lawyers and others profit from the fraudulent misapplication of the law, most of them are reluctant to admit the truth about the law even when confronted with it.

FACT #3-THE IRS ADMITS THAT THE "INCOME" TAX SYSTEM IS DEPENDENT ON THE VOLUNTARY FILING OF TAX RETURNS.

In the decision of **U.S. v. Flora, 362, U.S. 145 (1960),** on page 176, the U.S. Supreme Court stated: *Our system of taxation is based on voluntary assessment and payment, not upon distraint.* If a law requires you to do something, your compliance with the law is mandatory, not voluntary. But if a law requires certain other people (not you) to do something, then your compliance with that law is voluntary. The IRS has repeatedly stated that: "The mission of the Internal Revenue Service is to encourage and achieve the highest possible degree of voluntary compliance with the tax laws and regulations…(I.R. Manual Section 1111.1). (emphasis added)

Mr. Dwight E. Avis, the head of the Alcohol, Tobacco and Firearms Division of the Bureau of the Internal Revenue Service, testifying before the House Ways and Means Committee of the 83rd Congress in 1953 stated: *"Let me point this out now: Your income tax is a 100% voluntary tax, and your liquor tax is a 100% enforced tax. This situation is as different as night and day. Consequently your same rules just will not apply."* (emphasis added)

FACT #4-THE CONSTITUTION FORBIDS THE U.S. GOVERNMENT TO IMPOSE ANY DIRECT TAX ON THE PEOPLE IN THE STATES OF THE UNION.

Two provisions in the U.S. Constitution prohibit the imposition of direct taxes on the people or their property by the U.S. government. The first is Article 1, Section 2, Clause 3 which requires the amount of any direct tax to be billed to and divided among the state governments in proportion to the population of each state. The second provision is in Article 1, Section 9, Clause 4 which prohibits any capitation tax (a tax on people) or other direct tax unless apportioned among the states. Direct taxes have been imposed only five times in U.S. history. All were correctly and constitutionally imposed on state governments (not individuals). The last direct tax was imposed in 1861 by the union government to finance the Civil War.

FACT #5-THE U.S. SUPREME COURT RULED THAT THE "INCOME" TAX IS CONSTITUTIONAL AS AN INDIRECT (EXCISE) TAX, BUT NOT AS A DIRECT TAX (tax on general public).

In the 1916 decisions of **Brushaber v. Union Pacific R.R., 240 U.S. 1** and **Stanton v. Baltic Mining, 240 U.S. 103**, the U.S. Supreme Court ruled that the 16th Amendment (incorrectly called the "income tax" amendment) to the U.S. Constitution created **no new power of taxation** and that it did not amend or nullify the constitutional prohibition against direct taxation of the people within the states of the union. The Brushaber Court ruled that the "income" tax is constitutional only as an indirect **excise tax on corporations or on the receipts of foreigners**, but unconstitutional as a direct tax on U.S. citizens. In the decision of **Flint v. Stone Tracy Co., 220 U.S. 107 (1911)**, the U.S. Supreme Court defined an "excise" tax as a tax on **activities** involving the **exercise of a privilege**. (emphasis added)

FACT #6-THE IRS ADMITS THAT THE BRUSHABER DECISION RELATES TO "INCOME" ACCRUING TO NON-RESIDENT ALIENS ONLY - NOT TO U.S. CITIZENS!

Treasury Decision 2313, issued March 21, 1916 by the Commissioner of Internal Revenue to inform collectors of internal revenue of the significance of the Brushaber decision states: *"Under the decision of the Supreme Court of the United States in the case of* **Brushaber v. Union Pacific Railway Co.** *decided January 21, 1916, it is hereby held that income accruing to **non-resident aliens** in the form of interest from the bonds and dividends on the stock of domestic corporations is subject to the income tax imposed by the act of October 3, 1913."* (emphasis added)

FACT #7-FORM 1040 IS AN INCOME TAX RETURN FOR NON-RESIDENT ALIENS.

As previously stated, I.R. Code Section 871(a) imposes a tax of 30% on the amounts received by non-resident aliens from sources within the United States. Section 871(b) states that the non-resident alien shall be taxable under Section 1 thus authorizing the use of the charts in Section 1 to compute and reduce his tax so he can get a tax refund from the 30% which is withheld under the provisions of Section 1441. Also, under I.R. Code Section 874(a), the non-resident alien is entitled to the <u>benefit of deductions and credits</u> by filing or having his fiduciary agent <u>file a 1040</u> as stated in TD 2313. Again, these sections relate only to non-resident aliens or their agents-not to U.S. citizens acting for themselves.

FACT #8-"INCOME" IS MONEY RECEIVED ON BEHALF OF OR PAID TO A NON-RESIDENT ALIEN.

I.R. Code Section 1441(a) and (b) states that "...*interest...dividends, rents, salaries, wages, premium annuities, compensations, remunerations, emoluments, or other fixed or determinable annual or periodic gains, and profits...*" are "income" when received on behalf of or paid to a non-resident alien or other **foreign** entity. Also, courts have ruled that profits of corporations are "income". **There is no provision in the I.R. Code stating that receipts belonging to citizens or residents of the country are "income".** Thus, a U.S. citizen's own receipts <u>are not</u> "income", "gross income" or "taxable income" under the I.R. Code. Within the states, "income" is property derived from activities involving the exercise of a government-granted privilege. Working for a living is <u>not a privilege</u>. - It is a <u>non-taxable</u> constitutional <u>right</u>!

FACT #9-IT IS A PRIVILEGE FOR A NON-RESIDENT ALIEN TO DO BUSINESS, TO INVEST OR TO WORK IN THE U.S.A.

The U.S. government can prohibit foreigners from working, investing or doing business within this country; therefore, allowing such <u>activity</u> is a **privilege** subject to an **excise** tax similar to the government-granted privilege to do business as a corporation. But U.S. citizens have a non-taxable, constitutionally-protected RIGHT to work, invest or do business in this country. This <u>right</u> also extends to protect our citizens against state <u>taxation</u> of constitutional <u>rights</u> under the provisions of the fourteenth amendment. The U.S. Supreme Court in **Murdock v. Pennsylvania, 319 U.S. 105** stated: "*A state may not impose a tax for the enjoyment of a right granted by the Federal Constitution.*"

FACT #10-THE "INCOME TAX" IS AN INDIRECT EXCISE TAX ON PRIVILEGED ACTIVITIES, NOT ON "INCOME". THE "INCOME" IS MERELY THE MEASURE OF THE TAX.

The *Congressional Record*, Volume 89, Part 2 on page 2580 for March 27, 1943 states: *"The income tax is, therefore, not a tax on income as such. It is an **excise tax** with respect to certain **activities and privileges** which is measured by reference to the income which they produce. The income is not the subject of the tax; it is the basis for determining the amount of the tax."* (emphasis added) The U.S. Supreme Court in the decision of **Flint v. Stone Tracy Co., 220 U.S. 107** in discussing income tax as an excise tax stated on page 165: *"It is therefore well settled by the decisions of this court that when the sovereign authority has exercised the right to tax <u>a legitimate subject of taxation</u> as an exercise of a **franchise or privilege**, it is no objection that the <u>measure of taxation</u> is found in the income."* (emphasis added)

FACT #11-WITHHOLDING AGENTS ARE REQUIRED TO WITHHOLD FROM PAYMENTS OF "INCOME" TO FOREIGN PERSONS ONLY.

I.R. Code Section 7701(a)(16) states: *"The term 'withholding agent' means any person required to deduct and withhold any tax under the provisions of Sections 1441, 1442, 1443 or 1461."* These sections apply to money owed to, received on behalf of, or paid to, non-resident aliens, foreign partnerships, foreign corporations and other foreign entities only; not to money received by citizens on their own behalf. Because the U.S. government has no authority over foreign citizens living in a foreign country, the only individuals who are required to deduct and withhold the tax on foreigner's receipts and can be <u>made liable</u> for deduction and payment of the tax are the withholding agents for such foreigners.

FACT #12-THE ONLY PERSON MADE LIABLE IN THE INTERNAL REVENUE CODE FOR PAYMENT OF "INCOME" TAX IS A WITHHOLDING AGENT.

Subtitle A of the I.R. Code contains the provisions of the law imposing "income" tax. Subtitle A, Section 1461 is the <u>only</u> <u>section</u> making any person liable for (subject to) payment of "income" tax. The only individual made liable in Section 1461 is the "withholding agent" who is required to withhold from the "income" of foreign persons ONLY which is <u>identified</u> in I.R. Code Section 1441(b).

FACT #13-THE ONLY WAY A PERSON CAN BE "MADE LIABLE" FOR ANY INTERNAL REVENUE TAX IS BY A

PROVISION IN THE LAW (a statute).

In the decision of **Botta v. Scanlon, 288 F.2d 509 (1961),** the United States Court of Appeals explained that there is only one way that a tax liability can be created. It stated: *"Moreover, even the collection of taxes should be exacted only from persons upon whom a tax liability is imposed by some statute."* (emphasis added) In *Sutherland's Rules of Statutory Construction*, an authoritative reference book on interpretation of statutes, Section 66.03 states. *"…the obligation to pay taxes arises **only by force of legislative action…**".* (emphasis added) Legislative action is the passage of a statute (a law). For anyone to be "liable" for income tax it must be so stated in the I.R. Code. (emphasis added)

FACT #14-PROVISIONS MAKING ANYONE LIABLE FOR PAYMENT OF A TAX MUST BE STATED IN CLEAR UNDERSTANDABLE LANGUAGE.

In the decision of **Higley v. Commissioner of Internal Revenue, 69 F.2d 160**, head note 2 states: *"Liability for taxation **must clearly appear from statute** imposing tax."* (emphasis added) *Sutherland's Rules of Statutory Construction* under Section 66.01 titled, *"Strict Construction of Statutes Creating Tax Liabilities"* refers to the U.S. Supreme Court decision of **Gould v. Gould, 245 U.S. 151**, which states: *"In the interpretation of statutes levying taxes it is the established **rule not to extend their provisions by implication** beyond the clear import of the language used, or to enlarge their operation so as to embrace matters not specifically pointed out. In case of doubt they are construed most strongly <u>against the government, and in favor of the citizen</u>".* (emphasis added)

Fact #15-I.R. CODE PROVISIONS IMPOSING LIABILITY ARE CLEARLY STATED AND USE THE LORD "LIABLE".

The word "liable" is found in I.R. Code Section 4401(c), 5005(a), 5703(a) and 1461 which create liabilities for <u>wagering tax, distilled spirits tax, tobacco tax and "income" tax</u> respectively. Section 1461 is the ONLY section in the I.R. Code imposing liability for payment of "income" tax. That section applies to WITHHOLDING AGENTS ONLY (those required by Sections 1441 and 1442 to deduct and withhold from payments of "income" owed to foreign persons). Section 1461 states: *"Every person <u>required to deduct and withhold</u> any tax under this chapter* *is **hereby made liable** for such tax."* (emphasis added)

FACT #16-I.R. CODE CHAPTER #24 PROVIDES FOR VOLUNTARY WITHHOLDING FROM "EMPLOYEES". IT DOES NOT APPLY TO ANY NON-GOVERNMENT EMPLOYEE OR EMPLOYER. (See Section 3401 (c) and (d).

Chapter 24 of the I.R. Code contains provisions that authorize the U.S. Government, the District of Columbia, their agencies and instrumentalities ONLY to set up and administer a <u>voluntary</u> withholding system for <u>their</u> employees. Without such statutory authority, no official of the government could legally create a withholding system in government. Chapter 24 does <u>NOT</u> authorize or require withholding by any <u>non</u>-federal government employers, and this chapter does NOT impose any tax on any government employee or anyone else.

FACT #17-THERE IS NO AUTHORITY TO WITHHOLD MONEY FROM A CITIZEN OR RESIDENT OF THE UNITED STATES UNLESS HE AUTHORIZES IT.

The Fifth Amendment to the Bill of Rights of the U.S. Constitution states no individual can be deprived of property without due process of law (a hearing in a court of law). The ONLY way a United States citizen or resident alien can legally have "income" tax withheld from his pay is if he authorizes it by voluntarily signing an IRS W-4, "Employee's Withholding <u>Allowance</u> Certificate", thus indicating that he is in the same status as a non-resident alien. The Fifth Amendment protection is why the IRS pressures employers to obtain the <u>voluntary</u> execution of IRS Form W-4 by all people being hired. However, the Fifth Amendment <u>prevents</u> any law or regulation that <u>requires</u> any individual to sign a Form W-4 Withholding Allowance Certificate. I.R. code section 3402 (n) provides statutory reinforcement of the fifth amendment <u>right</u> by providing additional authority for citizens to stop voluntary withholding through submission of a signed statement that the employee owed no income tax in the current year and contemplated not owing any for the coming year.

FACT #18-TO UNDERSTAND THE I.R. CODE ONE MUST LEARN WHICH WORDS ARE USED IN THE CODE AS LEGAL TERMS.

In the I.R. Code, many words of common usage are used as legal terms that have meanings more limited in their application than when defined for common usage. Words such as *taxpayer, taxable income, taxable year, employee, employer, wages, United States, State, person, etc.* are legal terms that have limited meanings when used in the Code. Some legal terms have different meanings when used in different parts of the Code. As will be shown in detail in Chapters IV and V, to understand the true meaning of the Code, it is necessary to learn the various <u>limited</u> legal definitions of those terms and <u>where</u> in the Code <u>the definitions apply</u>.

FACT #19-THE I.R. CODE APPLIES TO "TAXPAYERS" ONLY (THOSE WHO ARE MADE LIABLE FOR A TAX BY A STATUTE).

This fact has been clearly stated through the years in many court decisions, some of which are repeatedly cited in this book, including **Long v. Rasmussen**, 281, F236 (1922), **Stuart v. Chinese Chamber of Commerce of Phoenix**, 168 F.2d 712 (1948), **First National Bank of Emlenton, Pa. v. U.S.**, 161 F. Supp. 847 (1958), **Botta v. Scanlon**, 288 F.2d 509 (1961) and **Economy Plumbing v. U.S.**, 470 F.2d 589 (1972). "Taxpayer" (one word not two) is a legal term defined in the I.R. Code, Section 7701(a)(14) which states: *"The term 'taxpayer' means any person <u>subject</u> to any internal revenue tax."* (emphasis added) As the court stated in **Botta v. Scanlon**, discussed earlier, for a person to be <u>subject to</u> a tax there must be a provision in the law stating clearly that his activity makes him "liable" for the tax. Paying a tax such as a sales tax, a license tax or real estate tax does not place one in the legal status of "taxpayer" as that term is used in the I.R. Code.

FACT #20-THE TERMS "TAXABLE INCOME" AND "TAXABLE YEAR" APPLY TO "TAXPAYERS" ONLY.

These terms defined in I.R. Code Section 441(a) (**taxable income**) and (b) (**taxable year**) apply to "**taxpayers**" only and to those who file returns thus stating (in effect) under penalty of perjury that they are "**taxpayers**". Also "**taxable year**" is a key legal term in Section 6012(a)(1) which is a section that the IRS cites when claiming that individuals are required to file income tax returns. Since a withholding agent is the only person in Subtitle A of the I.R. Code <u>"made liable"</u> for payment of income tax, he is the only individual in the legal status of "**taxpayer** in respect to "income tax";

thus a "withholding agent" is the only one who has a **taxable year** under Section 6012(a)(1).

FACT #21-CERTAIN "PERSON(S)" ONLY ARE SUBJEC TO CRIMINAL PENALTIES.

Those "person(s)" who are subject to the criminal penalties in the Code are defined and limited by I.R. Code Section 7343 to those required to act on behalf of a corporation or partnership. Section 7343 states: *"The term 'person' as used in this chapter includes an officer or employee of a corporation or a member or employee of a partnership who **as such officer, employer or member** is under a duty to perform the act in respect of which the violation occurs."* (emphasis added) Because the term "includes" is a word of limitation and not expansion, as we will see in Chapter IV, when an individual is not in a capacity as defined in this Section 7343 his prosecution under the Code is illegal.

FACT #22-A FILED TAX RETURN PROVIDES EVIDENCE FOR THE IRS TO USE AGAINST THE PERSON FILING TO PROVE LEGALLY THAT HE IS A "TAXPAYER" AND THEREBY SUBJECT TO ALL PROVISIONS OF THE I.R. CODE.

When an individual who is not a "taxpayer" as that term is defined in the I.R. Code files an income tax return signed under penalty of perjury, he has shown by his own act of filing that he is a "taxpayer" and thereby subject to all provisions of the Internal Revenue Code. Further, under the established legal doctrine of presumption by his own voluntary act of filing, he also subjects himself to the provisions of Title 28, Section 1746 of Federal law which states that his signature on the tax return which he signed under penalty of perjury has the same force and effect at law as a sworn oath or notarized affidavit. The very first thing that every IRS revenue agent learns when dealing with non-taxpayers who have not filed returns is to try to get them to file by deceiving them into believing that the law requires them to do so.

FACT #23-KARL MARX WROTE IN HIS COMMUNIST MANIFESTO TEN PLANKS NEEDED TO CREATE A COMMUNIST STATE. THE FIRST PLANK WAS THE ABOLITION OF THE RIGHT TO OWN PROPERTY. THE SECOND PLANK WAS A PROGRESSIVE INCOME TAX.

If the government could legally tax citizens' earnings, government would then have first claim on those earnings. His earnings are <u>compensation for his labor-the most precious of all his property</u>. His circumstances would be like the slave who is allowed to have only that which is left after the master takes whatever he wants.

CONCLUSION

It is morally wrong for our government (Congress) to intimidate and deceive the people into believing that they must pay an "income" tax that is forbidden by the U.S. Constitution to be imposed on our citizen's earnings or other receipts. All judges and government officials, <u>including all IRS agents,</u> are sworn to support, uphold and defend the Constitution. When they are notified or become aware of the IRS' illegal action to force ordinary citizens to pay a (so-called) "income" tax they do not owe, and they then do nothing to stop it, they violate their oaths of office to uphold and enforce the Constitution, and by so doing they subject themselves to dismissal and potential civil and criminal penalties as well.

CHAPTER II

THE SIXTEENTH AMENDMENT - THE MYTH AND THE REALITY

The Sixteenth Amendment to the Constitution of the United States of America, which was ratified by the states in 1913, and is generally referred to as the income tax amendment, is <u>the most misunderstood provision in the Constitution</u>. The misleading statements and publications of the IRS about the Sixteenth Amendment are completely different from the explanation of the Amendment's sponsor, President William Howard Taft in his message to a joint session of Congress on June 16, 1909. The President's complete message is published in the Congressional Record (Senate) on page 3344 and 3345 and at the end of this chapter. President Taft explained that the purpose and function of his proposed Sixteenth Amendment was to assure the constitutionality of his proposed Corporation Excise Tax Act that was passed in the same 1909 session of Congress. President Taft stated:

> *I recommend, then, first, the adoption of a joint resolution by two-thirds of both Houses, proposing to the States an amendment to the Constitution granting to the Federal government the right to levy and collect an...<u>EXCISE TAX</u> upon <u>ALL CORPORATIONS</u>, measured by 2 percent of their net income.* (emphasis added)

The proposed Amendment did not authorize any income tax on earnings or other receipts of U.S. citizens, which has always been, and still is, prohibited by our Constitution.

To better understand the Sixteenth Amendment, it is necessary to learn a few basic facts about the economic and political issues in America during the latter years of the 1800's and how they led up to the creation of the Sixteenth Amendment. In the years following the War Between the States, there was a great expansion of economic and industrial activity in the nation resulting in a concentration of power in the managements of corporations. This concentration of power was further increased by the joining together of corporations involved in the same line of business to form organizations called <u>trusts</u> which were formed to dominate the business or industry of their member corporations. Each trust had a management with central control over the corporations in the trust which eliminated competition and enabled the corporations to exploit the public by means of the <u>trust</u> monopolies that were created <u>to fleece the public</u> by expanding corporate trust member's profits.

These economic abuses caused a public reaction in a political movement to stop the trusts' exploitation of the public by enacting Federal laws designed to destroy the trusts. The first major reform law was the Sherman Anti-Trust Act enacted in 1890. This law declared illegal "every contract, combination in the form of trust or otherwise, or conspiracy, in restraint of trade or commerce among the several states, or with foreign nations"; it also included criminal penalties for violations of the laws' provisions. In Chapter I, we learned the difference between direct and indirect taxes and that the (so-called) "income" tax is an <u>indirect tax in the form of an excise</u> levied on the exercise of <u>privileges granted by government</u> to corporations such as limited liability of its stockholder-owners and perpetual life of the corporation. Also, the privilege granted by government to foreigners to work, invest or do business in the United States is another taxable privilege in the form of an excise. Until 1894 no "income" tax of any kind on corporations had ever been enacted into law. And, of course, no Federal tax on individual U.S. citizens or their the earnings or other receipts, including interest, dividends, capital gains, etc. had ever even been considered. As explained in Chapter I, any such direct tax on U. S. citizens is totally prohibited by the Constitution and also by the U.S. Supreme Court decisions which were quoted in Chapter I.

In 1894, in order to reach the huge corporate profits being earned at the time, Congress enacted an income tax law that imposed a tax on the income of corporations. The legality of the law was immediately challenged in court and the issue was decided in 1895 in the Supreme Court decision in the case of **Pollock v. Farmers Loan and Trust Co.** **(157 U.S. 420).** The United States Supreme Court, which at that time was considered very favorable to big business, ruled that the law was unconstitutional because it imposed a tax on income <u>derived</u> from property, and that to tax income <u>derived</u> from the use of property was the same as taxing the property itself, and, therefore, unconstitutional in violation of the constitutional prohibition against any direct tax, unless apportioned by population among the states, as set forth in Article 1, Section 2, Clause 3 of the Constitution. Some examples of income derived from property are income from rents, from real estate, profits from farming and profits from operation of a factory, all of which the Supreme Court said had never previously been taxed.

The Court's reasoning for their decision in the Pollock case was that to tax income, when the source of the income was property, imposes a Federal tax burden on the property itself, which is forbidden by limitations on direct taxation in the Constitution. The Court ruled that any tax on property, like <u>any direct tax upon an individual citizen, is a direct tax in the constitutional sense</u>, and therefore, since the tax was not apportioned among the states, they ruled the entire act to be unconstitutional. Again, as we learned in Chapter 1, a Federal direct tax is allowed by the Constitution to be imposed <u>only</u> <u>on the governments of the states of the union.</u> The amount of the tax on each state government is determined by apportioning (dividing) the total amount of the direct tax among the state governments, to be collected from all the states in proportion to the population of each state.

The 1895 <u>Pollock</u> decision of the U.S. Supreme Court effectively prevented the enactment of any new corporation income tax law until 1909 during the administration of President William Howard Taft. President Taft had been elected on a "trust buster" platform that obligated him to enact additional legislation to prohibit the existence of trusts. Taft wanted to get access to corporations' business records through the government's taxing power in order to uncover any corporations' abuses of the public by any secret violations of the Sherman Anti-Trust Act.

Being well-aware of the <u>Pollock</u> decision of 1895, in President Taft's June 16, 1909 message to a joint session of Congress, he called, first, for an amendment to the Constitution to override the effect of the <u>Pollock</u> court decision. The amendment, he reasoned, would accomplish this desired result, enabling Congress to enact a <u>corporation income tax</u> of 2%, measured by corporate profits, which he simultaneously proposed. President Taft reasoned that the amendment would prevent the proposed 2% tax on corporate profits from being overturned by the Supreme Court, because of the earlier <u>Pollock</u> court decision.

It is easy to understand how simply the wording in President Taft's proposed Sixteenth Amendment overrode the U.S. Supreme Court's ruling in the <u>Pollock</u> case. The <u>Pollock</u> ruling stated that the income could not be taxed if the <u>source </u>from which the income was derived was property. The Sixteenth Amendment states:

> **Congress shall have power to lay and collect taxes on incomes, from <u>whatever source derived</u>, without**

apportionment among the several states, and without regard to any census or enumeration. (emphasis added)

Obviously President Taft knew very well that any "income" tax would be restricted to an indirect excise tax subject to the rule of uniformity discussed in Chapter I. The underlined words clearly mean that income <u>derived</u> from <u>all sources</u>, including sources such as property and labor employed <u>by a corporation</u>, can be taxed by Congress, thus overriding the <u>Pollock</u> decision of the U.S. Supreme Court. However, the income tax authorized by the Sixteenth Amendment applies <u>only to income measured by profit or gain derived from the special privileges enjoyed by corporations and monies received by non-resident alien individuals, but not by citizen-individuals</u> who retained their inalienable rights as citizens against any taxation by government on their person or their property.

However, the **BIG LIE** that is spread by the IRS and even many, misinformed lawyers, is that the <u>Constitutional limitations</u> on the impositions of direct taxes were <u>changed by the Sixteenth Amendment</u>, thus authorizing income tax as a direct tax on citizens of the U.S. But the wording of the Amendment <u>does not repeal or change the Constitutional limitations against direct taxation of U.S. citizens contained in Article 1, Section 2, Clause 3 or in Article 1, Section 9, Clause 4</u> which still remain in effect today limiting the "income" tax to a tax on the profits or gains earned from the privileges exercised by government-created corporations or other privileged entities such as non-resident aliens investing in the U.S.

By contrast, the Eighteenth Amendment (the so-called "prohibition" amendment) which prohibited the manufacture, sale or distribution of alcoholic beverages was specifically <u>repealed</u> by the Twenty-First Amendment which stated in Clause 1: *"The eighteenth <u>article</u> of amendment to the Constitution of the United States <u>is hereby repealed</u>."* (emphasis added) Again, <u>no such repeal</u> of Article 1, Section 2, Clause 3 or Article 1, Section 9, Clause 4 was enacted in the Sixteenth Amendment! Consequently, U.S. citizens <u>remain protected</u> by these constitutional limitations against any direct tax on their earnings or other receipts.

The U.S. Supreme Court in a 1913 decision in the case of **Stratton's Independence v. Howbert, 231 U.S. 399** explained in a discussion of the Income Tax Act of 1909 that the income tax is:

> ...*an <u>excise tax</u> upon the <u>conduct of business</u> in a <u>corporate capacity</u>, measuring however, the amount of the tax by the income (profits or gains) of the corporation...* (emphasis added)

A corporation is a legal entity created by government and its activities are controlled and limited by the provisions in its charter. The corporation, however, enjoys the privileged benefits of perpetual life and limited liability for its stockholder-owners. The Supreme Court in the <u>Stratton</u> decision explained that it was these <u>privileges granted by government</u> to do business in the corporate form that is subject to tax; that the <u>income</u> is <u>not</u> the subject but merely the <u>measurement</u> for determining the amount of the tax <u>on the corporate privileges</u>. Also, monies earned by non-resident aliens, who have no rights (unlike U.S. citizens) under our Constitution, to work, invest, do business in or even to enter the country are also taxable <u>privileges</u> granted by the U.S. government. Because of these privileges, the activities of non-resident aliens measured by monies earned are also subject to the same indirect-<u>excise</u> income tax as corporations as will be shown in Chapter III. By contrast, however, U.S. citizens have the natural, God-given, constitutionally-protected <u>right</u> to do these things <u>without government permission</u>, and are, therefore, <u>not subject to</u> government income/excise taxes on their earnings. (See Chapter I.)

The decision of the U.S. Supreme Court in the case of **Brushaber v. Union Pacific Railroad, Inc., 240 U.S. 1 (1916)** is the cornerstone decision relied upon by the IRS that established the constitutionality of the income tax <u>but only as an indirect excise tax</u> on government-privileged entities such as corporations and non-resident aliens by reason of the Sixteenth Amendment. This case involved withholding from monies by Union Pacific Railroad, Inc. owing (meaning payable) to <u>non-resident aliens</u>, but <u>not to U.S. citizens</u>. It is interesting to note that <u>nothing in the Court's decision exposes this very important fact, but this fact is admitted by the IRS itself in their Treasury Decision Ruling #2313 (T.D. #2313) which is quoted later in Chapter III</u>.

The <u>Brushaber</u> court decision explained that the 16th Amendment states that the income tax authorized by the Amendment could only be imposed "<u>without apportionment</u>", because the Constitution still required that <u>all direct taxes</u> <u>be</u> <u>apportioned among the states</u>. The income tax <u>could not stand constitutionally as a direct tax on the income of citizens</u>. The

Brushaber court stated that the income tax is constitutional <u>only as an indirect tax in the nature of an excise</u> which <u>limits its application to corporations and other privileged entities</u>, such as non-resident aliens, who are not protected against taxation of their earnings or other receipts as are U.S. citizens.

Other decisions by the U.S. Supreme Court have also ruled that the income tax authorized by the Sixteenth Amendment is an <u>excise tax imposed on activities</u> involving the exercise of a government-granted <u>privilege</u>. This includes the activities of corporations doing business in this nation, and that <u>income</u> (as profit or gain) is merely the measurement for determining the amount of the tax imposed on the privileges of such corporations. Non-resident aliens, however, who, unlike citizens, have no constitutional protection against direct taxation, can lawfully be taxed on <u>all monies</u> in whatever form received by them from any sources within the United States.

In 1916 the U.S. Supreme Court in the decision of **Stanton v. Baltic Mining, 240 U.S. 102** held:

...that the provisions of the 16th Amendment conferred <u>no new power of taxation</u>, but simply prohibited the previous complete and plenary power of income taxation passed by Congress from the beginning from being taken out of the <u>category of indirect taxation to which it inherently belonged</u>, and being placed in the category of direct taxation subject to apportionment...(emphasis added)

In the 1918 U.S. Supreme Court decision of **Peck & Co. v. Lowe, 247 U.S. 165**, this Court decision also explained the limited application of the Sixteenth Amendment. The Court stated in its decision as follows:

The Sixteenth Amendment... does <u>not extend the taxing power to new or excepted subjects</u>...
(emphasis added)

The "<u>excepted subjects</u>" wording in this Court decision is a clear reference to capitation taxes (taxes on citizens or their earnings) which are still forbidden by Article 1, Section 9, Clause 4 of the Constitution!

The IRS' own Treasury Decision #2313 which is a notification bulletin sent to all Internal Revenue collectors acknowledges that the Brushaber case involved the withholding of tax on monies accruing to non-resident aliens, but not to citizens and that the IRS Form 1040 is to be used for reporting "income" of non-resident alien individuals! IRS Treasury Decision #2313 states:

> *Under the decision of the Supreme Court of the United States in the case of Brushaber...it is hereby held that income accruing to non-resident aliens in the form of interest from the bonds and dividends on the stock of domestic corporations is subject to the income tax imposed by the Act of October 3, 1913....The responsible heads, agents, or representatives of non-resident aliens, who are in charge of the property owned or business carried on within the United States, shall make a full and complete return of the income therefrom on Form 1040, revised, and shall pay any and all tax, normal and additional, assessed upon the income received by them in behalf of their non-resident alien principals.* (emphasis added)

Summary

Nothing in the Sixteenth Amendment repealed or nullified the Constitutional limitations on the imposition of direct taxes which still prohibit the imposition of any federal taxes on individual citizens of this country or on their property. This book shows why there is no provision in the Internal Revenue Code imposing any federal tax on real estate or making any individual U.S. citizens liable for payment of income tax on their personal earnings or other receipts. No U.S. citizen is required by law to file any 1040 U.S. Individual Income Tax Return or to pay any "income" tax on his or her earnings, or on any profits or gains derived from business, investments or from buying or selling any form of property.

Because there has never been an "income" tax imposed on individual citizens or their earnings, the mistaken idea that repealing the Sixteenth Amendment would eliminate income tax on individual citizens is totally erroneous because the Sixteenth Amendment did not authorize any tax on U.S. citizens or their earnings. Instead, a repeal of the Amendment would simply restore the legal force of the Pollock decision of 1895 and make any tax on the privileged activities of corporations unconstitutional.

It is this writer's opinion that the intent of President Taft in his speech to Congress was very clearly limited to passage of an amendment which would provide Congress with the authority to levy an excise tax on <u>only corporate</u> income (profit or gain) earned through the privileged activities of incorporation. No suggestion was ever made by the president in this proposal that the limitations and prohibitions against direct taxation of U.S. citizens on their own earnings or other receipts would become taxable by reason of the amendment. This writer's underlinings in the following speech by President Taft merely emphasize and support that conclusion.

A judicially recognized rule of law which is stated by *Sutherland's Rules of Statutory Construction* is also supportive of this conclusion. It states as follows:

> ***One of the most readily available intrinsic aids to the interpretation of statutes is the action of the legislature on <u>amendments</u> which are proposed to be made during the course of consideration in the legislature. Both the state and federal courts will refer to proposed changes in a bill in order to interpret the statute as finally enacted. The journals of the legislature are the usual source for this information. Generally, <u>the rejection of an amendment</u> indicates that the legislature does not intend the bill to include the provisions in the rejected amendment. (Sutherland on Statutory Construction),*** *Sec. 48.18 (5th Edition)* (emphasis added)

Sutherland's legal maxim quoted above is a well established rule of law in determining the legislative intent of any statute or (as in this case) an amendment to the Constitution. Accordingly, the congressional debates preceding enactment of the amendment must be reviewed to clarify the amendment's intent. Any changes to the proposed amendment that were rejected during these congressional debates prior to its passage must then also be rejected as not being consistent with the intent of the amendment. In the case of the Sixteenth Amendment, there were, prior to its final enactment, two proposed amendments by Senator McLaurin of Mississippi and then later another by Senator Bristow of Kansas, both of which would have effectively eliminated the constitutional provisions in Article 1, Section 2, Clause 3 and Article 1, Section 9, Clause 4 of the Constitution, thereby allowing <u>direct</u> taxation of citizen's earnings or other receipts. These rejected amendments clearly showed that Congress had no intent whatsoever to eliminate these long-standing provisions limiting direct taxation. These decisions to reject these proposed amendments in the congressional debates were in harmony with President Taft's limited intent to authorize a corporate excise/income tax statute only that would not be struck down by the courts because of the existence of the ruling in Pollock v. Farmers Loan and Trust Co., discussed earlier in this chapter. The full history of these proposed and rejected amendments is available by internet research in the Congressional Record (44 Cong. Rec. 4109 (1909)).

For the reader's education, the entire text of President Taft's speech to Congress on June 16, 1909 is reproduced as follows with underlinings for emphasis as explained in this chapter:

The Secretary (of the Senate) read as follows from the President (copied from the Congressional Record-pages 3344 and 3345):

To the Senate and House of Representatives:

It is the constitutional duty of the President from time to time to recommend to the consideration of Congress such matters as he shall judge necessary and expedient. In my inaugural address, immediately preceding this present extraordinary session of Congress, I invited attention to the necessity for a revision of the tariff at this session, and stated the principles upon which I thought the revision should be effected. I referred to the then rapidly increasing deficit and pointed out the obligation on the part of the framers of the tariff bill to arrange the duty so as to secure an adequate income, and suggested that if it was not possible to do so by import duties, new kinds of taxation must be adopted, and among them I recommended a graduated inheritance tax as correct in principle and as certain and easy of collection. The House of Representatives has adopted the suggestion, and has provided in the bill it passed for collection of such a tax. In the Senate the action of its Finance Committee and the course of the debate indicate that it may not agree to this provision, and it is now proposed to make up the deficit by the imposition of a general income tax, in form and substance of almost exactly the same character as that which in the case of Pollock v. Farmers' Loan and Trust Company (157 U.S. 420) was held by the Supreme Court to be a direct tax, and therefore not within the power of the Federal Government to impose unless apportioned among the several States according to population. This new proposal, which I did not discuss in my inaugural address or in my message at the opening of the present session, makes it appropriate for me to submit to the Congress certain additional recommendations.

The decision of the Supreme Court in the income-tax cases deprived the National Government of a power which, by reason of previous decisions of the court, it was generally supposed that Government had. It is undoubtedly a power the National Government ought to have. It might be indispensable to the Nation's life in great crises. Although I have not considered a constitutional amendment as necessary to the exercise of certain phases of this power, <u>a mature consideration has satisfied me that an amendment is the only proper course for its establishment to its full extent. I therefore recommend to the Congress that both Houses, by a two-thirds vote, shall propose an amendment to the Constitution conferring the power to levy an income tax upon the National Government without apportionment among the States in proportion to population.</u>

This course is much to be preferred to the one proposed of reenacting a law once judicially declared to be unconstitutional. For the Congress to assume that the court will reverse itself, and to enact legislation on such an assumption, will not strengthen popular confidence in the stability of judicial construction of the Constitution. It is much wiser policy to accept the decision and <u>remedy the defect by amendment</u> in due and regular course.

Again, it is clear that by the enactment of the proposed law the Congress will not be bringing money into the Treasury to meet the present deficiency, but by putting on the statute book a law already there and never repealed will simply be suggesting to the executive officers of the Government their possible duty to invoke litigation. If the court should maintain its former view, no tax would be collected at all. If it should ultimately reverse itself, still no taxes would have been collected until after protracted delay.

It is said the difficulty and delay in securing the approval of three-fourths of the States will destroy all chance of adopting the amendment. Of course, no one can speak with certainty upon this point, but I have become convinced that a great majority of the people of this country are in favor of vesting the National Government with power to levy an income tax, and that they will secure the adoption of the amendment in the States, if proposed to them.

Second, the decision in the Pollock case left power in the National Government to levy an excise tax, which accomplishes the same purpose as a corporation income tax and is free from certain objections urged to the proposed income tax measure.

I therefore recommend an amendment to the tariff bill imposing upon all corporations and joint stock companies for profit, except national banks (otherwise taxed), savings banks, and building and loan associations, an excise tax measured by 2 percent on the net income of such corporations. This is an EXCISE TAX upon the privilege of doing business as an artificial entity and of freedom from a general partnership liability enjoyed by those who own stock.

I am informed that a 2 percent tax of this character would bring into the Treasury of the United States not less than $25,000.000.

The decision of the Supreme Court in the case of Spreckels Sugar Refining Company against McClain (192 U.S. 397) seems clearly to establish the principle that such a tax as this is an EXCISE TAX UPON PRIVILEGE and not a direct tax on property, and is within the federal power without apportionment according to population. The tax on net income is preferable to one proportionate to a percentage of the gross receipts, because it is a tax upon success and not failure. It imposes a burden at the source of the income, at a time when the corporation is well able to pay and when collection is easy.

Another merit of this tax is the federal supervision which must be exercised in order to make the law effective over the annual account and business transactions of all corporations. While the faculty of assuming a corporate form has been of the utmost utility in the business world, it is also true that substantially all of the abuses and all of the evils which have aroused the public to the necessity of reform were made possible by the use of the very faculty. If now, by a perfectly legitimate and effective system of taxation, we are incidentally able to possess the Government and the stockholders and the public of the knowledge of the real business transactions and the gains and profits of every corporation in the country, we have made a long step toward that supervisory control of corporations which may prevent a further abuse of power.

I recommend, then, first, the adoption of a joint resolution of *two-thirds of both Houses, <u>proposing to the States an amendment to the Constitution granting to the Federal Government the right to levy and collect an income tax without apportionment among the States according to population; and, second, the enactment, as part of the pending revenue measure</u>, either as a substitute for, or in addition to, the inheritance tax, <u>of an EXCISE TAX UPON ALL CORPORATIONS, measured by 2 percent of their net income.</u>* (emphasis added) ~ **William Howard Taft**

CHAPTER III

WHOSE RECEIPTS ARE "INCOME"?

There is much confusion and misunderstanding as to the meaning of the term "income" when it is used in tax law to describe monies received by individuals. People who study the Internal Revenue (I.R.) Code, (Title 26 of the U.S. Code, available in public libraries) to find the meaning of "income" are surprised when they cannot find a definition of the term "income" in the Code. It cannot be found because it is <u>not there</u> as explained in the decision in the case of **<u>U.S. v. Ballard</u>, 535 F2d 400, p. 404 (1976)**. The court states:

> *The general term 'income' is <u>not defined</u> in the Internal Revenue Code.* (emphasis added)

The <u>Ballard</u> court's statement can easily make people accept the false idea promoted by the IRS that all monies that "come in" to <u>all individuals</u> are "income". This conclusion sounds logical, but, as we will see in this chapter, further research shows it is legally taxable only when the "income" is earned by, and payable to, certain entities-specifically corporations or non-resident aliens-who are not protected against such taxation by our Constitution as are U.S. citizens.

Those individuals who study further often rely on court decisions that make statements about "income" such as the words of the U.S. Supreme Court in the decision of **<u>Stratton's Independence v. Howbert</u>, 231 U.S. 399, p. 415 (1913)**, a corporation case arising under the <u>Corporation</u> Excise Tax Act of 1909. The Court stated:

> *Income may be defined as the gain derived from capital, from labor, or from both combined.* (emphasis added)

It is essential for a proper understanding of this definition that we remember that this case involved <u>corporation</u> income-<u>not</u> "individual" income. In Chapter II we showed that the Sixteenth Amendment had been proposed by President Taft only a few years before the Stratton case, and its purpose was to tax <u>corporate profits only</u>. The President had no thought of taxing citizens' earnings or other receipts. So the Stratton court's "income" definition related specifically and <u>only</u> to corporate gains earned and <u>derived</u>

from the use of capital and labor. An income tax on the earnings of U.S. citizens had never even been considered by our legislature at this time in our nation's history, making it even more obvious that the Stratton court's definition related only to corporate "income" ("income" being profit derived from the use of capital and labor).

However, because the definition of "income" in the Stratton case did not specifically exclude individuals, it could lead to the erroneous conclusion that if there is a profit or gain to any individual, then it is "income". As will be shown, however, this may or may not be true depending on the citizenship and legal residence of the recipient-individual. Many of the court decisions on which justice department lawyers and IRS personnel rely involve corporations, all of whose "income" measured by their profits are legally taxable, by I.R. Code Section 11. Also, those individuals who have voluntarily signed and filed returns, thereby acknowledging under penalty of perjury on the return that their receipts are "income" and that they owe "income" tax, have created documentary evidence by their voluntary filing and signing the return under the legal doctrine of "presumption" that they are "taxpayers"!

I.R. Code Is Tricky

Most people, including many accountants and attorneys, do not know that the taxes on "income" apply only to government-created entities such as corporations that are taxed under Section 11 of the I.R. Code, and also under Section 1441 to the receipts of a certain legal class of individuals (not to all individuals) called "non-resident aliens" who are not protected by our Constitution against direct taxation because they are not U.S. citizens. The I.R. Code identifies that legal class of individuals to whom the income tax laws apply. In order to understand the true meaning of the I.R. Code, it is absolutely necessary to learn whose monies are "income" and whose monies are not "income" according to the Code. The Internal Revenue Service's own Publication 1140 (Rev. 4-87) even instructs us how to determine facts about the tax laws. It states:

> *Research the Internal Revenue Code to determine if it allows the issue. The Code is the highest authority you can cite and should be used in lieu of any other legal instrument.*

Since there is no definition of the term "income" in the I.R. Code (see **U.S. v. Ballard** above) to find an answer to this key question, we must see if receipts of any kind are either listed or <u>identified</u> as being "income" in the Code. Any such provision would answer the key question, "Whose earnings are income?" without being a definition of the <u>term</u> "income".

Sec. 1461 in Chapter 3 of the I.R. Code is well known by those who have studied the Code to be the <u>ONLY</u> section making a "person" (a defined <u>term</u> with many definitions-see Chapter IV) <u>liable</u> for the payment of "income tax". Therefore, Sec. 1461 is a logical place to start in determining <u>what monies</u> are involved in the creation of liability for payment of "income" tax. Section 1461 states:

> *Every <u>person</u> required to deduct and withhold any tax under this chapter is hereby <u>made liable</u> for such tax...* (emphasis added)

The words "this chapter" mean Chapter 3 which is titled "Withholding Of Tax On Nonresident Aliens, Foreign Partnerships and Foreign Corporations".

SECTION 1441 ANSWERS KEY QUESTIONS

The only Code section in Chapter 3 requiring any "person" to "deduct and withhold any tax" from "income" accruing to non-resident aliens is Sec. 1441 which states under Sub-Section (a):

> *...all <u>persons</u>...<u>having</u> the control, receipt, custody, disposal, or payment of any of the <u>items of income specified in subsection (b)</u> to the extent that any of such items constitutes gross income from sources within the United States, <u>of any nonresident alien individual, or of any foreign partnership</u> shall...deduct and withhold from such items a tax equal to 30 percent thereof...*(emphasis added)

> *Sub-section 1441(<u>a</u>) applies to "items of income specified in subsection 1441(<u>b</u>)...<u>of any non-resident alien individual</u>, or of <u>any foreign partnership</u>", <u>only</u>, but **NOT TO RECEIPTS OF A CITIZEN**.* (emphasis added)

> Sub-section 1441(<u>b</u>) identifies the receipts of non-resident aliens

and foreign partnerships as being "income". It states:

> *Income items. <u>The items of income referred to in subsection (a) are</u> interest…, dividends, rents, <u>salaries, wages</u>, premiums, annuities, compensations, remunerations, emoluments, or other fixed or determinable annual or periodical gains, profits, and income…* (emphasis added)

This section of the law very clearly shows that the monies listed are "<u>income</u>" <u>only</u> when received by or payable to a non-resident individual or foreign partnership, but <u>not by or to a U.S. citizen</u> who IS constitutionally immune from direct taxation as is repeatedly shown in Chapter I and elsewhere in this book.

Law Means Only What Is Stated

Of equal importance is the fact that there is <u>nothing in Sec. 1441 or elsewhere in the I.R. Code</u> that identifies receipts belonging to or owing to an individual U.S. citizen as being "income". Some people who learn about Section 1441 <u>mistakenly assume</u> that, because the receipts of non-resident aliens are "income" when received from sources within the U.S., that the receipts of individual citizens must also be "income" as well. However, the U.S. Supreme Court has ruled that the <u>tax laws mean only that which is stated and nothing more</u>. As stated in Chapter I, in the decision in **Gould v. Gould, 245 U.S. 150 (1917)** the U.S. Supreme Court stated:

> *In the interpretation of <u>statutes levying taxes</u> it is the <u>established rule not to extend their provisions</u>, by implication, <u>beyond the clear Import of the language used</u>, or <u>to enlarge their operations so as to embrace matters not specifically pointed out</u>. In case of doubt they are construed most strongly against Government, and in favor of the citizen.* (emphasis added)

When discussing the meaning of the term "income" as used in the I.R. Code, IRS agents sometime cite Section 61(a) as being a section defining "income". That section defines "<u>gross</u> income" as being all "income" from all sources, but it does <u>not</u> define the term "income". Section 61(a) lists fifteen <u>sources</u> from which taxable "income" could be <u>derived</u>, but we now know that this list of fifteen "sources" of income can be "income" <u>only</u> if received by or payable to a non-resident alien, a foreign partnership or foreign corporation according to the I.R. Code, Sections 1441(a) or 1442(a).

According to the law, money from these sources would <u>not</u> be income if received by a citizen because NOWHERE IN THE I.R. CODE DOES IT STATE THAT RECEIPTS OF CITIZENS ARE "INCOME". Code Section 61(a) does not explain that for the monies coming from the various sources to legally be "income" to an individual the individual-recipient must be a foreign person, foreign partnership or foreign corporation only (as stated in Sections 1441 or 1442), not a U.S. citizen who is protected against any such direct capitation tax by Article 1, Section 9, Clause 4 of the Constitution as shown in Chapter I.

IRS Says Taxing Foreigners' Receipts Is Constitutional

Those who have studied the legality of the "income" tax know that the IRS frequently cites the decision of the U.S. Supreme Court in **Brushaber v. Union Pacific R.R. Co., Inc., 240 U.S. 1 (1915)** as the decision which established the constitutionality of the "income" tax, but only when applied as an indirect excise tax upon corporate profits or gains, or on money received by an <u>alien</u>-individual-<u>but not against a citizen-individual</u> who is constitutionally protected against any such tax as shown in the previous paragraph. It is particularly important to understand that the <u>IRS itself</u> relies on the <u>Brushaber</u> decision when, or if, the constitutionality of the "income tax" is ever challenged.

In its <u>own</u> document, I.R.S. T.D. (Treasury Decision) #2313, issued soon after the <u>Brushaber</u> decision, Mr. W.H. Osborn, then Commissioner of the Internal Revenue Service, refers specifically to the <u>Brushaber</u> decision and clearly shows in T.D. #2313 that the "<u>income</u>" involved in that decision was <u>corporate profits and gains in the form of</u> MONIES ACCRUING TO NON-RESIDENT ALIEN INDIVIDUALS. Such non-resident alien-individuals whose receipts from investments in United States securities were the subject of the <u>Brushaber</u> court's decision. The court ruled that such monies were taxable as "income". This Treasury Department decision was an obvious <u>recognition</u> by the IRS that the <u>Brushaber</u> court's decision had ruled that the income tax authority which was established by the Sixteenth Amendment included authority to tax the privilege granted to foreigners to invest in United States securities. It is revealing that <u>no mention</u> was made in this decision of any authority to tax earnings or other receipts of U.S.

citizens!

The T.D. 2313 ruling even specifies use of IRS Form 1040 for the purpose of reporting such "income" of non-resident aliens by those having control of such monies. No suggestion was made in the decision of any taxing authority by the Brushaber court to tax the earnings or receipts of U.S. citizens!

T.D. 2313 states in part:

*Under the decision of the Supreme Court of the United States in the case of **Brushaber v. Union Pacific Railway Co.**, decided January 21, 1916, it is hereby held that **income accruing to nonresident aliens** in the form of interest from the bonds and dividends on the stock of domestic corporations **is subject to the income tax** imposed by the act of October 3, 1913. "The responsible heads, **agents** or **representatives of non-resident aliens, who are in charge of the property owned** or business carried on in the United States, shall make a full and complete return of the income therefrom on **Form 1040**, revised, and **shall pay any** and **all tax**, normal and additional, assessed upon the income **received by them in behalf of their nonresident alien principals...*** (emphasis added)

The wording in the Brushaber decision issued by the U.S. Supreme Court did not reveal that the "income" at issue in this case was, in fact, money being paid to Mr. Brushaber as a fiduciary in the form of interest and/or dividends owing to Mr. Brushaber's non-resident alien client! This IRS document, dated March 21, 1916, only two months after the Supreme Court ruled in the Brushaber case, shows that IRS lawyers knew that Mr. Brushaber was acting as a fiduciary, holding stocks and bonds in Union Pacific Railway Co. for his non-resident alien principal.

Since the Brushaber decision is the primary case relied upon by the IRS to prove the constitutionality of the income tax when applied to receipts of an individual, the IRS has, through the issue of this Treasury Department Decision #2313 explained that the "income" involved in the case was money owing to non-resident alien individuals ONLY. The IRS, however, did not, because they know that they could not lawfully claim that the receipts of

U.S. citizens could constitutionally be taxed. They knew very well that the U.S. Constitution in Article 1, Section 9, Clause 4 pointedly states:

No capitation...

This means <u>no tax on individual citizens</u>. *Black's Law Dictionary* defines a capitation as:

Capitation: A tax or imposition upon the person.

In the decision in the case of **Peck v. Lowe, 247 U.S. 165 (1918)**, the U.S. Supreme Court, commenting on the "income" tax, stated:

The Sixteenth Amendment does <u>not</u> extend the power of taxation to new or <u>excepted</u> subjects... (emphasis added)

This U.S. Supreme Court decision clearly confirms retention of the constitutional prohibitions against any tax on U.S. citizen's earnings. Use of the term "excepted subjects" in this court's decision is a clear reference to capitation taxes (a tax on the person) which the court knew were prohibited by Article 1, Section 9, Clause 4 of the Constitution. In Chapter I of this book we cited several Supreme Court decisions which support this "excepted subject" rule. Without quoting again from these court decisions, we call attention to them again with the suggestion that, for better understanding, the court quotes from these decisions which are shown in Chapter I be read again. These Supreme Court decisions are from: **Butchers Union v. Crescent City Co., 111 U.S. 746 (1883), Allgeyer v. Louisiana, 165 U.S. 578 (1897)** and **Coppage v. Kansas, 236 U.S. 1 (1915).**

I.R. Code Section 1 does not impose an income tax on U.S. citizens. Section 1 states, in part, as follows:

Part I.-TAX ON INDIVIDUALS

Sec. 1. Tax imposed.
(a) Married individuals <u>filing joint returns</u> and surviving spouses.
There is hereby <u>imposed</u> on the <u>taxable income</u> of -
(1) every married individual (as defined in section 7703) <u>who makes a single return</u> jointly with his spouse under section

6013, and...

(d) Married individuals filing separate returns...
(emphasis added)

Despite the contrary suggestion by the IRS and many tax preparation forms, accountants and even some lawyers, I.R. Code Section 1 does not and cannot impose an income tax on the earnings or receipts of U.S. citizens. First, Section 1 of Part 1 has the deceptive, meaningless heading, "TAX ON INDIVIDUALS", also this Code section shows that it imposes a tax on "taxable income"-not on individuals as falsely implied by the heading of Part 1. The adjective "taxable" which modifies "income" proves that not all "income" is taxable. And, as we will see, only a very select few "individuals" can be "liable" for income tax in any event. I.R. Code Section 7806(b) shows that there is no legal value to a Code section heading. It states:

> **Sec. 7806. Construction of title.**
> **(b) Arrangement and classification.**
> No inference, implication, or presumption of legislative construction shall be drawn or made by reason of the location or grouping of any particular section or provision or portion of this title, nor shall any table of contents, table of cross references, or similar outline, analysis, or descriptive matter relating to the contents of this title be given any legal effect...(emphasis added)

This Code section means that the words in the heading of Section 1 which states "TAX ON INDIVIDUALS" in Section 1 has no legal effect because they are clearly "descriptive matter" as shown and underlined for emphasis in the above quotation. This writer believes that such words used as headings in this and other code sections are intentionally placed there by the I.R.S. in order to confuse and deceive citizens into believing that the taxes are imposed on them personally, even though the laws impose all "income" taxes only on the "income" of corporations, limited partnerships, trusts, etc. and certain foreign entities but not on individual citizens who are protected by the constitutional prohibition against any capitation tax under Article 1, Section 9, Clause 4.

This imposition statute is clearly limited by Section 1(a) to an imposition only on "individuals" who either have filed or are filing income tax returns-not to U.S. citizens who know the truth and have stopped filing. Also, this section imposes a tax on "taxable income" which is defined in Section 441(a) and (b) as something that can be computed on the basis of a "taxpayer's taxable year". Therefore, as we have previously stated, the "individual" described in this Code Section 1 must be a "taxpayer" in order to have a "taxable year" which creates "taxable income". All of these terms are shown in either Section 1 or in Section 441 which is referred to in Section 1 by use of the term "taxable income". As shown earlier in this chapter, Section 1441 is the only section of the Internal Revenue Code which refers to a non-resident alien "individual" as the individual whose receipts are identified in that Code section as "income". It is very revealing that a U.S. citizen's earnings or other receipts are not identified anywhere in the I.R. Code as being "income".

Further, the use of the wording "who makes a single return" in section (1)(a)(1) limits application of this section to those who have made a return. Section 1(d) also refers to married individuals "filing separate returns". Consequently, this Section 1 applies only to U.S citizen "individuals" who have made or filed returns-not to U.S. citizen-individuals who have learned the truth, have stopped filing returns altogether because they know they have no liability for payment of any income tax on their earnings! For all these reasons, Section 1 can only apply to U.S. citizen-"individuals" who voluntarily continue to self-impose the income tax upon themselves by filing returns, or to those custodians or withholding agents who have a statutory (Code section) responsibility under Sections 1461 or 1442 of the I.R. Code to deduct and withhold monies payable to non-resident alien individuals, foreign partnerships or foreign corporations and are thereby "liable for" tax under Section 1461 of the I.R. Code. Remember that "tax payer" is a defined term under the internal revenue code under section 7701 (a)(14) as "any person subject to any internal revenue tax."

Careful reading also shows that I.R. Code, Chapter 21, Section 3101 which imposes the so-called, but miscalled "payroll tax", often also miscalled the "employment", FICA (Federal Insurance Contributions Act) or "Social Security" tax does not impose any tax on payroll or employment but rather imposes the tax on "income" which, as we explained earlier in this chapter, is not a defined term anywhere in the I.R. Code. It is also not imposed on "wages" as many people mistakenly believe. Wages are merely used as a measurement of the amount of the so-called FICA tax which as will be shown in Chapter V, is actually only a flat-rate <u>income</u> tax that applies only in the four island possessions! Chapters IV and V will explain in detail that "wages" is a defined term in the I.R. Code which limits its application in such a manner that it cannot be considered even as a <u>measurement</u> of any "income" tax on U.S. citizens' earnings or other receipts. The Social Security tax is also <u>not</u> a "TAX ON EMPLOYEES" as deceptively stated in the <u>heading</u> of Sub-Chapter A in the table of contents at the beginning of Chapter 21, because of the limitation contained in Code Section 7806(b) stated earlier in this chapter which forbids any legal meaning to be given to words such as "descriptive matter" in the <u>headings</u> of Code sections.

Summary

The term "income", by law (I.R. Code), applies to receipts of non-resident alien individuals, foreign partnerships and foreign corporations but not to receipts of citizens, according to the I.R. Code.

As is stated repeatedly in this book, I.R. Code, Section 1461 is the <u>ONLY</u> section making anyone <u>liable</u> for payment of "income" tax. Section 1461 makes certain "persons" only-such as corporations or those individuals acting for corporations, non-resident aliens or other government-privileged entities <u>liable</u> for payment of "income" taxes which are required by Section 1441 to be withheld from receipts payable to non-resident alien individuals, foreign partnerships or, under Section 1442, payable to foreign corporations, but <u>not</u> from the earnings or receipts of U.S. citizens.

Unfortunately, most citizens have been deceived and misled by the IRS, their lawyers, accountants and tax preparers into believing incorrectly that the law says that <u>their</u> receipts <u>are</u> "income", and that they <u>are liable</u> for payment of a tax on that "income". Consequently, they sign and file returns and/or Form W-4 Employees' Withholding Allowance Certificates, thinking that they are required by law to do so. When they sign and file Form 1040 "income" tax returns (voluntary actions), they <u>certify by their signature under penalties of perjury</u> that their receipts <u>are</u> "income" and that they <u>are</u> liable for payment of "income" tax. These certifications can be considered by the IRS and by the courts under authority of Title 28, Section 1746 to be legal grounds under the legal doctrine (rule) of "presumption" for the IRS to claim that the citizens' receipts <u>are</u> "income" by their own admission and <u>are</u>, therefore, subject to the "income" tax. *Black's Law Dictionary, 5th Edition* defines "presumption" as follows:

A presumption is a rule of law, statutory or judicial, by which finding of a basic fact gives rise to existence of presumed fact, <u>until presumption is rebutted</u>... (emphasis added)

Because this definition allows (as underlined in the definition shown above) for a rebuttal, in order to legally rebut such presumptions, many citizens who have learned the truth have stopped allowing the IRS to deceive them into being "volunteers". They prepare and file in the record office of the court house of the county of their residence an affidavit stating that they had been misled and deceived by constructive fraud-that such false belief had previously required them by law to sign and file, under penalties of perjury, IRS forms. These forms, which citizens are <u>not</u> required to file, include but are not limited to the IRS' 1040 tax returns and W-4 Employees' Withholding Allowance Certificates. The 1040 and 1040A income tax forms which are signed and filed under penalties of perjury indicate incorrectly that the signer was <u>required</u> to file income tax returns and make payment of "income" tax. The AFFIDAVIT OF REVOCATION AND RECISSION, which is discussed in detail in Chapter VIII of this book, <u>revokes the signatures</u> on all these previously-filed forms and returns, making it difficult, if not impossible, for the IRS to use them against the citizen in order to claim that they either <u>allowed</u> withholding in the case of the W4 Employees' Withholding Allowance Certificate, or that they acknowledged that they were "taxpayers" who owed a tax in the case of Form 1040 returns! The Affidavit rebuts all such evidence and creates a convincing reason for the IRS to forego any criminal charge which they might otherwise consider bringing against a citizen who had not filed such an affidavit. A sample AFFIDAVIT OF REVOCATION AND RESCISSION document which has been used appears at the end of Chapter VIII of this book. Contact this author for information on when and how the AFFIDAVIT can be inexpensively filed publicly for future use.

The above facts may surprise many people but millions of citizens have already learned the truth about the misapplication of the income tax laws by the IRS, and they have stopped filing income tax returns according to a report in *USA Today* on September 30, 1992. The report stated:

As many as 10 million people and businesses didn't file for 1990, the IRS says.

In subsequent years there have been greatly increased numbers of educated non-filers reported. It is this writer's hope that, as knowledge of IRS deception spreads, perhaps, in part, through wide reading of this book, that many more U.S. citizens will join the steadily increasing numbers whose anger at being victimized for so many years will finally be heard by Congress resulting in legislation to require the IRS to cease their misapplication of the I.R. Code to the earnings and other receipts of U.S. citizens..

CHAPTER IV

THE INTERNAL REVENUE CODE-
A MASTERPIECE OF TRICKERY AND DECEPTION

The previous chapters have shown the constitutional limitations against the imposition of any Federal taxes on United States citizens. In this chapter, we will show how the I.R. Code uses words of common usage as "terms", and which have definitions (meanings) for usage in the Code that are far different from the meanings of those words in common usage which leads us to the wrong understanding of the law. The very well-trained and clever writers of the wording in the I.R. Code relating to income tax were fully aware of the necessity to write the law in such a way that there was no conflict with the constitutional prohibitions against the imposition of any Federal tax on U.S. citizens. In order to avoid constitutional conflict, they have intentionally worded the income tax law in such a manner that it incorrectly <u>appears</u> to the average reader that the income tax is imposed upon the earnings of U.S. citizens even though a careful study of the I.R. Code shows that, in fact, <u>no</u> income tax <u>is</u> imposed on the earnings or other receipts of U.S. citizens.

Unfortunately, there is no way the ordinary reader can easily identify the words that are used as "terms" in the I.R. Code. Words that are defined in the Code that are "terms" are not printed in italics, bold print, underlining or other styles of print that differ from ordinary print and are hard to identify without intense study of the Code.

As an example, the word "taxpayer" (one word, not two) which is widely used throughout the Code in IRS publications and in news articles relating to income tax is a word that is used as a <u>term</u> in the Code. It is legally defined in the Internal Revenue Code in Section 7701(a)(14) as *"... any person <u>subject to</u> any internal revenue tax."* (emphasis added) Note that this definition does not state that one is a "taxpayer" simply because he has paid a tax. To the contrary, a person who has paid any tax is, in fact, a "tax payer" (two words not defined in the I.R. Code) but doing so does not put one within the legal definition of the term "taxpayer" (one word) as that term <u>is</u> legally used and <u>defined</u> in Section 7701(a)(14) of the I.R. Code as *"any person <u>subject to</u> any internal revenue tax"*. (emphasis added) Such a person must be <u>made "subject to"</u> the tax under another Code section. It is important to know that the words "subject to" (a tax) means "liable for"

62

as the Court of Appeals stated in headnote #2 of <u>Houston Street Corp. v. Commissioner of Internal Revenue</u>, 84 F2d, 821 as follows: Phrases "liable for such tax" and "subject to a tax" are interchangeable and connote payment of a tax. Also *Black's Law Dictionary*, 5th Edition, states that "subject to" means "liable". This is important because nowhere in the I.R. Code is it stated that any person is "subject to" any tax. Those persons upon whom a tax is imposed are described in the Code as "being liable" for the tax. For example, I.R. Code Section 1461, the only section of the Code requiring any person to pay income tax, uses the word "made liable". Section 1461 states: *"Every person required to deduct and withhold any tax under this chapter is hereby <u>made liable</u> for such tax."* (emphasis added)

There are many other words in common usage which are used and defined as <u>terms</u> in the Internal Revenue Code which have legal definitions different from their meaning in common usage. Some of these terms are: "person", "United States", "States", "includes" and "including", "trade or business" "wages", "employer", "employee" and "employment". The terms "wages", "employer", "employee" and "employment" will also be discussed in Chapter V.

When one reads the many Code sections where these words are used extensively, the difference is striking between the generally understood meaning of the word in common usage and their true, legal meaning when they are used as "terms" in the Code which governs in legal proceedings. Consider the term "United States" as an example. <u>Amazingly, there are fourteen different definitions of the term "United States" in the I.R. Code.</u> One might understandably ask, "How can this be? Everybody knows what "United States" means. When we see this apparent verbal trickery repeated in the Code over and over again, it becomes obvious that the deception has to be intentional; that is, the true, legal meanings of the terms are intentionally hidden in the definitions which are generally found in separate Code sections apart from where the terms are used so that the reader will have an incorrect understanding that the law applies to him. Trickery? Deception? Oh yes-unquestionably so, because if the true, legal meaning of the terms were known to the reader (including most lawyers) when he first reads the Code section, he would recognize that the law does not apply to ordinary citizens-a correct conclusion that the IRS doesn't want him to have. At the same time the limited meanings of the true, legal definitions make the statute and the I.R. Code provisions constitutional because they limit the application of the law, often geographically, in order to assure their constitutionality. As an example, Code Section 3121(e)(2) defines "United States" as used in the so-called "Social Security" tax chapter as the four island possessions-Puerto Rico, the Virgin Islands, Guam and American Samoa only.

The IRS unlawfully administers the Social Security tax as a direct tax on the wages of citizens of the fifty states. As we previously stated in Chapter I, the only Federal direct tax that can constitutionally be levied must be apportioned by relative population on the governments of the states of the union and not on American citizens. In Chapter V, we will show that the Social Security tax is simply another "income" tax in the form of an indirect excise tax on the receipts of non-resident aliens only which may legally and constitutionally be imposed only in the specified four island possessions. Because of this territorial restriction in the definition of the "term" "United States" contained in Section 3121(e)(2) the so-called "Social Security" tax applies in the stated four island possessions only, and not in the fifty states of the union. This limited territorial application keeps the Social Security tax constitutional. An in depth discussion of the very limited application of both the Social Security tax and the withholding of money for tax are included in Chapter V of this book titled *Social Security A Flat-Rate Income Tax And Voluntary Witholding.*

The IRS' statutory drafters know very well how to define terms in order to make the law constitutional. For instance, Code Section 4612(a)(4), which relates only to a tax on crude oil, defines the term "United States" as: "*the fifty states, the District of Columbia, the Commonwealth of Puerto Rico, any possession of the United States, the Commonwealth of the Northern Mariana Islands and the trust territory of the Pacific Islands.*" This defining Code section shows that when the law includes the fifty states of the union, they are specifically named as such in the defining section! However, it is important to understand that this broad wording in Section 4612(a)(4)(A) limits this definition of the term "United States" to its use in Sub-Chapter A of Chapter 38 only which imposes a tax on specific crude oil and petroleum products! This definition of the term "United States" doesn't apply elsewhere in the I.R. Code.

Code Section 7701(a)(9) is also among the fourteen separate definitions of the term "United States". It states: "The term 'United States' includes only the States and the District of Columbia." Immediately following this definition is the definition of the term "State" (singular) which is defined in Section 7701(a)(10) as the District of Columbia (only). One might very well ask: How can "State" mean the District of Columbia? The answer, very simply, is because that is exactly how it is specifically defined, and, in fact, the "term" "State" must be so defined because the Federal government has no constitutional authority or jurisdiction in or over the separate fifty states of the union or their governments! For this reason the word "States" as used in Section 7701(a)(9) also can not mean the fifty states of the union. However, the Federal government does have total governmental authority and jurisdiction in and over the District of Columbia and the island possessions because these are outside the boundaries of any of the fifty states of the union!

In order to understand the apparent confusion in the wording of Sections 7701(a)(9) and (10) previously defined, let's again take a closer look at the word States (plural) as used in the body of Section 7701(a)(9) and the word State (singular) as used in Section 7701(a)(10). We have already shown that the word "State" (singular) is defined in 7701(a)(10) as the District of Columbia only. Section 7701(m)(1) explains that singular terms are to be defined as including the plural. Therefore, "States" as used in the body of Section 7701(a)(9) must also mean the same as State (singular). Since State (singular) is defined in Section 7701(a)(10) as the District of Columbia, this means that the legal definition of States (plural) in the body of Section 7701(a)(9) also means the District of Columbia. Therefore, both Code sections limit the definitions of both State (singular) and States (plural) to mean the same thing-the District of Columbia only. The following paragraph will show why this must be true to keep the meanings of these terms constitutional.

Those analyzing the true meaning of Section 7701(a)(10) often question the meaning of the words at the end of this Code section which read: *"where such construction is necessary to carry out provisions of this title."* As we have explained in an earlier chapter of this book, the taxing statutes must be written in conformity with the constitutional prohibitions limiting direct federal taxation to taxes that are imposed by apportionment among the fifty state governments. Therefore, these words must mean *"in order to insure the constitutionality of the taxing statutes."* This gives us even more understanding of why State and States both legally mean ONLY the District of Columbia and the island possessions where jurisdiction of the federal government is applicable.

Another misunderstanding of these I.R. Code sections arises from an incorrect assumption of the meaning of the <u>terms</u> "includes and "including". Section 7701(c) is the I.R. Code section defining these terms which states as follows: "The <u>terms</u> 'include' and 'including', when used in a definition contained in this title, shall not be deemed to exclude things otherwise within the meaning of the term defined." We first must see what the courts have to say about the words "include" and "including". The Supreme Court has given us the answer to this question in the case of **Montello Salt v. Utah, 221 U.S. 452** wherein they noted that "including" is the participle of the word "include" which they state is defined in the New Century Dictionary as to "confine within something", "to hold as in an inclosure", "inclose", "contain". Quite clearly these definitions show that <u>"includes" and "including" are words of limitation or confinement and not of expansion</u>. This is in conformity with *Sutherland's Rules of Statutory Construction,* an authoritative legal guidebook, often referenced in law schools, which under Section 6601 titled *Strict Construction of Statutes Creating Tax Liabilities,* explains the limited application of tax laws. It refers to the U.S. Supreme Court decision of **Gould v. Gould**, **245 U.S. 151** which states: "*In the interpretation of statutes levying taxes it is the established rule <u>not</u> to extend their provisions by implication beyond the clear import of the language used, <u>or to enlarge their operation so as to embrace matters not specifically pointed out</u>. In case of doubt, they are construed most strongly against the government and in favor of the citizen.*" (emphasis added) So the Supreme Court tells us in this decision that the I.R. Code sections mean <u>only that which is stated</u>. Nothing else can be added to that which is stated in the Code section. Also, the Supreme Court stated in the decision of U.S. Merriam, 263 U.S. 179 (1923) :

But in <u>statutes levying taxes</u> the literally meaning of the words employed is most important, for such statutes are not to be extended by implication beyond the clear import of the language used. If the words are doubtful, the doubt must be resolved against the government and in favor of the tax payer.

Some tax code researchers have suggested that the wording of Section 7701(c) defining "includes" and "including" gives the words an expanded meaning. However, this conclusion is not shared by either the U.S. Supreme Court as previously shown in the **Montello Salt v. Utah** , **Gould v. Gould and U.S. v. Merriam** cases. Other court cases also support the **Montello Salt and Gould** Supreme Court decisions which limit the meaning of taxing statutes to that which is stated in the statute only. One such case is **U.S. v. Missouri Pacific Railroad 278 U.S. 269 (1929)** wherein the Supreme Court stated that *"When the language of an enactment is clear, and construction, according to its terms does not lead to absurd or impracticable consequences, the words employed are to be taken as the final expression of the meaning intended."* (emphasis added) Another U.S. Supreme Court decision affirmed this same limited interpretation principle in the case of **Dickerson v. New Banner Institute, Inc., 460 U.S. 103 (1983)** in which the Court stated: *"In determining the scope of a statute one is to look first at its language. If the language is unambiguous, ordinarily it is to be regarded as conclusive, unless there is 'a clearly expressed legislative intent to the contrary'."*

An authoritative maxim of statutory construction which is recognized in legal jurisprudence as the PLAIN MEANING RULE is "expression unius est exclusion alterius". Roughly translated, this phrase means that whatever is omitted is understood to be excluded. With this rule and the confirming Supreme Court decisions already discussed, let us consider again the wording in Section 7701(c) which can easily be misunderstood when we consider the meaning of the last clause of the statute which reads: "shall not be deemed to exclude other things otherwise within the meaning of the term defined." To this writer, this wording raises two questions immediately. First, what, if anything, other than what is stated in the statute could be included as being "within the meaning of the term defined"? Common sense as well as court decisions already quoted tell me that the answer to this question is that nothing can be included other than what is stated in the law. This conclusion is supported by the U.S. Supreme Court decisions in U.S. v. Missouri Pacific Railroad and Dickerson v. New Banner Institute, previously shown, the Plain Meaning Rule from *Sutherland's Rules of Statutory Construction* and the legal maxim of "expression unius est exclusion alterius" (whatever is omitted is understood to be excluded). After all, if there is or was something which should be considered or read into the statute other than what is stated therein, why was it not stated specifically therein? Second, would such an interpretation mean that I can read into the law anything else that I wish? If so, this would also lead us to the unthinkable conclusion that anyone, including judges, prosecutors, defense attorneys and all citizens can add whatever unstated provision they may wish to the meaning of the statute. So, clearly the answer to this question is "no". The I.R. Code sections mean ONLY what is stated and both the Supreme Court and *Sutherland's Rules of Statutory Construction* agree.

The word "person" is another word which is used as a <u>term</u> in the I.R. Code and as a <u>term</u> is defined in Section 7701(a)(1) as follows: *"The <u>term</u> "person" shall be construed to mean and include an <u>individual</u>, a trust, estate, partnership, association, company or <u>corporation</u>."* (emphasis added)

We notice that a "person" under this definition is very broad- being defined by seven separate meanings including "corporation". So a corporation is within the meaning of the "term" "person". Corporations are taxable persons which are specifically taxed under Section 11 of Part II of the I.R. Code. How interesting that, legally, a "person" can be a corporation!

However, the term "person" also includes an "individual", and the prefix to all the definitions in Section 7701 has revealing wording which states: "...*when used in this title, where not otherwise distinctly expressed <u>or manifestly incompatible with the intent thereof</u>.*" (emphasis added) To understand the meaning of this wording, we must remember that it is necessary for Congress to write all laws so that they are in conformity with the limitations and restrictions on taxing power within the Constitution. Remembering this, it is this writer's opinion that this portion of the prefix clause which is underlined above limits the inclusion of the word "individual" to those particular "persons" who come within the meaning of the term "taxpayer" which is defined in Section 7701(a)(14) as *"any person subject to any Internal Revenue tax"*. Such a "taxpayer" is only identified in the Code under Section 1461 which names those "persons" who are "made liable" for payment of income tax and, as such, they are within the meaning of the term "person", and they satisfy the restricted meaning of "individuals" within the meaning of the words *"not...manifestly incompatible with the intent thereof."*

Another blatant example of the difference between common understanding of the meaning of words in general usage and the legal definition of those words when used as a <u>term</u> in the I.R. Code is shown by the definition of the <u>term</u> "trade or business" which is defined in the I.R. Code Section 7701(a)(26) as follows: "The <u>term</u> trade or business <u>includes</u> the performance of the functions of a public office." (emphasis added) Because "includes" is a word of confinement and not expansion, "trade or business" is not <u>at all</u> what we thought it was, but rather it is limited to the functions of elected or appointed officials of government! How totally confusing this is to the average reader!

There are also many statutory headings in both the table of contents and elsewhere throughout the I.R. Code that use words which lead readers to incorrectly think that the law applies to them when, in fact, a careful examination of other Code section regulations, court cases and the Constitution show this not to be true. The wording of Section 7701(c) which defines "includes" and "including" also previously pointed out is just one example of the tricky misleading provisions in the Code.

Many other words used of common usage when used as terms in the I.R. Code have legal definitions in the Code that are different from their ordinary meaning or are defined as terms which also give the words different meanings from the customary or ordinary meaning. One such very important word is "shall".

"Shall" Means "May"

In general use, the word "shall" is a word of command with a generally mandatory meaning. In the IRS Code, "shall" is a directory word that has a mandatory meaning when applied to corporations or to individuals such as withholding agents acting on behalf of corporations or non-resident aliens who do not have the protection of our Constitution as do U.S. citizens. The IR Code contains many Code sections using the word "shall" which is part of the verb describing the actions called for in those sections of the law. The provisions of these Code sections are requirements for corporations because corporations are created by government and, consequently, are subject to government direction and control. Corporations are granted the privilege to exist and operate by government-issued charters, and its stockholder-owners are given the privilege of not being personally liable for the obligations of the corporation. Corporations do not have the constitutionally-guaranteed rights of citizens. This government-granted privilege legally obligates corporations to make a "return" of profits and gains earned in the exercise of their privileged operations when directed to do so by law. This is why the tax form is called a "return". No "return" to government is required, however, of citizens whose right to earn a living is God-given and protected by our Constitution as we have discussed in depth in Chapter I.

However, a directory word such as "shall" when used in the Code merely implies that citizens are required to perform certain acts, but a directory word such as "shall" is not a requirement for citizens when a mandatory interpretation of the directory word would conflict with a citizens' constitutionally-guaranteed rights such as those taxing limitations contained in Article 1, Section 2, Clause 3 and Article 1, Section 9, Clause 4 already discussed. Courts have repeatedly ruled that in statutes, when a mandatory meaning of the word "shall" would create a constitutional conflict, "shall" must be defined as meaning "may". The following are quotes from a few of these decisions:

In **Cairo & Fulton R.R. Co. v. Hecht,** **95 US 170**. the U.S. Supreme Court stated: *"As against the government the word 'shall' when used in statutes, is to be construed as 'may', unless a contrary intention is manifest."* (emphasis added)

In **George Williams College v. Village of Williams Bay,** **7 N.W. 1d 891**, the Supreme Court of Wisconsin stated: *"'Shall' in a statute may be construed to mean 'may' in order to avoid constitutional doubt."* (emphasis added)

In **Gow v. Consolidated Coppermines Corp., 165 A 136**, the court stated: *"If necessary to avoid unconstitutionality of a statute, 'shall' will be deemed equivalent to 'may'…"*. (emphasis added). Clearly these court cases show that for U.S. citizens who enjoy the protection of our Constitution under the Fourth, Fifth and Thirteenth Amendments "shall" has a voluntary meaning. (emphasis added)

The Disclosure, Privacy Act and Paperwork Reduction Act Notice is a legally required part of the IRS instruction booklet covering the filing of income tax returns. The notice states that the IRS gets its' legal authority to "ask for information" on the income tax form from IR Code Sections 6001, 6011 and 6012 and their regulations.

Section 6001 states: *"Every person liable for any tax imposed by this title, or for the collection thereof, shall keep such records, render such statements, make such returns and comply with such rules and requirements as the Secretary may from time to time prescribe."* (emphasis added)

Section 6011 states: *"When required by regulations prescribed by the Secretary any person made liable for any tax imposed by this title, or for the collection thereof, shall make a return or statement according to the forms and regulations prescribed by the Secretary."* (emphasis added)

Section 6012 (a) states: *"Returns with respect to income taxes under Sub-Title A <u>shall</u> be made by the following..."*. (emphasis added) As we have shown, the use of the word <u>shall</u> in all three of these Code sections cannot be mandatory but must have a <u>voluntary</u> meaning for U.S. citizens. (emphasis added)

Because a U.S. citizen's Fourth Amendment right to be secure against unreasonable searches or seizures of their personal papers and effects, his Fifth Amendment right not to be required to be a witness against himself, and the Thirteenth Amendment protection against involuntary servitude, all lock the door against any mandatory compliance with Section 6001, 6011 or 6012 shown above.

Section 6012(a)(1)(A) further states: *"Every individual <u>having</u> for the <u>taxable year</u> gross income..."* (emphasis added).

Section 441(b) states that the <u>term</u> "taxable year" is identified under sub-section (1) as "(1) the <u>taxpayers</u> annual accounting period...". (emphasis added). The term "taxpayer" is defined in I.R. Code Section 7701(a)(14) as follows: *"The term 'taxpayer' means any person 'subject to any Internal Revenue tax'."* The U.S. Court of Appeals decision in the case of **Houston Street Corp. v. Commissioner, 84F2d 821 (1936)** states that "subject to" a tax and "liable for" a tax mean the same thing.

The words "<u>having...income</u>" as used in Section 6012 are identical to those used in Section 1441 which identifies those persons who <u>shall</u> deduct and withhold a tax on items of income listed in Code Section 1441(b) owing and/or paid to non-resident alien individuals or foreign partnerships. It is important to understand that monies and other receipts received by non-resident aliens and foreign partnerships are <u>identified</u> in this Code section as "INCOME" <u>but nowhere in any I.R. Code section</u> is there any provision or statement identifying the receipts of U.S. citizens as being "INCOME".

Section 1461 of the I.R. Code is the <u>ONLY</u> section of Sub-Title A that makes anyone "liable for" income tax and applies only to those who are <u>required to deduct and withhold</u> under Chapter 3 which applies to withholding from foreign persons, partnerships or foreign corporations This Section (1461) identifies <u>only</u> "every person" (this includes a corporation or an individual acting for a corporation) required to deduct and withhold any tax" (a withholding agent) as <u>the person</u> "...made liable" for such tax.

If you are not such a person, you are NOT LIABLE for the tax!

The subject of the <u>limited application</u> of income taxes to withholding agents acting on behalf of non-resident aliens, foreign partnerships or foreign corporations was covered in great detail in Chapter III of this book. Because IRS prosecutors mistakenly use I.R. Code Section 6012 to <u>improperly</u> attempt to show the courts that citizens' are <u>required</u> by that section to file returns, it is important for us to understand the very <u>limited</u> application of this Code section-that is that the filing requirement of Section 6012 does not apply to U.S. citizens acting on their <u>own</u> behalf but only to corporations or those individuals acting on behalf of corporations or other privileged entities who have a witholding requirement as stated in section code 1461. These persons have no constitutional protection for their requirement to withhold monies owing to non-resident aliens or foreign partnerships. Rather, they <u>can be</u> and <u>are</u>, in fact, "persons" "made liable" under Code Section 1461 and are, therefore, "subject to" income tax filing and payment requirements. <u>THERE IS NOT AND CANNOT CONSTITUTIONALLY BE ANY SECTION IN THE IRS CODE THAT MAKES THE U.S. CITIZENRY LIABLE FOR PAYMENT OF INCOME TAX ON THEIR OWN EARNINGS OR OTHER RECEIPTS.</u> Any law imposing a Federal tax on citizens would be unconstitutional because it would violate the taxing limitations in the U.S. Constitution discussed in Chapter I which prohibit direct taxation of citizens by the Federal government.

People are often confused when reading the I.R. Code because under Subtitle A, Chapter 1 which covers income taxes, Part 1 of Subchapter A has the misleading title – "Tax on Individuals". I.R. Code Section 7806(b) states in part that no "descriptive matter relating to the content of this title be given any legal effect." Hence, the <u>intentionally deceptive</u> capitalized heading "TAX ON INDIVIDUALS" which describes Section 1 of the Code has no legal effect. This reading is also misleading because Part 1 imposes the tax on "income" but contains no requirements for "citizen-individuals" to pay it. However, even citizens can be "presumed" by a judge to be a "person liable" for the tax under the rule of law covering a "presumption (Title 28, section 1746)" when they file a 1040 income tax form, thereby stating under penalty of perjury that they are liable for income tax when, by law, they are <u>not</u>, in fact, liable for it! If, however, a citizen has never filed any Internal Revenue form, all of which are signed under penalty of perjury, the rule of presumption cannot be used against him! Early in their training all IRS revenue agents are trained to always first ask all non-filers of returns to file a Form 1040 return which gives the IRS the legal advantage of the rule of presumption whereby the IRS gains legal teeth in their contention that <u>the filer legally acknowledged that he knew he was a "taxpayer" by his act of filing a return</u>!

The Disclosure, Privacy Act and Paperwork Reduction Act notice in the IRS income tax return instruction booklet also shows that disclosure of information by individuals is <u>not</u> required. The notice states: *"Our legal right to <u>ask</u> for information is located in Internal Revenue Code Sections 6001 and 6011 and their regulations."* (emphasis added) IRS does <u>not</u> say, because they <u>know</u> they cannot say, that those sections <u>require</u> individuals to submit the information; those sections only give the IRS the authority to <u>ask</u> for it! As we have seen, the law imposes a requirement only on those who are "liable" for a tax, such as those acting on behalf of certain "persons" such as corporations or non-resident aliens, as we have seen in this chapter and in Chapters I and III of this book.

As we stated earlier, any requirements compelling individual citizens acting on their own behalf to keep records, make returns and statements, or to involuntarily perform any other services for tax collectors would be violations of constitutionally-guaranteed rights under the Fourth, Fifth & Thirteenth Amendments.

The Fourth, Fifth & Thirteenth Amendments to our Constitution protect citizens from defining the word "shall" as meaning "is required to". Thus, "shall" in the above-mentioned Code sections <u>must</u> be interpreted as meaning "may" when applied to ordinary citizens. Consequently, for ordinary citizens keeping records, making statements and making returns for government are clearly <u>voluntary</u> actions that are not required by law.

Earlier, we noted that the word "person" is another "term" defined in I.R. Code Section 7701(a)(1), which also uses the word "shall" as follows: *"The <u>term</u> 'person' <u>shall</u> be construed to mean* and include an <u>individual</u>, a trust, estate, partnership, association, company, or corporation." (emphasis added) Note that this definition includes five <u>privileged</u> entities in addition to an "individual". However, as we have shown, to be an <u>individual</u> subject to government jurisdiction for any tax obligation because of the use of the word "shall" and because of the constitutional protections already discussed, the word "individual", as used in this definition (7701(a)(1), must be confined to a citizen acting on behalf of a privileged entity. A couple of examples would be the "individual" treasurer of a corporation acting on behalf of the corporation. Another example would be an "individual" such as Frank Brushaber, the petitioner in the U.S. Supreme Court case of **Brushaber v. Union Pacific RR Co., Inc., 240 U.S. 1 (1916).** Mr. Brushaber was a fiduciary in this case, holding stocks and bonds and collecting dividends and interest for his non-resident alien principals. Therefore, the word "individual" as used in this definition has very limited and restricted meaning.

Another grossly misleading but obviously intentional bold-face heading in the I.R. Code is the heading which introduces the so-called Social Security Chapter 21 in bold letters as: **CHAPTER 21-FEDERAL INSURANCE CONTRIBUTIONS ACT.** Although this heading may be the technically correct name for the so-called "Social Security" law, it is misleading because the tax has nothing whatsoever to do with insurance, and there are no "<u>contributions</u>"-it is a very constitutionally <u>limited</u> flat-rate "income" tax law which, as we shall see in Chapter V, is legally applicable by law to aliens <u>only</u> (not U.S. citizens) "in the four island possessions of Puerto Rico, the Virgin Islands, Guam and American Samoa". Beneath this misleading heading, the Code incorrectly lists subchapter A "Tax on Emplo<u>yees</u>". Again the tax is not on the employee, but rather it is a tax on "income" which is <u>measured</u> by <u>wages</u>. Section 3101(a) also misleads the reader by the heading "Old-age, Survivors and Disability <u>Insurance</u>" to believe incorrectly that the tax on "income" mandated by this section somehow guarantees some future benefit by inclusion of the word "insurance". As we will see in Chapter V, there are <u>no guarantees</u> of any sort in the Social Security program. In fact, we hear almost daily in the news how our Social Security system is going bankrupt and that those paying into it today may never see any return of their investment at retirement age. Whether this prediction is true or not, there is no vestige of "insurance" in the social security tax. The payor can only<u> hope</u> for a benefit at his or her retirement age. In Chapter V we will learn about the limited application of the tax and show how U.S. citizens can lawfully opt out of this "income" tax which is misapplied unlawfully against their earnings.

<u>Summary</u>

There are many words used in the I.R. Code that are used as terms whose true legal meanings as "terms" are defined in various sections of the Internal Revenue Code far apart from the sections where they are used. These legal definitions give the terms a different meaning from that which is commonly understood for the word in general usage. It is often these limited legal definitions of the "terms" which make the code sections constitutional by not making ordinary citizens "subject to" (liable for) income tax. Also there are numbers of titles, headings, tables of contents and descriptive matter describing some sections or parts of the Code which also use words that mislead the reader to believe that a taxing section applies to him or her when, in fact, this is not true because such descriptive words have no legal effect. In fact, <u>only the bodies of the I.R. Code sections</u> have legal effect.

It is apparent to this writer that the use of these "terms" which <u>create</u> true legal meaning to the Code sections, as well as the use of misleading non-binding headings and phrases describing other Code provisions, are tactics <u>intended to deceive</u> and confuse the public about the true meaning of the law. The Code is written in such a manner as to <u>intentionally deceive</u> ordinary citizens into believing that the law applies to him when, in fact, it does not! This deception, as it relates to the so-called (but <u>mis</u>stated) Social Security tax is a flagrant example which will next be exposed in Chapter V.

CHAPTER V

SOCIAL SECURITY-A FLAT-RATE INCOME TAX AND VOLUNTARY WITHHOLDING

The Social Security Act, which is part of Title 42 of the United States Code, was enacted in 1935 as a U.S. government-sponsored, <u>voluntary</u> (so-called) pension program for the benefit of individuals who wished to <u>voluntarily</u> participate in the program. The Act is administered by the Social Security Administration which handles the administration and payment of benefits under the provision of the law. The withholding provisions in Chapter 24 of Title 26, United States Code and its implementing regulations create the required authorization for the U.S. government to set up and administer a voluntary withholding system for <u>Federal employees</u> who voluntarily authorize the deduction and withholding of money from their pay. These withholding laws are necessary in order for any Federal official to operate a withholding system for their employees. By contrast, a private employer would not need such statutory authority to set up and administer such a program for his employees as is required by the U.S. government. The IRS, however, has unlawfully misapplied the provisions of this voluntary withholding program to private employers and employees as this chapter will show.

The so-called Social Security tax, upon which the old-age benefits are supposedly based, is imposed and collected by the Internal Revenue Service under the provisions of Chapter 21 the Internal Revenue Code, which is Title 26 of the United States Code. Contrary to common belief, monies collected by the IRS are <u>not</u> sent to the Social Security Administration to fund their administrative and disbursement activities. In fact, they go into the general fund along with other taxes collected. An accounting "gimmick" is created to lead the public to believe that the monies paid in are held in a (so-called) "trust fund". Although it may be technically correct that a so-called "trust fund" exists, the truth is that it contains no monies or other assets-only governmental IOU's promising to pay money to itself. Monies disbursed by the SSA must be appropriated by Congress each year as needed. Since no contractual obligation exists for the payment of any benefits, technically the benefits could be terminated at any time, if Congress did not appropriate the necessary funds. Congress' potential failure to order this annual appropriation has created great concern by millions of Americans-both those oldsters who are now living on their Social Security check as well as the younger workers who have no guarantee that there will be funds available to pay them when they reach retirement age.

This chapter deals with the I.R. Code sections relative to the imposition and collection of the so-called Social Security tax in Chapter 21 and the laws relating to withholding in Chapter 24. References to Code sections are those in Title 26 of the United States Code, which is a codification of the statutes at large as enacted by Congress. All code sections shown herein are copied from Title 26, United States Code. All Internal Revenue taxes, including the personal and corporate income taxes, the so-called self-employment taxes, as well as the <u>so-called</u> Social Security tax, are imposed and collected under Title 26, United States Code. This (Social Security) flat-rate income tax is imposed by Code Section 3101 in Chapter 21 deceptively titled: *FEDERAL <u>INSURANCE</u> CONTRIBUTIONS ACT*. However, I.R. Code Section 7806 tells us that <u>titles</u> have no legal effect:

Sec. 7806. Construction of title.
(a) Cross References.
The cross references in this title to other portions of the title or other provisions of law, where the word "see" is used, are made only for convenience, and shall be given no legal effect.
(b) Arrangement classification.
No inference, implication, or presumption of legislative construction shall be drawn or made by reason of the location or grouping of any particular section or provision or portion of this title, nor shall any table of contents, table of cross-references, or similar outline, analysis, <u>or descriptive matter relating to the contents of this title be given any legal effect</u>. The preceding sentence also applies to the side notes and ancillary tables contained in the various prints of this Act before its enactment into law. (emphasis added)

Hence, the title of Chapter 21, which deceptively includes the word <u>INSURANCE,</u> is obviously intended by the drafters to deceive the readers by suggesting that there is, by use of the word "insurance", some provision creating an <u>insurance</u> guarantee in the law. As will be shown later in this chapter, this not true.

It is noteworthy that this flat-rate income/excise tax, which is imposed by Chapter 21 of the I.R. Code, is almost always mistakenly referred to by accountants, lawyers and tax preparers as a "payroll" or "FICA" tax. The use of the non-word "FICA" in describing the tax is confusing to the public because there is no such word as "FICA" in the English language. By using the first letter in each of the four words which comprise the title of Chapter 21 of the I.R. Code, which is *FEDERAL INSURANCE CONTRIBUTIONS ACT*, to create the non-word "FICA", it appears that the IRS has encouraged use of this non-word to describe this excise tax in order to intentionally give the erroneous impression that there is some kind of "insurance" benefit created by the imposition of this so-called Social Security flat rate/income tax. The first two letters of the non-word "FICA" are the first letters for the words "FEDERAL INSURANCE" that strongly imply (erroneously) that there is a Federal insurance program encompassed in this flat-rate income tax.

Before examining the actual wording contained in these I.R. Code sections, it is important to understand that courts have repeatedly held that a statute means only that which is stated in the statute and nothing more. Since the Code sections are copied from the statutes, the meanings of the Code sections, like the statutes, are limited to that which is stated therein.

Sutherland's Rules of Statutory Construction, an authoritative legal guidebook, under Section 66.01 titled *Strict Construction of Statutes Creating Tax Liabilities* explains the limited application of tax laws. The guidebook refers to the U.S. Supreme Court decision of **Gould v. Gould, 245 US 151 (1917)**, previously quoted, which states:

Gould v. Gould, 245 US151 (1917)

In the interpretation of statutes levying taxes it is the established rule not to extend their provisions by implication beyond the clear import of the language used, or to enlarge their operation so as to embrace matters not specifically pointed out. In case of doubt, they are construed most strongly against the government and in favor of the citizen.
(emphasis added)

So the U.S. Supreme Court tells us in this case that the I.R. Code sections, the wording of which is taken from the statutes, mean only that which is stated; nothing else can be added to that which is stated in the Code section.

With this Supreme Court ruling in mind, let's look at the wording of Code Sections 3101(a) and 3111(a) which are imposition statutes for the so-called Social Security or FICA (Federal Insurance Contributions Act) tax- Section 3101(a) applying to "every individual" and 3111(a) to employers:

Section 3101. Rate of tax
(a) Old-Age, survivors and disability insurance.
In addition to other taxes, there is hereby imposed on the income of every individual a tax equal to the following percentages of the wages (as defined in section 3121(a) received by him with respect to employment (as defined in section 3121(b) (emphasis added)

(b) Hospital insurance.
In addition to the tax imposed by the preceding sub-section, there is hereby imposed on the income of every individual a tax equal to the following percentages of the wages (as defined in section 3121(a) received by him with respect to employment (as defined in section 3121(b))....(emphasis added)

Sec. 3111. Rate of tax.
(a) Old-age, survivors, and disability insurance.
In addition to other taxes, there is hereby imposed on every employer an excise tax, with respect to having individuals in his employ, equal to the following percentages of the wages (as defined in section 3121(a)) paid by him with respect to employment (as defined in section 3121(b)) (emphasis added)

Sec. 3111. Rate of tax.
(b) Hospital insurance.
In addition to the tax imposed by the preceding sub-section, there is hereby imposed on every employer an excise tax, with respect to having individuals in his employ, equal to the following percentages of the wages (as defined in section 3121(a) paid by him with respect to employment (as defined in section 3121(b))- (emphasis added)

First, the word "insurance" is used four times <u>in the descriptive headings</u> of Code Sections 3101(a) and (b) and also 3111(a) and (b). As shown in Section 7806(b) previously quoted in this chapter: "…nor shall any…<u>descriptive matter</u> relating to the contents of this title be given any legal effect…". (emphasis added) So this Code Section 7806(b) tells us that there is <u>no</u> <u>insurance</u> of any sort created by these Code sections; they impose an <u>income/excise tax</u> only!

Second, we will see from the <u>defined words wages, employee, employment and United States</u>, as used in this chapter, and particularly in Sections 3101(a) and (b), that the "income" of the "individual" referred to in these sections who is being taxed is measured by his "wages" which is a <u>defined term</u> as shown below in Section 3121(a). This definition of the <u>term</u> "wages" is tied to the term "employment" which is another <u>defined term</u> as shown below in Section 3121(b). This term "employment" is <u>defined</u> as "a service performed by an 'employee' which is another <u>defined term</u> in Section 3121(d) also reproduced below in pertinent part:

Sec. 3121. Definitions.
(a) Wages.
For purposes of this chapter, the term "<u>wages</u>" means all remuneration for <u>employment</u>…
(b) Employment.
For purposes of this chapter, the term "<u>employment</u>" means any service, of whatever nature, performed (A) by an "<u>employee</u>" for the person employing him,…(1) <u>within the United States</u>... (four island possesions)
(d) Employee.
For purposes of this chapter, the term "<u>employee</u>" means...
(2) any <u>individual</u> who, under the usual common law rules applicable in determining the employer-employee relationship has the status of an employee, or…(emphasis added)

Therefore, by properly connecting one Code section to a second and then to a third, we must conclude that the word "individual" as used in Code Sections 3101(a) and (b) can only be the "individual" <u>employee</u> identified in Code Section 3121(d)(2).

Third, the popular <u>mistaken belief</u> is that the flat-rate income tax, which is imposed on the <u>income</u> of "every individual" (employee) under Section 3101(a), is a "wage" tax. However, a reading of Section 3101(a) (above) shows clearly that the tax is <u>not</u>, in fact, a <u>wage tax, but instead, is imposed on "income"</u> which is merely <u>measured</u> by "wages". Hence, the tax is simply another income/excise tax. However, what is of <u>vital importance</u> in <u>both</u> these sections is the limited application of the terms "<u>wages</u>: (as defined in Section 3121(a)) and "<u>employment</u>" (as defined in Section 3121(b). The definitions of these terms create a <u>territorial</u> limitation on the application of the tax, shown in Code Section 3121(e)(2) which limits application of the tax to "income" of non-resident aliens working in the four island possessions!

As shown, the <u>term</u> "employment" means a service performed by one identified by the <u>term</u> "employee" within the "<u>United States</u>...". "<u>United States</u>" is also a <u>term</u> used in this chapter which also has a very restricted definition in Section 3121(e) as follows:

> **(e) State, United States, and citizen.**
> For purposes of this chapter...
> **(2) United States.** <u>The term "United States" when used in a geographical</u> sense includes the <u>Commonwealth of Puerto Rico, the Virgin Islands, Guam and American Samoa</u>...
> (emphasis added)

The definition of the <u>term</u> "United States" lists the <u>precise geographical area</u> in which the activity described by the <u>term</u> "employment" takes place. The definition lists <u>only</u> the Commonwealth of Puerto Rico, the Virgin Islands, Guam and American Samoa as the areas in which the tax imposed by this chapter applies-the fifty states of the union are <u>not included</u>! Before examining the provisions of this law, it is essential to understand the use of words as "terms" when used in laws. When words are used as <u>terms</u> in order to establish their clear legal meanings, precise definitions of those terms are necessary to be included in the law. These definitions state the exact limited meanings of terms used in the I.R Code. These meanings are often different from the meanings of the words in common, customary usage. (See Chapter IV of this book.)

Finally, as was shown in Chapter III, "income" is not <u>defined</u> in the Internal Revenue Code. However, it is <u>identified</u> in Code Section 1441 as monies received or owing to non-resident aliens <u>only</u>! Consequently, only non-resident alien "individuals" are taxable under Sections 3101(a) and (b) on their "income" measured by the "wages" they receive from "employment" only within the four island possessions, which is the geographical area identified in which the (so-called FICA or Social Security) tax applies through the definition of this area in Section 3121(e)(2) shown above!

As quoted in this and earlier chapters, the U. S. Supreme Court in the decisions of **Gould v. Gould and U.S. v. Merriam** established that, in taxing statutes, definitions of terms used in the statutes cannot be expanded by implication. Nothing can be added to the definition of a term; it means only that which is stated, regardless of any belief to the contrary. At first, it may be hard to believe that the definition of the term "United States" could be limited to mean only the four island possessions of Puerto Rico, the Virgin Islands, Guam and American Samoa. But that is exactly what this definition means because the statutes mean only that which is stated, nothing more, as explained by the Supreme Court in the decisions listed above. Also, there are other decisions where our courts have addressed the principle of the limited meaning of statues. The U.S. Court of Appeals for the 9th Circuit explained two such Supreme Court decisions in the case of:

United States v. Varbel, 780 F2d 758 at Page 761 (9th Cir.) (1986) which stated:

> *We begin our interpretation by reading the statutes and regulations for their plain meaning. The plain meaning rule has its' origin in U.S. v. Missouri Pacific Railroad, 278 U.S. 269 (1929). There the Supreme Court stated that "where the language of an enactment is clear and construction according to its' terms does not lead to absurd or impracticable consequences, the words employed are to be taken as the final expression of the meaning intended...". The principle was more recently affirmed in Dickerson v. New Banner Institute, Inc., 460 U.S. 103, 103 S.Ct. 986, 74 L.Ed.2d 845 (1983), rehearing denied, 461 U.S. 911, 103 S.Ct. 1887, 76 L.Ed.2d 815 (1983), where the Court stated, "In determining the scope of a statute, one is to look first as its language. If the language is umambiguouos...it is to be regarded as conclusive unless there is a clearly expressed legislative intent to the contrary."* (emphasis added)

Also, Code Section 3121(e)(2) uses the term "includes" which, in law, is a word of confinement and not expansion. This is exactly what the U.S. Supreme Court said in the decision of Montello Salt v. Utah, 221 U.S. at page 455, wherein they stated:

Montello Salt v. Utah, 221 U.S. at page 455

"Include" or the participal form therof, is defined; 'to comprise within'; 'to hold'; 'to contain'; 'to shut up' and synonyms are 'contain'; 'enclose'; 'comprise'; 'comprehend'; 'embrace'; 'involve'. (emphasis added)

This Montello Salt decision and others such as the case of **U.S. v. Missouri Pacific Railroad Co.** quoted above all support the ruling that 'includes" is a word of limitation as was stated in the Supreme Court's decision in **Gould v. Gould** that there can be no broadening of the statute by implication. Legislative drafters in the Internal Revenue Service who write the tax bills know very well this "plain meaning rule" of statutory interpretation. If the term "United States" could constitutionally include the fifty states of the union, they would have specifically included them in the definition. As an example of this, Code Section 4612, which relates to a tax on crude oil, defines the term "United States" under **Code Section 4612(a)(4)(A)** as follows:

Sec. 4612. Definitions and special rules.
(a) Definitions.
For purposes of this sub-chapter… (emphasis added)
(4) United States.
(A) In general, the term "United States" means the 50 States, the District of Columbia, the Commonwealth of Puerto Rico, any possession of the United States, the Commonwealth of the Northern Mariana Islands, and The Trust Territory of the Pacific Islands,…(emphasis added)

It is important to note that this definition of the term "United States" applies only to Sub-Chapter A of Chapter 38 which is titled "ENVIRONMENTAL TAXES" relevant to the tax on petroleum only! There is no way that the definition of the term "United States in Code Section 4612(a)(4) can be extended to apply to the Code Sections pertaining to income tax because the Code section pointedly and specifically limits this broad definition to the tax on petroleum only. This shows that when the term "United States" means to include the fifty states of the union in a definition, it says so!

Consequently, it is very clear that the term "United States", when used to describe the areas where the miscalled "Social Security" tax applies, means, and is limited to, the four island possessions which are the only areas listed in the term's definition under Code Section 3121(e)(2) quoted earlier in this chapter. Therefore, according to the wording of the law itself, this flat-rate income tax does not apply within the fifty states of the Union. This makes sense when one understands the limitations of the direct taxing authority of the Federal government as contained in the Constitution under Article 1, Section 2, Clause 3 and Article 1, Section 9, Clause 4. Article 1, Section 2, Clause 3 limits any Federal direct tax to be imposed only on the states of the union in proportion to their populations. The second, Article 1, Section 9, Clause 4, forbids any capitation tax which is a tax on the person or his property (earnings) anywhere-not just in the fifty states! The Social Security flat-rate income tax is unconstitutionally administered by the IRS as if it were a direct tax on all individuals everywhere. To be constitutional, any direct tax on individuals can be imposed by law only outside the fifty states of the union-in this case those specified four island possessions only despite the IRS' deception of the public into falsely believing the tax applies in the fifty states of the union. Even then, imposition of this flat-rate income tax cannot be imposed even in the four island possessions on the earnings of U.S. citizens who are protected against such taxation by the prohibition in Article 1, Section 9, Clause 4 of the Constitution. Therefore, by law, the so-called Social Security tax can constitutionally be applied only against the earnings of non-resident aliens who may be living in the four island possessions! Because natives of the possessions are also U.S. citizens, either by birth or naturalization, they are protected by our Constitution equally with citizens of the fifty states of the union. Therefore, the misnamed FICA tax which is an excise tax on "income" can apply only to the earnings of non-resident aliens whose "income" is identified and taxed as such by Section 1441 of the I.R. Code when received by such non-resident aliens who may be living in the four island possessions! Obviously, the drafters of these imposition statutes (Code sections) were aware of the constitutional restrictions against taxation of the earnings of U.S. citizens which is the reason why these territorial limitations on the misnamed FICA tax are written into this chapter of the Code.

I.R. Code Section 7655 also supports even further the limited meaning of the term "United States" as respects both the self-employment tax imposed in Chapter 2 of the Code as well as the flat-rate income tax imposed in Chapter 21. Section 7655 states:

> **Sec. 7655. Cross references.**
> **(a) Imposition of tax in <u>possessions.</u>**
> For provisions <u>imposing tax in possessions,</u> see
> (1) Chapter 2, relating to <u>self-employment</u> tax;
> (2) Chapter 21, relating to the tax under the <u>Federal</u> Insurance Contributions Act. (emphasis added)

This Code section clearly shows the limited geographical application of both the self-employment tax (Section (a)(1)) and the Social Security flat-rate income tax (Section (a)(2)) imposed under Chapters 2 and 21 to be limited to "possessions" (Puerto Rico, Virgin Islands, Guam and American Samoa as listed in I.R. Code Section 3121(e)(2) defining the <u>term</u> "United States") in respect to these taxes.

The self-employment tax, which is imposed by I.R. Code Section 1401(a) states as follows:

> **Sec. 1401. Rate of tax.**
> **(a) Old-age, survivors, and disability insurance.**
> In addition to other taxes, there shall be imposed for each <u>taxable year,</u> on the <u>self-employment income</u> of every <u>individual</u> a tax equal to the following percent of the amount of the self-employment <u>income</u> for each <u>taxable year.</u> (emphasis added)

The words "taxable year" underlined in this Code section clearly show the requirement for the "individual" referenced in this Code section to be a "taxpayer" because only a "taxpayer" has a "taxable year", and, as we showed in Chapter IV, a "taxpayer" is a person who is "subject to" or "liable for" income tax, and as we have also shown throughout this book, the only person who is "<u>subject to</u>" or "<u>liable for</u>" such tax is a withholding agent for a non-resident alien who is identified in Code Section 1461 only!

Also, as respects the tax imposed on so-called "self-employment income" by Section 1401(a), it is noteworthy that the hyphenated term "self-employment" is derived from the word "employment" which is defined under Section 3121(b) as "any service of whatever nature, performed by an 'employee'…within the "United States." And "United States" is defined just two sections further in I.R. Code Section 3121(e)(2) as the aforementioned four island possessions <u>only</u>! Therefore, the I.R. Code says that <u>self</u>-employment is a word describing <u>an activity that occurs only in the four island possessions</u> of Puerto Rico, Guam, the Virgin Islands and American Samoa. Even then, if such self-employment is conducted by a U.S. citizen in these four island possessions, he is protected and immune from application of the tax by the prohibition against any capitation tax (a tax on people) in the Constitution under Article 1, Section 9, Clause 4. By law, therefore, only <u>non</u>-citizens of the United States working for themselves in these possessions would be subject to the self-employment tax imposed under Section 1401(a)!

Section 1402(d)-The Key to Understanding
The Geographical Limitations of Chapters 2, 21 & 24

In the Code there are many definitions that are limited in their applications by words such as "for purposes of this chapter", "for purposes of this <u>sub</u>-chapter" and "for purposes of this <u>sub-part</u>". In contrast, Section 1402 contains definitions of terms upon which there are <u>no such limitations</u> upon their application; therefore, the definitions therein apply <u>throughout</u> the <u>entire</u> Code. Section 1402(d) states as follows:

> **Sec. 1402. Definitions.**
> **(d) Employee and wages.**
> The term "<u>employee</u>" and the term "<u>wages</u>" shall have the same meaning as <u>when used</u> in Chapter 21 (sec. 3101 and following related to Federal Insurance Contributions Act). (emphasis added)

Note the <u>absence</u> in this Code definition of any words of limitation such as "for purposes of this chapter" or "for purposes of this sub-chapter". This definition means, therefore, that <u>whenever and wherever</u> the <u>terms</u> "employee" and "wages" are used <u>anywhere</u> throughout the Code, <u>their applications are limited to those people involved in activities within the four island possessions</u>, the same as in Chapter 21, the Social Security flat-rate income tax chapter.

All Withholding Is Voluntary

The Internal Revenue Code, Chapter 24, relates to <u>withholding</u> by the Federal government from Federal government employees only. This chapter is deceptively titled "COLLECTION OF INCOME TAX AT SOURCE". It is extremely important to note that this chapter contains <u>no section imposing any tax</u>. Rather, the entire chapter was written many years ago merely to establish a convenient method for <u>Federal</u> employees (only) to make <u>voluntary</u> smaller, easier payments for income tax on a weekly, semi-weekly or monthly basis rather than having to exercise the discipline required to <u>voluntarily</u> set aside funds from each paycheck sufficient to make a single annual payment of tax at the end of the year.

In enacting this legislation, Congress was aware of the very natural temptation which we all have to spend our money as soon as received, making collection of taxes in one lump payment on an annual basis difficult, if not impossible. To remedy this problem, Congress passed the <u>voluntary</u> withholding system to make it much easier for <u>Federal employees</u> to pay the tax in small increments as they received their periodic paychecks. Note that we have stressed the word "voluntary" by underlining because it is of vital importance that the reader understand that all United States citizens, <u>including Federal employees,</u> have an <u>absolute constitutional right</u> to keep the <u>entire</u> fruits of their labor in the form of their paycheck without interference by their employer, whether their employer is the Federal government <u>or</u> a private employer. The Fifth Amendment right of <u>all</u> U.S. citizens, including Federal citizen-employees, not to be deprived of their property (their paycheck) without due process of law cannot be interfered with by government. It is in recognition of this absolute right that the <u>voluntary</u> withholding system was established for the benefit of Federal employees to merely make it possible for them to <u>volunteer</u> by means of the W-4 withholding <u>Allowance</u> Certificate to pay an income tax that they, like all others U.S. citizens, <u>do not owe</u> on their wages, salaries or other receipts!

The terms "employ<u>ee</u>" and "employ<u>er</u>" are defined in the witholding chapter under I.R. Code Sections 3401(c) and (d) reproduced below showing that, for the purposes of the entire withholding chapter, the employ<u>ee</u> is a <u>Federal worker</u> and the employ<u>er</u> is the <u>Federal government</u>. Such definitions that apply within this withholding Chapter 24 are necessary because, obviously, the Federal government <u>has no control</u> over the paychecks of <u>non</u>-government workers. And despite these clear <u>limiting definitions</u> of "employer" and "employee", the IRS has been amazingly successful, through their propaganda efforts, to erroneously convince private employers and employees that the provisions of this withholding chapter are mandatory, and that they apply to them as well as to government employers and workers. As this chapter will show, there is only one short reference to voluntary withholding in Chapter 24 as respects non-government workers. This is shown in Code Section 3402(p)(3)(B) which will be quoted and explained following in this chapter. As we will see, however, the voluntary nature of the entire withholding program is emphasized in both the Code sections passed by Congress and the implementing Regulation 31.3402.(p) published by the IRS, which is in keeping with every citizen's Fifth Amendment right to keep the fruits of his labor (paycheck) without interference by government or any other employer unless the employee grants permission for the withholding by signing a W-4 Withholding Allowance (permission) Certificate.

IRS Regulation 31.3402(p)(2), the law which we will quote later, shows every government-employee's right to cancel voluntary withholding. It is this writer's opinion that this regulation is really necessary only for government workers who may be aliens because they would not have the same Fifth Amendment protection as citizen-government workers. Every citizen's right to stop all withholding by giving his employer a signed, written notice to stop withholding is his constitutionally-secured right under the Fifth Amendment, as we have previously explained. This fifth amendment constitutional right is also recognized statutorily in the IR code section 3402(n) of the witholding chapter which says in summary that if the person completing the W-4 certificate states that he had no income tax liability for the preceeding or the current year, his employer is relieved from the withholding requirement. Because of the Fifth Amendment, the entire withholding system is totally dependent upon a voluntary action of a worker who authorizes withholding by signing and submitting the IRS form "W-4 Employee's Withholding Allowance Certificate". This allows (permits) the employer to deduct and withhold money from his pay. The creation of withholding is voluntary, and the cancellation is also voluntary because these rights under our Fifth Amendment accrue to all citizens regardless of whether they are Federal employees or non-Federal employees because they are still citizens, and they are protected by the Fifth Amendment of the Constitution to keep all the fruits of their labor!

The terms "employee" and "employer" have very limited definitions in the withholding Chapter 24 as follows:

Sec. 3401. Definitions.
(c) Employ__ee__.
For purposes of this chapter, the term "employee" includes an officer, employee, or elected official of the United States, a State, or any political sub-division thereof, or the District of Columbia or any agency or instrumentality of any one or more of the foregoing. The term "employee" also includes an officer of a corporation. (emphasis added)

Sec. 3401. Definitions.
(d) Employer.
For purposes of this chapter, the term "employer" means the person for whom the individual performs or performed any service, of whatever nature, as the "employer" of such person except that... (emphasis added)

In addition to the District of Columbia Section 3401(c), by referring to "an officer, employee or elected official of the United States", is a clear reference to the United States government and not to a geographical area. Hence, this statute embraces all Federal employees of the United States wherever domiciled, including the District of Columbia, the fifty states of the union and the four island possessions.

It is revealing that the definition of "employee" shown in Code Section 3401(c) includes the term "State" which is also a term that is defined in Code Section 7701(a)(10) as follows:

Sec. 7701. Definitions.
(a) (10) State.
The term "state" shall be construed to include the District of Columbia, where such construction is necessary to carry out the provisions of this title. (emphasis added)

The word "include" in this definition needs an explanation showing the definition of the terms "includes" and "including" as follows:

Sec. 7701(c). Definitions.
(c) "Includes" and "including".
The terms "includes" and "including" when used in a definition contained in this title shall not be deemed to

exclude other things otherwise within the meaning of the term defined. (emphasis added)

This Code section suggests at first reading that these could be some unstated meaning of the term "includes". However, the wording of this section immediately raises the question: "What can be included other than what is stated?" And the obvious answer to this question is "nothing". And this answer/conclusion is in keeping with *Sutherland's Rules of Statutory Construction* and the U.S. Supreme Court in the decisions of Gould v. Gould, U.S. v. Missouri Pacific Railroad, Dickerson v. New Banner Institute, Inc. and Montello Salt v. Utah, quoted earlier in this chapter and elsewhere. Therefore, this definition limits the application of the term "employee" to those working for the Federal government, for the District of Columbia, for U.S. possessions and officers of a government-owned corporation. Section 3401(d) identifies the "employer" as one for whom the "employee" works. This means that the meaning of the term "employer" is limited to those entities listed in Section 3401(c)-the U.S. government, District of Columbia, etc. The term "employer" does not apply to any non-government employer or business. On the basis of these definitions alone, most of the nation's population is not subject to the withholding provisions in this chapter! This is understandable because, like all citizens (including Federal employees), they have their own fifth amendment constitutional right to their property (paycheck), but they don't need any special statutory program to negotiate a withholding plan with their employers as do Federal employees.

In addition to these limitations on the application of the term "employee" shown above, as is shown earlier in this chapter, Section 1402(d) limits the meaning and the application of the term "employee" and the term "wages" to activities taking place within the specific four island possessions only. Therefore, the I.R. Code states that the withholding provisions of Chapter 24 apply only to Federal employees in the four island possessions.

I.R. Code Section 3402(a)(1) contains tricky wording which could easily lead businesses and individual employers to erroneously believe that they are required to deduct and withhold taxes from the pay of those they hire. It is worded as follows:

Sec. 3402. Income tax collected at source.
(a) Requirement of withholding.
(1) In general. Except as otherwise provided in this section,

every employer making payment of wages shall deduct and withhold upon such wages a tax determined in accordance with tables or computational procedures prescribed by the Secretary. Any tables or procedures prescribed under this paragraph shall... (emphasis added)

Note that this Section 3402(a)(1) states that the term "employer" (defined in Section 3401(d) as the Federal government, District of Columbia or the four island possessions of Puerto Rico, Virgin Islands, Guam and American Samoa) who are under Federal jurisdiction and control shall deduct and withhold from "wages" a tax determined in accordance with the Secretary's tables and computational procedures. We previously showed that the meaning of the term "wages" is limited by Section 1402(d) to payments for activities occurring within the four island possessions only, the same as provided in Chapter 21 imposing the so-called Social Security flat-rate income tax. These "tables and procedures" are authorized to be provided by the Secretary under I.R. Code Section 3402(p)(3) for both government and non-government workers as follows:

Sec. 3402. Income tax collected at source.
(p) Voluntary withholding agreements.
(3) Authority for other voluntary withholding.
The Secretary is authorized by regulations to provide for withholding-
(A) from remuneration for services performed by an employee for the employee's employer which (without regard to this paragraph) does not constitute wages, and
(B) from any other type of payment with respect to which the Secretary finds that withholding would be appropriate under the provisions of this chapter, if the employer and employee, or the person making and the person receiving such other type of payment, agree to such withholding. Such agreement shall be in such form and manner as the Secretary may by regulations prescribe. For purposes of this chapter (and so much of sub-title F as relates to this chapter), remuneration or other payments with respect to which such agreement is made shall be treated as if they were wages paid by an employer to an employee to the extent that such remuneration is paid or other payments are made during the period for which the agreement is in effect. (emphasis added)

Because we have previously shown that by definitions under Code Sections 3401(c) and (d) the <u>terms</u> "employ<u>ee</u>" and "employ<u>er</u>" used in the above Code section refer <u>only</u> to Federal employees and the Federal government respectively, we should note that, by contrast, the words "<u>person making</u>" and "<u>person receiving</u>" used in the middle of this Code section 3402(p)(3)(B) is a clear reference to private, <u>non</u>-government employers and employees.

It is particularly noteworthy that this section refers to both <u>government</u> and <u>non-government</u> employees and employers. The Federal government in referenced by use of the term "employ<u>er</u>" and the Federal workers by the term "employ<u>ee</u>". By contrast, private <u>non</u>-government workers are referred to in Section 3402(p)(3)(B) as "the <u>person making</u> and the <u>person receiving</u> such other type of payment." However, the important thing to note and remember about this statute is that, <u>both</u>, the government employer and employee, as well as the <u>non</u>-government employer and employee "must <u>agree</u> to such withholding". Reference is made to the remuneration or other payments with respect to which such <u>agreement</u> is made. Again, by multiple refernces to the required "<u>agreement</u>", this Code Section proves the voluntary nature of withholding for everybody!

It is also interesting to note that this Code Section 3402(p)(3)(B), refers to the "remunaration or other payments..." "<u>as if </u>they were wages paid by an employer to an employee." Which is an acknowledgement of the provisions in Section 1402(d) discussed earlier in this chapter and which identifies the terms "employee" and "wages" as <u>persons</u> and <u>renumeration</u> earned only in the four island possessions!

Note also that the start of Code Section 3402(p)(3) states that "the Secretary is 'authorized' by regulations to <u>provide</u> for withholding...". Again, these words clearly imply <u>no requirement</u>; in fact "to provide for means "make available" - words which obviously stipulate and confirm the voluntary nature of all withholding.

An agreement exists only when an individual (either a government or a non-government employee) who is hired <u>voluntarily requests</u> it by using Form W-4 Employees Withholding Allowance Certificate which he <u>voluntarily </u>executes and submits as a request for withholding from his pay. The "employer" is considered to agree to the request by <u>voluntarily</u> withholding money from the employee's pay.

Despite the general mistaken belief that the deduction and withholding of money for taxes is required by law, a simple reading of this Code section shows that such is not the case. The lawyers who included the word "voluntary" in the heading of Code Section 3402(p)(3), quoted above, are well aware that mandatory withholding would conflict with two key provisions in the U.S. Constitution: the <u>Fifth Amendment</u> right to <u>due process</u> states that no person shall be deprived of property (having his pay withheld) <u>without due process of law</u> (a ruling by a court) and for individual <u>citizen</u>-employers the Thirteenth Amendment prohibition against slavery or <u>involuntary servitude</u>, such as being forced to be a Federal worker or a Federal tax collector.

<u>Regulation</u> Number 31.3402(p)(1) which is <u>added</u> protection against compulsory withholding for <u>government</u> employees states:

Sec. 31.3402(p)-1. Voluntary withholding agreements.
(T.D. 7096, filed 3-17-71; amended by TD 7577, filed 12-19-78).
(a) In general. An <u>employee</u> and his <u>employer</u> <u>may</u> enter into an <u>agreement</u> under section 3402(p) to provide for the withholding of <u>income tax</u> upon payments of amounts described in paragraph (b)(1) of sub-sec. 31.3401(a)-3, made after December 31, 1970. An <u>agreement</u> may be entered into under this section only with respect to amounts which are includable in the gross income of the <u>employee</u> under sec. 61, and must be applicable to all such amounts paid by the <u>employer</u> to the <u>employee</u>. The amount to be withheld pursuant to an <u>agreement</u> under section 3402(p) shall be determined under the rules contained in section 3402 and the regulations thereunder.
(b) Form and duration of <u>agreement</u>.
(1)(i) Except as provided in sub-division (ii) of this sub-paragraph, an employee who <u>desires to enter into an agreement</u> under section 3402(p) shall furnish his employer with Form W-4 (Withholding Exemption Certificate) executed in accordance with the provisions of section 3402(f) and the regulations thereunder. The furnishing of such Form W-4 shall constitute a <u>request</u> for withholding.
(ii) In the case of an employee who <u>desires</u> to enter into an <u>agreement</u> under section 3402(p) with his employer, if

the employee performs services (in addition to those to be the subject of the agreement) the remuneration for which is subject to mandatory income tax withholding by such employer, or if the employee wishes to specify that the agreement terminate on a specific date, the employee shall furnish the employer with a request for withholding which shall be signed by the employee and shall contain-

(a) The name, address, and social security number of the employee making the request,

(b) The name and address of the employer,

(c) A statement that the employee desires withholding of Federal income tax and, if applicable, of qualified State individual income tax (see paragraph (d)(3)(i) of sub-section 301.6361-1 of this chapter (Regulations on Procedure and Administration)), and

(d) If the employee desires that the agreement terminate on a specific date, the date of termination of the agreement. If accepted by the employer as provided in sub-division (iii) of this sub-paragraph, the request shall be attached to, and constitute part of, the employee's W-4. An employee who furnishes his employer a request for withholding under this sub-division shall also furnish such employer with Form W-4 if such employee does not already have a Form W-4 in effect with each employer.

(iii) No request for withholding under section 3402(p) shall be effective as an agreement between an employer and an employee until the employer accepts the request by commencing to withhold from the amounts with respect to which the request was made. (emphasis added)

Note the wording in sub-sections (b)(1)(ii) and (iii) of this regulation: "…an employee who desires to enter into an agreement" and "request for withholding", "desires withholding" and "mutually agree upon", all of which clearly and unambiguously show the voluntary nature of withholding for all government employees. The significance of a Form W-4 "Employee's Withholding Allowance Certificate" is clearly explained in this regulation's wording which states in Section 31.3402(p)-1.(b)(1)(i):

The furnishing of such Form W-4 shall constitute a request for withholding. (emphasis added)

The printed heading on the Form W-4 itself confirms the voluntary nature of withholding; it states "Employee's Withholding Allowance Certificate". If withholding were mandatory, why would the form be called an "Allowance" Certificate? To "allow" means to "permit"-if the law required the withholding of tax from your pay, withholding would be mandatory, and no permission or request form would be needed! To have a non-deceptive, clear-meaning heading, the words could and should be rearranged to read "Employee's Certificate Permitting Withholding" which wording would clearly show that withholding is voluntary. Again, the Fifth Amendment right to due process (not having his pay withheld without a ruling from a court authorizing the withholding) ALONE protects the citizen's paycheck (property) from withholding without his permission-hence the necessity for the Withholding Allowance Certificate. The following regulation is an even stronger specific acknowledgement that withholding is voluntary for all government employers and employees (Again, note the "voluntary" words for emphasis):

Regulation Section 31.3402(p)(2) states:

Sec. 31-3402(p)(2). Voluntary withholding agreements.
An agreement under section 3402(p) shall be effective for such period as the employer and employee mutually agree upon. However, either the employer or the employee may terminate the agreement prior to the end of such period by furnishing a signed written notice to the other. Unless the employer and the employee agree to an earlier termination date, the notice shall be effective with respect to the first payment of an amount in respect of which the agreement is in effect which is made on or after the first "status determination date" (January 1, May 1, July 1, and October 1 of each year) that occurs at least 30 days after the date on which the notice is furnished. If the employee executes a new Form W-4, the request upon which an agreement under section 3402(p) is based shall be attached to, and constitute a part of, such new Form W-4. (emphasis added)

This regulation states that the agreement "shall be effective for such period as the employer and employee mutually agree upon" (emphasis added) and that either the employer or the employee "may terminate the agreement prior to the end of such period by furnishing a signed written notice to the other." (emphasis added) Therefore it is obvious that if cancellation of withholding is <u>requested</u> by the employee, <u>it must be agreed to</u> by the employer and, in fact, it <u>MAY BE TERMINATED BY EITHER THE EMPLOYER OR THE EEMPLOYEE BY GIVING WRITTEN NOTICE TO THE OTHER</u>. The regulations merely state that the notice terminating withholding should be a signed, written notice. No particular form is even required!

How Non-Government Employers Are Deceived And Intimidated

Because employers have possession and control over their employees' earnings before the money is paid over to the employees, the key to the operation of the withholding scam is in IRS' deception and intimidation of the employers to withhold money from their employees' pay even if their employees object to the withholding. Most employers, as well as their accountants and attorneys, have never studied the I.R. Code carefully enough to understand its complexity. They are not aware of the geographical and other limitations of the flat-rate income tax imposed by Chapter 21 (so-called Social Security tax) which doesn't even use the words "Social Security" which do not appear anywhere in Chapter 21. There is no such thing as a "Social Security" or "payroll" tax imposed anywhere in the I.R. Code! Employers do not understand (as explained earlier in this chapter) that this flat-rate income tax and the withholding provisions apply statutorily only within the island possessions-Puerto Rico, the Virgin Islands, Guam and American Samoa; that under Chapter 24 withholding is not mandatory for either employer or the employee, and that withholding applies <u>only</u> to cases where <u>both</u> the employer and the employee <u>voluntarily agree</u> to withholding on a signed W-4 Withholding Allowance Certificate.

If an employer considers <u>not</u> withholding when his employees demand that they stop withholding and receive their full pay and the employer consults his accountant, tax lawyer or the IRS about the matter, his attention is usually called to I.R. Code Section 3403. This section contains a psychologically-intimidating, but <u>legally useless</u> wording designed to intimidate the employer into ignoring and defying any employee's refusal to agree to withholding. I.R. Code Section 3403 states:

Sec. 3403. Liability for tax.
The <u>employer</u> shall be liable for the payment of the tax <u>required</u> to be deducted and withheld under this chapter, and

shall not be liable to any person for the amount of any such payment. (emphasis added)

This section could <u>erroneously</u> convince employers that they are personally liable to pay to the IRS the amount the withholding tables specify if they do not withhold the money from their employees' pay. Non-government employers rarely understand that the <u>term "employer"</u> used in this section does not apply to them because the <u>term "employer"</u>, as defined in the withholding provisions, <u>means only the Federal government or Federal government-related</u> agencies and instrumentalities (listed in Section 3401(c) quoted earlier in this chapter). <u>Even then, withholding applies only when there is a voluntary mutual agreement</u> for withholding requested by the Federal "employee" and agreed to by the Federal government "employer". Consequently, the word "required" as used in this Code section, <u>has no legal effect</u>. There is <u>no</u> withholding "requirement". Because of these facts there is no way <u>any</u> non-government employer within the fifty states can be required to withhold tax under Chapter 24 because the term "employer" doesn't apply to him. Also, if an employ<u>er</u> is a U.S. citizen, he cannot be "<u>liable</u>" for payment of the tax because the Thirteenth Amendment of our Constitution protects him against being forced into <u>involuntary servitude</u> as an unpaid tax collector unless he <u>voluntarily</u> acts as such a tax collector for the government.

Summary

The flat-rate income tax (misnamed Social Security tax) imposed in Chapter 21 is a territorial <u>income</u> tax. It applies only to foreigners (not U.S. citizens) in the four island possessions. Usually <u>mis</u>named as a FICA, payroll, employment or Social Security tax, it is actually a flat-rate <u>income</u> tax that is specifically identified as such in I.R. Code Section 3101(a) and (b). Despite the common <u>mis</u>identification in the press, on the news and in public usage of this flat-rate income tax, in order not to be unconstitutional, the tax applies only to foreigners working within a limited geographical area as defined in Section 3121(e)(2) as <u>only</u> the four island possessions of Puerto Rico, Guam, the Virginia Islands and American Samoa! Wherein the <u>term</u> "United States" is defined.

This geographically-restricted definition in the Code often raises the question: "Why is this tax so restricted, both as to <u>whom</u> it applies and as to <u>where</u> it applies?" First, we must remember that our Constitution authorizes only two kinds of taxation-either direct or indirect, and any tax on a U.S. citizen or his earnings has always been ruled to be a <u>direct</u> tax. As respects the first question-"To whom does the tax apply?", we have previously stated in this book that Article 1, Section 2, Clause 3 of our Constitution requires direct taxes to be apportioned by population and levied only <u>on the states of the union</u>-and Article 1, Section 9, Clause 4 prohibits capitation taxes <u>anywhere</u>. "Capitation" is defined by *Black's Law Dictionary, 5th Edition* as "a tax or imposition on the person", and this definition includes a citizen/person's earnings and other receipts. For this reason, the tax can apply only to foreigners who, unlike citizens, are not protected against capitation taxation by Article 1, Section 9, Clause 4 of the Constitution.

As respects the second question-"<u>Where</u> does the tax apply?", the answer of <u>only</u> in the four island possessions because that is the <u>constitutionally-necessary</u> territorial restriction that Congress wrote into the law when they defined the <u>term</u> "United States" in I.R. Code Section 3121(e)(2) for purposes of the application of the tax to be limited by this Code Section to mean <u>only</u> the four island possessions of Puerto Rico, Guam, the Virgin Islands and American Samoa. Even then, application of the tax is limited to foreigners who have no constitutional immunity against direct taxation, but <u>not</u> to U.S. citizens residing in the possessions!

Both the I.R. Code and the regulations implementing the withholding provisions in the I.R. Code clearly show that <u>all withholding</u> is voluntary for <u>all citizens, both government employees under Code Section 3402(p)(1)(2) and (3) and non-government</u> <u>employees</u> under 3402(p)(3)(B). In order to institute any withholding, a <u>voluntary</u> <u>request</u> must be made by the employee and <u>acceptance</u> must be made by the employer, and either can exercise their rights to stop withholding at any time.

After studying these Code sections and their regulations carefully and understanding that they say what they mean and mean what they say, the complexity of the Code becomes much easier to understand. Terms, such as "United States", as defined in Section 3121(e)(2), show the restricted meaning of the term "United States" in Chapter 21 imposing the erroneously called Social Security tax to mean the four island possessions only. A student of the Code will find at <u>least thirteen other definitions</u> of the <u>term</u> "<u>United States</u>" in the I.R. Code. Sections 168, 217, 911, 927, 993, 3306, 4121, 4132, 4612, 4662, 4672, 7651 and 7701(a)(9) also define the <u>term</u> "United States" differently for <u>restricted use</u> in various sections of the Code. But, as discussed previously, when a particular Code section intends to include "the fifty states" in its definition, it says so – as in Section 4612(a)(4). But the <u>term</u> "United States", as defined in Section 3121(e)(2), limits application of the so-called Social Security flat-rate income tax to apply to "wages" received by <u>foreigners</u> (not U.S. citizens) only when they are working in the four island possessions!

Because of the disbursed placement of I.R. Code sections defining <u>words that are used as terms</u> in the Code, most people who read the Code without thorough study are unaware of the unique I.R. Code definitions of these terms. These definitions limit the applications of the tax laws so that they do not conflict with the Fifth or Thirteenth Amendments or with the constitutional prohibition against unapportioned direct taxes in the fifty states or against capitation taxes <u>anywhere</u>. The highly paid and well-trained attorneys who write the tax bills which are given to Congress for enactment are smart guys-they know very well the necessity of drafting these statutes in conformity with these Constitutional limitations forbidding direct taxation of citizens or their earnings. But, through careful wording of statutes and the use of confusing and misleading words, terms and definitions, they made the Code almost impossible to understand without deep study. Such actions perpetuate the <u>intentionally created, false, popular belief</u> that the Federal government has the constitutional authority to tax citizens directly. But once these Code sections are carefully analyzed, one is reminded of the old adage which points the finger at the writers of the tax code: "Oh what a tangled web we weave when first we practice to deceive."

CHAPTER VI

IRS' ILLEGAL COLLECTION ACTIVITES

Millions of citizens across the nation are learning the truth about the verbal trickery in the income tax laws and how the public is deceived by the IRS' misapplication of the law into believing that the income tax applies to the general citizenry. Most of these citizens who are learning about the income tax scam are not aware that the income tax <u>regulations</u> (Title 26 Code of Federal Regulations) are necessary to <u>implement</u> (give force of law to) the provisions in the Code. By law, the IRS gets its authority from the regulations-not from the Code. As will be shown in this chapter, the Code of Federal Regulations (CFR) authorizes actions for enforcement of alcohol, tobacco and firearms taxes only, but <u>not for income tax</u>!

The Internal Revenue Code (Title 26, United States Code) is a compilation according to subject matter of the many provisions in the taxing statutes for easy finding of the law. It is created by a government commission from the provisions relating to internal taxes in the various bills enacted into Federal law called the U.S. Statutes at Large. According to footnotes on charts listing the fifty titles in the United States Code (U.S.C.) found in law books, the I.R. Code (Title 26, U.S.C.) has never been enacted into <u>positive</u> law. The I.R. Code is only prima facie evidence of law. The law actually is in the U.S. Statutes at Large, all of which have been enacted into law by Congress.

IRS' <u>Regulations</u> Implement (Give Force Of Law To) I.R. Code Provisions

The regulations (Title 26 Code of Federal Regulations) are written by the IRS itself and are based on the provisions in the I.R. Code. When they are published in the Federal register for ninety days, as required by law, they then have the force of law, which is imposed <u>only on those persons specified in the Code</u>, as being subject to its provisions.

Black's Law Dictionary (5th Edition) defines the I.R. Code's limitations as follows:

> Internal Revenue Code (I.R.C.)
> That body of law which <u>codifies</u> all federal tax laws

including income, estate, stamp, gift, excise, etc. taxes. Such laws comprise Title 26 of the U.S. Code and are <u>IMPLEMENTED BY TREASURY REGULATIONS AND RULINGS</u>. (emphasis added)

I.R. Code Section 7805(a) explains the <u>necessity for regulations</u> to authorize and require certain actions specified in the Code. Section 7805(a) states:

Sec. 7805. Rules and regulations.
(a) Authorization.
Except where such authority is expressly given by this title to any person other than an officer or employee of the Treasury Department, the <u>Secretary shall prescribe all needful rules and regulations for the enforcement of this title</u>, including all rules and regulations as may be necessary by reason of any alteration of law in relation to internal revenue. (emphasis added)

The word "SECRETARY" (as used above) is a word used as a <u>term</u> in the I.R. Code which has an expanded meaning, as defined in Code Section 7701(a)(11)(B) as follows:

Sec. 7701: Definitions
(a) When used in this title, <u>where not otherwise distinctly expressed or manifestly incompatible with the intent thereof-</u>
(11) **Secretary of the Treasury and Secretary.**
(B) Secretary. The <u>term</u> "Secretary" means the Secretary of the Treasury <u>or his delegate</u>. (emphasis added)

The I.R. Code defines the <u>term</u> "or his delegate" in Section 7701(a)(12)(A)(i) to include virtually any Treasury Department employees whom the Secretary might authorize to act on his behalf:

Sec. 7701 Definitions.
(a) When used in this title, where not otherwise distinctly expressed or manifestly incompatible with the intent thereof-
(12) **Delegate**
(A) In general. The term "or his delegate"-

(i) when used with reference to the Secretary of the Treasury, means any officer, employee, or agency of the Treasury department duly authorized by the Secretary of the Treasury directly, or indirectly by one or more redelegations of authority, to perform the function mentioned or described in the context; ...(emphasis added)

The U.S. Supreme Court explained the essential nature of regulations created by the Secretary or his delegate of the Treasury in two decisions as follows:

<u>**California Bankers Assn. v. Schultz, et al.**</u>, **416 U.S. 21 (1974)**

*...we think it's important to note that the Act's <u>**CIVIL AND CRIMINAL PENALTIES ATTACH ONLY UPON VIOLATION OF REGULATIONS**</u> promulgated by the Secretary; if the Secretary were to do nothing, <u>the Act itself would impose no penalties on anyone.</u>* (emphasis added)

<u>**Caha v. U.S., 152 U.S. 211**</u> **(1894)**

<u>*Regulations prescribed...by the head of Departments...may thus have,*</u> *in a proper Sense,* <u>*the force of law*</u>*...* (emphasis added)

As shown above, the regulations that are written by the I.R.S. and published in the Federal Register, as required by Code Section 7805(a), are based upon the I.R. Code. The Code is taken from the <u>Statutes at Large</u> which are enacted into law by Congress. Consequently, if ever a regulation is published which exceeds the provisions of the Code, then the provisions of the Code and <u>not</u> the regulation govern its implementation.

Regulation Prefix Numbers Identify Taxes

All the regulations implementing the I.R. Code sections have <u>prefix numbers</u> that identify the <u>kind of tax to which the regulation applies</u>. In volume one of the *Federal Income Tax Regulations* (Title 26, Code of Federal Regulations) published by law book publisher, Prentice Hall, the "Introduction" contains a paragraph <u>explaining the various taxes to which</u>

the prefix numbers apply. It states:

> **Government Regulation System**
> *Treasury Regulations that follow relate to: <u>Income Tax (prefixed 1)</u>; Employment Taxes and Collection of Income Tax at source (prefixed 31); Windfall Profit Excise Taxes (prefixed 51); Private Foundation Excise Taxes (prefixed 53); Qualified Pension, etc., Plan (prefixed 54); Procedure and Administration (prefixed 301)* (emphasis added)

The prefix numbering system shows that for a regulation to apply to income tax, it must have a prefix of "1". There is an <u>official volume</u> of the regulations titled *CFR INDEX AND FINDING AIDS*. In this volume is a chart titled *PARALELL TABLE OF AUTHORITIES AND RULES* which lists the I.R. Code sections that authorize or require actions; it also lists the <u>regulations</u> that implement (<u>give force of law to</u>) those Code sections. This chart shows that the key I.R. Code sections authorizing the collection and enforcement of taxes are <u>not implemented</u> in the regulations that apply to income tax (<u>26 CFR</u>). Instead, the implementing regulations are listed as being a part of <u>27 CFR only</u>, the regulations that apply to alcohol, tobacco and firearms (ATF) taxes ONLY!

The CFR PARALLEL TABLE OF AUTHORIES AND RULES shows that the I.R. Code sections applying to the MAKING OF RETURNS (6020), ASSESSMENTS (6201), COLLECTIONS (6301), LIENS (6321), LEVIES (6331), SUMMONS FOR RECORDS (7602), SEIZURES (7608) AND CIVIL SUITS (7401 and 7403) are implemented in <u>27 CFR ONLY</u>, the regulations that apply to ATF (alcohol, tobacco and firearms) taxes <u>ONLY</u>. Thus, <u>FOR INCOME TAX</u> all of these actions by any IRS personnel are <u>ILLEGAL and FRAUDULENT</u> because they are not authorized by any regulation. It is important to remember that this PARALLEL TABLE OF AUTHORITIES AND RULES, which shows the regulations authorizing collection and enforcement for payment of taxes, <u>IS PUBLISHED BY THE OFFICE OF THE FEDERAL REGISTER FROM THE IRS REGULATIONS WRITTEN BY THE SECRETARY OF THE TREASURY OR HIS DELEGATE</u>! Therefore, all the above-listed Code sections may, <u>by IRS' own direction</u>, be implemented only in connection with taxes imposed under Title 27-Alcohol, Tobacco and Firearms!

My page numbers 106-109 show the actual printed pages of the CFR INDEX AND FINDING AIDS, including the PARALLEL TABLE OF AUTHORITIES AND RULES.

The reader's attention is called specifically to those Title 26 Code Sections cited above-namely, 6020, 6201, 6301, 6321, 6331, 7602, 7608, 7401 and 7403-all of which have implementing regulations for their enforcement in Title 27 pertaining to alcohol, tobacco and firearms ONLY-NOT income tax!

code of federal regulations

CFR Index and Finding Aids

Revised as of January 1, 1997

Published by
the Office of the Federal Register
National Archives and Records
Administration

as a Special Edition of
the Federal Register

(Except for Editors' Notes and the identifying arrows with descriptions, the information herein is copied from the CFR Index and Finding Aids)

PARALLEL TABLE OF AUTHORITIES AND RULES

The following table lists rulemaking authority (except 5 U.S.C. 301) for regulations codified in the *Code of Federal Regulations*. Also included are statutory citations which are noted as being interpreted or applied by those regulations.

The table is divided into four segments: United States Code citations, United States Statutes at Large citations, public law citations, and Presidential document citations. Within each segment the citations are arranged in numerical order:

For the United States Code, by title and section;
For the United States Statutes at Large, by volume and page number;
For public laws, by number; and
For Presidential documents (Proclamations, Executive orders, and Reorganization plans), by document number.

Entries in the table are taken directly from the rulemaking authority citation provided by Federal agencies in their regulations.* Federal agencies are responsible for keeping these citations current and accurate. Because Federal agencies sometimes present these citations in an inconsistent manner, the table cannot by considered all-inclusive.

The portion of the table listing the United States Code citations is the most comprehensive, as these citations are entered into the table whenever they are given in the authority citations provided by the agencies. United States Statutes at Large and public law citations are carried in the table only when there are no corresponding United States Code citations given.

This table is revised as of January 1, 1997. (emphasis added)   Page 705

EDITORS' NOTES

*   IRS is the Federal agency providing the regulations and citations used to create the table identifying the regulations that implement the various sections in the Internal Revenue Code.

UNDERSTANDING IRS REGULATIONS

IR code section 7805 explains the functions and necessity of regulations to authorize and enforce the provisions in the IR Code. It states:

> **Except where such authority is expressly given by this title to any person other than an officer or employee of the Treasury Department, the Secretary shall prescribe all needful rules and regulations for the enforcement of this title...** (emphasis added)

The U.S. Supreme Court explained the need for and the effect of regulations in the following two decisions:

> **Regulations prescribed...by the head of departments...may thus have, in a proper sense, the force of law...**
> Caha v. U.S., 152 U.S. 211 (1894)

> **...we think it important to note that the Act's civil and criminal penalties attach only upon violation of regulations promulgated by the Secretary; if the Secretary were to do nothing, the Act itself would impose no penalties on anyone.**
> California Bankers Association v. Schultz, et al., 416 US 21 (1974)

On the back of this page the chart of the PARALLEL TABLE OF AUTHORITIES AND RULES has arrows added to show the key code sections and implementing regulations which apply to the activities listed. All of these key collection and enforcement sections are given force of law in regulations under 27 CFR only, which applies to alcohol, tobacco and firearms taxes only

CFR INDEX

26 U.S.C. (1986 I.R.C.)---Continued	CFR
5688	19 Part 162
5691	27 Part 194
5701	27 Parts 270, 275, 290
5703---5705	27 Parts 270, 275, 290, 295
5707	27 Part 270
5708	27 Part 275, 296
5711---5713	27 Parts 270, 290
5712	27 Part 200
5721---5723	27 Parts 270, 290
5722---5723	27 Part 275
5723	19 Part 19
	27 Part 295
5731	27 Parts 270, 290
5741	27 Parts 70, 270, 275, 290, 295
5751	27 Parts 270, 290, 295, 296
5752	19 Part 19
5753	27 Part 270
5761---5763	27 Parts 270, 275, 296
5761---5762	27 Part 270
5761	27 Part 70
5762---5763	27 Part 295
5801 et seq	27 Part 179
5802	27 Part 70
6001	26 Parts 1, 31, 55, 156
	27 Parts 19, 53, 194, 250, 296
6011---6012	26 Part 1
6011	26 Parts 17, 31, 40, 55, 156, 301
	27 Parts 25, 53, 194
6015	26 Part 1
6020	27 Parts 53, 70
6021	27 Parts 53, 70
6031	26 Part 1
6033	26 Part 301
6036	26 Part 301
6038---6038B	26 Part 1
6038A	26 Part 1
6039A	26 Part 7
6041	26 Part 1
6043	26 Part 1
6045	26 Parts 1, 5f
6047	26 Part 35
6048	26 Part 404
6049	26 Part 1
6050D	26 Parts 1, 602
6050H---6050I---1	26 Part 1
6050K---6050L	26 Part 1
6050M	26 Parts 1, 301
6050P	26 Part 1
6051	26 Part 31
6053	26 Part 31
6056	27 Part 22
6059	26 Part 301
6060	26 Part 1
6061	26 Parts 156, 301
	27 Parts 22, 25, 53, 194, 270, 290
6064	27 Part 70
6065	26 Part 1
	27 Parts 17-20, 22, 24, 25, 194, 252, 270, 290
6071	26 Parts 1, 31, 49, 55, 154, 156

749

26 U.S.C. (1986 I.R.C.)---Continued	CFR
	27 Parts 53, 194
6081	26 Parts 1, 301
	27 Part 53
6090	26 Part 43
6091	26 Parts 1, 40, 44, 46, 55, 156
	27 Parts 17, 24, 25, 53, 194
6101---6104	27 Part 53
6101	26 Part 40
6102	27 Part 70
6103---6104	26 Part 301
6103	20 Parts 401, 422
	42 Part 401
6109	26 Parts 35a, 40, 150, 301
	27 Parts 17, 19, 22, 24, 25, 53, 194, 270
6111---6112	26 Part 301
6151	27 Parts 17, 22, 25, 53, 194, 270, 290
6154	26 Part 1
6155	27 Parts 53, 70
6157	26 Part 31
6158	26 Part 301
6159	27 Part 70
6161	26 Part 156
	27 Part 53
6201	27 Part 70
6203---6204	27 Part 70
6205	26 Part 31
6223	26 Part 301
6227	26 Part 301
6230---6231	26 Parts 1, 301
6232	26 Parts 41, 150
6233	26 Part 301
6241	26 Part 301
6245	26 Part 301
6301---6303	27 Part 53
6301---6302	27 Parts 24, 25, 250, 270, 275
6301	27 Part 70
6302	26 Parts 1, 31, 40
	27 Parts 19, 251
	31 Parts 203, 214
6303	27 Part 70
6311	27 Parts 19, 24, 25, 53, 70, 194, 270
6313---6314	27 Part 70
6313	27 Parts 25, 270, 275, 295
6314	27 Part 194
6321	27 Part 70
6323	26 Part 1
	27 Part 70
6324A---6324B	26 Part 301
6325	26 Part 401
	27 Part 70
6326	26 Part 301
	27 Part 70
6331---6343	27 Part 70
6334	26 Part 404
6343	26 Part 301
6364	26 Part 31
6401---6404	27 Part 70
6402	27 Parts 17, 25, 53, 194, 270, 290

750

CFR INDEX

26 U.S.C. (1986 I.R.C.)---Continued	CFR
6404	26 Part 301
	27 Parts 53, 270, 275, 290
6407	27 Part 70
6416	27 Parts 53, 70
6423	27 Parts 70, 270
6426	26 Part 154
6427	26 Part 48
6501---6503	27 Part 70
6511	27 Parts 17, 70, 194
6513---6514	27 Part 70
6532	27 Part 70
6601---6602	27 Part 70
6601	27 Parts 170, 194, 296
6611	27 Part 70
6621---6622	27 Parts 70, 170, 296
6621	26 Part 301
	27 Part 194
6651	27 Parts 24, 25, 70, 194
6653	27 Part 70
6654---6655	26 Part 1
6656---6658	27 Part 70
6656	27 Part 25
6657	27 Part 194
6662	26 Part 1
6665	27 Part 70
6671---6672	27 Part 70
6676	26 Part 35a
	27 Parts 19, 24, 25, 270
6689	26 Part 301
6701	27 Part 70
6721	26 Part 35a
6723	27 Part 70
6801	27 Part 70
6804	27 Part 250
6806	27 Parts 19, 22, 25, 270, 290
6851	26 Part 1
6862---6863	27 Part 70
6867	26 Parts 1, 301
6901	27 Part 70
7011	27 Parts 17, 19, 22, 24, 25, 70, 194, 270, 290
7025	27 Part 197
7101---7102	27 Part 250
7101	26 Part 403
	27 Parts 70, 72, 275
7102	27 Parts 70, 250
7121---7122	27 Part 70
7207	27 Part 70
7209	27 Part 70
7212	27 Parts 170, 270, 275, 290, 295, 296
7213	27 Part 17
7214	5 Part 3101
	27 Part 70
7216	26 Parts 1, 301
7302	27 Parts 24, 252
7304	27 Part 70
7322---7327	26 Part 403
7322---7326	27 Part 72
7325	27 Part 270
7326	27 Part 72
7327	27 Part 72
7342	27 Parts 24, 25, 170, 270, 275, 290, 295, 296

Lien Enforcement

26 U.S.C. (1986 I.R.C.)---Continued	CFR
7401	27 Part 70
7403	27 Part 70
7406	27 Part 70
7423---7426	27 Part 70
7429---7430	27 Part 70
7432	27 Part 70
7502---7503	27 Parts 24, 70, 270
7502	27 Part 53
7505---7506	27 Part 70
7510	27 Part 19
7513	27 Part 70
7519	26 Part 1
7520	26 Parts 1, 20, 301
7601---7606	27 Part 70
7602	27 Parts 170, 296
7606	27 Parts 24, 25, 170, 270, 275, 290, 295, 296

Summons of Records

Seizure Authority

7608	27 Parts 70, 170, 296
7609	27 Part 70
7610	27 Part 70
7622---7623	27 Part 70
7624	26 Part 301
7651 et seq	40 Part 76
7651---7652	27 Part 250
7652	27 Parts 17, 275
7653	27 Part 70
7654	26 Part 1
7701	26 Parts 1, 31, 301
7804	26 Part 1
7805	20 Part 615
	26 Parts 1-5, 5c, 5e, 5f, 6a, 7, 8, 9, 11-13, 14a, 15, 15a, 16, 16a, 17-20, 22, 25, 26, 27, 31, 32, 35, 35a, 36, 40, 41, 43-49, 52-55, 141, 143, 145, 148, 156, 301-303, 305 400, 401, 403, 404, 420, 502-505, 509-511, 514-517, 601, 602, 701, 702
	27 Parts 3, 5, 17-22, 24, 25, 30, 70, 72, 170, 179, 194, 200, 250-252, 270, 275, 290, 295, 296
7851	27 Part 24
7872	26 Part 1
9002	11 Part 9002
9003	11 Part 9003
9004	11 Part 9004
9005	11 Part 9005
9006	11 Part 9005
9007	11 Parts 301, 9007
9008	11 Parts 201, 9008
9009	11 Parts 201, 9001-9008
9012	11 Part 9012
9031	11 Part 9031
9032	11 Part 9032
9033	11 Part 9033
9034	11 Part 9034
9035	11 Part 9035
9036	11 Part 9036
9037	11 Part 9037
9038	11 Parts 201, 9038
9039	11 Part 9031-9039
9701---9708	20 Part 422

27 U.S.C.

202	27 Parts 6, 8, 10, 11
203---204	27 Part 1
203	19 Part 1

751

IRS Response To Non-Filers Who Have Stopped Withholding

In Chapters I through V we have learned that a U.S. citizen who merely exercises his constitutional right to earn a living is protected by both the Constitution and the I.R. Code against imposition or collection of an income tax on those receipts. After gaining the knowledge of law and fact contained in this book, when a citizen makes the decision to stop submitting to the extortion by stopping withholding, recording an AFFIDAVIT OF REVOCATION AND RECISSION (which will be discussed in Chapter VIII) and no longer files income tax returns, the question arises as to what response the IRS will have to his actions. The IRS' erroneous position is that all citizens owe money in the form of income taxes on their earnings that exceed the amount of their exemptions.

As we explained in the prologue and preface to this book, however, IRS' <u>policy</u> is to try to find a way, despite the law, to <u>intimidate citizens</u> into <u>voluntarily</u> paying income tax on their receipts. The IRS falsely claims that the Sixteenth Amendment (the income tax amendment) authorized Congress to impose taxes on citizens' earnings. The IRS trains their employees to believe the commonly accepted lie that the SIXTEENTH Amendment authorized Congress to directly tax the earnings and other receipts of U.S. citizens despite the overwhelming evidence to the contrary that we have explained in the earlier chapters of this book. However, the IRS has some major problems with their claim. First the law, supported by the U.S. Supreme Court in the case of **Bull v. United States**, requires, as we will show, that the IRS must make a list showing the names and amounts of taxes assessed against each person whose name appears on the list, and then must create a signed and recorded assessment certificate for any tax to be owed. The United States Supreme Court decision in the case of **Bull v. United States, 295 U.S. 247 (1935)** stated the importance of the <u>requirement</u> of an <u>assessment</u> for a tax be owed. In this decision the U.S. Supreme Court stated:

Bull v. United States, 295 U.S. 247 (1935)

The assessment may be a valuation of property subject to taxation, which valuation is to be multiplied by the statutory rate to ascertain the amount of tax. Or it may include the calculation and fix the amount of tax payable, and assessments of federal estate <u>and income taxes</u> are of *this type. Once the tax is assessed, the taxpayer will owe the sovereign the amount when the date fixed by law for payment arrives...* (emphasis added)

Clearly, this decision shows the necessity for an assessment of any tax for it to be owed. However, there is no assessment statute anywhere in the I.R. Code relating specifically to income tax as is the case in other types of taxes such as alcoholic beverages which we will see in our examination of Code Section 5061 following in this chapter.

Also, the United States Court of Appeals for the Fifth Circuit in the decision of **Brafman v. United States, 384 F2d 863 (1967)** ruled in their decision that the required assessment certificate must be signed by an authorized assessment officer in order to be valid. Therefore, the Court said in that decision that both preparation of the assessment certificate and a signature thereon are required in order for any tax to be owed:

Brafman v. United States, 384 F2d 864 (1967)

The date of the assessment is the date the summary record is signed by an assessment officer. ****Tres. Reg. #301.6203 (1955)*

It is obvious from this wording and from these Court decisions that no tax indebtedness can be created until the tax is assessed and an assessment certificate is prepared and signed by an authorized assessment officer. Therefore, we must next look at the limited assessment authority set forth in I.R. Code Section 6201 to show how the IRS tries to stretch its provisions to include authority to assess income taxes.

I.R. Code Section 6201 which is headed ASSESSMENT AUTHORITY in Sub-Sections (a) and (a)(1) states as follows:

Section 6201. Assessment authority.
(a) Authority of Secretary.
The Secretary is authorized and required to make the inquiries, determinations and assessments of all taxes (including interest, additional amounts, additions to the tax, and assessable penalties) imposed by this title, or accruing under any former internal revenue law which have not been

duly paid by stamp at the time and in the manner provided by law. Such authority shall extend to and include the following: (emphasis added)
(1) Taxes shown on return.
The Secretary shall assess all taxes determined by the taxpayer or by the Secretary as to which returns or lists are made under this title. (emphasis added)

Section 6201(a)(1) appears at first reading to be a "catch all" statute which, it seems the IRS has included, in order to give the mistaken belief that the Secretary of the Treasury or his delegate has authority to make assessments for income taxes. The wording in Section 6201(a) on line five "which have not been duly paid by stamp" is a reference to taxes on alcohol or tobacco products which are usually paid by stamp, but not to income taxes for which the IRS has no assessment authority as was shown earlier in this chapter on the PARALLEL TABLE OF AUTHORITIES AND RULES which limits such authority to taxes on alcohol, tobacco and firearms under Title 27 only!

For purposes of analysis and comparison a reference to I.R. Code Section 5061 is revealing. This Code section reads as follows:

Sec. 5061. Method of collecting tax.
(a) Collection by return.
The taxes on distilled spirits, wines, and beer shall be collected on the basis of a return. The Secretary shall, by regulation, prescribe the period or event for which such return shall be filed, the time for filing such return, the information to be shown in such return, and the time for payment of such tax.
(b) Exceptions.
Notwithstanding the provisions of sub-section (a), any taxes imposed on, or amounts to be paid or collected in respect of, distilled spirits, wines, and beer under-…shall be immediately due and payable at the time provided by such provisions (or if no specific time for payment is provided, at the time the event referred to in such provision occurs). Such taxes and amounts shall be assessed and collected by the Secretary on the basis of the information available to him in the same manner as taxes payable by return but with respect to which no return has been filed… (emphasis added)

Paragraph (a) of this Code section states an initial necessity for the taxes on distilled spirits, wines and beer to be collected, as underlined above, "on the basis of a return". However, sub-section (b) **Exceptions** states that "such taxes…shall be assessed…in the same manner as taxes payable by return but with respect to which no return has been filed." (emphasis added) Since Section 5061 clearly authorizes assessment of taxes on alcoholic products with or without a return, this writer is of the opinion that Section 6201 is really an unnecessary Code section because this broad assessment authority is totally covered by Section 5061. This writer thinks that Section 6201 was enacted in order to create the false impression that this Section 6201 authorizes an income tax assessment that obviously does not exist in Section 5061 which is pointedly limited to alcoholic products. It really makes no difference whether this is correct or incorrect because the IRS' own PARALLEL TABLE OF AUTHORITIES AND RULES specifically limits any application of Code Section 6201 in its entirety to enforcement under Title 27 alcohol, tobacco and firearms taxes only! Also, any tax on citizens of the United States or their earnings which we have discussed in depth in earlier chapters of this book would be a capitation tax, which is prohibited by Article 1, Section 9, Clause 4 of the Constitution.

I.R. Code Section 6203 is titled Method of Assessment and explains the necessity for recording the liability of the taxpayer as follows:

Sec. 6203. Method of assessment.
The assessment shall be made by recording the liability of the taxpayer in the office of the Secretary in accordance with rules or regulations prescribed by the Secretary. Upon request of the taxpayer, the Secretary shall furnish the taxpayer a copy of the record of the assessment. (emphasis added)

As is shown by this Code section, an assessment document of recordation must be prepared by the Secretary or his delegate and made available upon request by the taxpayer. The wording in Code Section 6203 which reads: "shall furnish the 'taxpayer' a copy of the record of the assessment" is clearly intended to include a record of the taxpayer's name, and the amount of tax assessed in order that the "taxpayer" might be able to confirm that they have been personally assessed. A simple copy of the record of the assessment which did not include the taxpayer's name and the amount of tax he had been assessed would provide no "record of the assessment" that would satisfy the requirement of Code Section 6203.

The U.S. Supreme Court's decision in the case of <u>Gould v. Gould,</u> quoted repeatedly in this book, supports and confirms this conclusion. It is important because the IRS knows that they have no authority to assess income taxes. Therefore, assessments against citizens who have stopped voluntary filing and withholding are not made because the IRS knows that they would be illegal and fraudulent. Such exposure of the IRS' illegal actions would be politically unacceptable at best, which explains why they don't make these unlawful assessments.

As we pointed out earlier in this chapter, the PARALLEL TABLE OF AUTHORITIES AND RULES which is prepared by the Office of the Federal Register from the IRS' regulations written by the Secretary of the Treasury or his delegate also shows that the <u>entire assessment authority</u> including the making of the assessment, and the preparation of a recordation assessment document is applicable only to taxes imposed by regulations in Title 27 for Alcohol, Tobacco and Firearms-<u>not</u> for income taxes under Title 26 regulations!

Common Misuse of the Levy Authority
All Levy Notices For Income Tax Are Unlawful And Fraudulent

The word "levy" is incorrectly assumed by most people to mean "a claim". However, *Black's Law Dictionary* (5th Edition) defines the word "levy" as follows:

> **Levy, n.** *A <u>seizure</u>. The obtaining of money by legal process through <u>seizure</u> and sale of property...* (emphasis added)

Note that the legal definition of "levy" is "seizure"-meaning physical acquisition or possession of the property levied upon. The use of the term "levy" in connection with alcohol, tobacco and firearms taxes makes sense because for such taxes the IRS has the power to "seize" the taxable property in contrast to the misapplication of the word "seize" to income taxes where monies in bank accounts or paychecks are <u>not property susceptible to "seizure"</u>. In addition, as we have previously shown, the PARALLEL TABLE OF AUTHORITIES AND RULES, which is prepared by the Office of the Federal Register <u>from IRS regulations</u>, limits all levy authority which is authorized by Code Section 6331 to Title 27-Alcohol, Tobacco and Firearms taxes only. Consequently, when the IRS sends out a so-called NOTICE OF LEVY to a U.S. citizen's employer or bank, falsely alleging income tax due they are improperly misapplying the law in two different ways. First, the IRS' own PARALLEL TABLE OF AUTHORITIES AND RULES shows that use of the levy authority is limited to alcohol, tobacco and firearms taxes. Ignoring these limitations, the IRS illegally sends thousands of these fraudulent levy notices to the employers and banks of U.S. citizens in attempts to illegally collect income taxes which are not owed. Second, over and above this limitation (which is sufficient in and of itself) the statutory limitations on the power of levy require a seizure.

Section 6502 Collection after assessment.
(b) Date when levy is considered made.
The date on which a levy on property or right to property is made shall be the date on which the notice of seizure provided in Section 6335(a) is given. (emphasis added)

Sec. 6335. Sale of seized property.
(a) Notice of Seizure.
As soon as practicable after seizure of property, notice in writing shall be given by the Secretary to the owner of the property...(emphasis added)

These provisions clearly show that there must first be a "seizure", followed by a "Notice of Seizure" to the property owner in order for a "levy" to be created. However, when the I.R.S. agent mails the "Notice of Levy" form to an employer or a bank, even though they obviously have not "seized" the pay (of an employee) or the bank account of the depositor (in the bank), the notice contains a lie that a levy (seizure) has already been made in order to fraudulently induce the recipient of the notice to voluntarily surrender the individual's money to the I.R.S. The IRS agent who sends out this notice also clearly ignores the statutory requirements of the I.R. Code Sections 6502(b) and 6335(a) which show that when no seizure has been made and the required Notice of Seizure has not been sent, no levy is created.

A third statutory limitation on the I.R.S.' power of levy is contained in Code Section 7608 which authorizes seizures.

Sec. 7608. Authority of internal revenue enforcement officers.
(a) Enforcement of subtitle E and other laws pertaining to liquor, tobacco, and firearms.

Any investigator, agent, or other internal revenue officer by whatever term designated, whom the Secretary charges with the duty of enforcing any of the criminal, seizure, or forfeiture provisions of <u>subtitle E</u> or of any other law of the United States <u>pertaining to the commodities subject to tax under such subtitle</u> for the enforcement of which the Secretary is responsible may-…(emphasis added)

(b) Enforcement of laws relating to internal revenue other than subtitle E: (includes sub-title A)
(1) Any <u>criminal investigator</u> of the Intelligence Division or of the Internal Security Division of the Internal Revenue Service whom the Secretary charges with the duty of enforcing any of the <u>criminal</u> provisions of the internal revenue laws or other <u>criminal</u> provisions of law relating to internal revenue for the enforcement of which the Secretary is responsible, in the performance of his duties, is authorized to perform the functions described in paragraph (2).
(2) The <u>functions authorized</u> under this subsection to be performed <u>by an officer referred to in paragraph (1)</u> are:
(A) to execute and serve search warrants and arrest warrants,…
(B) to make arrests without warrant for any offense against the the United States relating to the internal revenue laws.
(C) to make <u>seizures</u> of <u>property subject to forfeiture</u> under the internal revenue laws.

Note that under sub-section (a) of Section 7608, the seizure authority is limited to enforcement of sub-title E, relating to alcohol, tobacco and firearms <u>only</u>. Sub-section (b)(1) provides no enforcement authority for income tax; rather it is restricted to criminal provisions found in Sub-Title F which contains Chapter 75 that specifies penalties for various crimes.

It is important to note that sub-section (b) of Code Section 7608 applies to the to enforcement of the <u>criminal</u> provisions of sub-title F which includes Chapter 75 citing penalties for criminal violations of various tax laws. Consequently, this Code section extends <u>no authority</u> to enforcement of <u>civil</u> provisions which are involved in the IRS' unlawful lien and levy collection efforts against U.S. citizens for income tax.

Therefore, sub-sections (a) or (b), by their own wording as shown above, provide no authority for any investigator, agent or other Internal Revenue officer, whether a revenue or a criminal agent, to engage in civil collection activity for income tax! Over and above this, as we have previously shown, the PARALLEL TABLE OF AUTHORITYIES AND RULES provides yet another reason why this statute (Code Section) has no application for enforcement to taxes other than for those in Title 27-alcohol, tobacco and firearms and confirms the lack of authority for income tax under IR Code Section 7608.

Finally, the seizure authority in Section 7608 is limited by sub-section (b)(2)(C) to "property subject to forfeiture". Such property is specifically limited and defined in Code Sections 7301(a), (b), (c), (d) and (e) and in Sections 7302 and 7303 as follows:

PART I.-PROPERTY SUBJECT TO FORFEITURE

Sec. 7301. Property subject to tax.
Sec. 7302. Property used in violation internal revenue laws.
Sec. 7303. Other property subject to forfeiture.

Sec. 7301. Property subject to tax.
(a) Taxable articles.
Any property on which, or for or in respect whereof, any taxes imposed by this title which shall be found in the possession or custody or within the control of any person, for the purpose of being sold or removed by him in fraud of the internal revenue laws, or with design to avoid payment of such tax, or which is removed, deposited or concealed, with intent to defraud the United States of such tax or any part thereof, may be seized, and shall be forfeited to the United States.
(b) Raw materials.
All property found in the possession of any person intending to manufacture the same into property of a kind subject to tax for the purpose of selling such taxable property in fraud of the internal revenue laws, or with design to evade the payment of such tax, may also be seized, and shall be forfeited to the United States.
(c) Equipment.
All property whatsoever, in the place or building, or any yard

or enclosure, where the property described in subsection (a) or (b) is found, or which is intended to be used in the making of property described in subsection (a) with intent to defraud the United States of tax or any part thereof, on the property described in subsection (a) may also be seized, and shall be forfeited to the United States.
(d) Packages.
All property used in a container for, or which shall have contained, property described in subsection (a) or (b) may also be seized, and shall be forfeited to the United States.
(e) Conveyances.
Any property (including aircraft, vehicles, vessels, or draft animals) used to transport or for the deposit or concealment of property described in subsection (a) or (b), or any Property used to transport or for the deposit or concealment of property which is intended to be used in the making or packaging of property described in subsection (a) may also be seized and shall be forfeited to the United States.

Sec. 7302. Property used in violation of internal revenue laws.
It shall be unlawful to have or possess any property intended for use in violating the provisions of the internal revenue laws, or regulations prescribed under such laws, or which has been so used, and no property rights shall exist in any such property. A search warrant may issue as provided in chapters 205 of title 18 of the United States Code and the Federal Rules of Criminal Procedure for the seizure of such property. Nothing in this section shall in any manner limit or affect any criminal or forfeiture provision of the internal revenue laws, or of any other law. The seizure and forfeiture of any property under the provisions of this section and the disposition of such property subsequent to seizure and forfeiture, or the disposition of the proceeds from the sale of such property shall be in accordance with existing laws or those hereafter in existence relating to seizures, forfeitures, and disposition of property or proceeds, for violation of the internal revenue laws.
Sec. 7303. Other property subject to forfeiture.
There may be seized and forfeited to the United States the

following:

(1) Counterfeit stamps. Every stamp involved in the offense described in section 7208 (relating to counterfeit, reused, cancelled, etc., stamps), and the vellum, parchment, document, paper, package, or article upon which such stamp was placed or impressed in connection with such offense.

(2) False stamping of packages. Any container involved in the offense described in section 7271 (relating to disposal of stamped packages), and of the contents of such container.

(3) Fraudulent, bonds, permits, and entries. All Property to which any false or fraudulent instrument involved in the offense described in section 7207 relates.

Section 7301, which defines properties subject to forfeiture, states that seizures may be made of taxable property upon which tax has not been paid which is held under 7301(a) "<u>for the purpose of being sold or removed</u>" (<u>from a bonded warehouse</u>) and under Sub-Titles (b), (c), (d) and (e) respectively-raw materials, equipment, packages and conveyances used in the manufacture or transport of such taxable property (alcohol and tobacco products). From these definitions, clearly property subject to seizure and forfeiture does <u>not</u> <u>include monies held by banks, employers, agents, creditors, etc. which are owned by, due or owed to any individual</u>. On the basis of these Code Sections, a Notice of Levy sent to such parties (usually employers and/or banks) demanding the turnover of money for income tax allegedly owed by their employees or depositors is fraudulent because it contains a <u>false statement</u> that a levy has been made when such is not the case because there has been <u>no seizure</u> and no notice of seizure given, as required by Section 6335(a) in order to create a levy as provided in Section 6502(b). Again, the IRS' own PARALLEL TABLE OF AUTHORITIES AND RULES restricts both Code Sections 6335(a) and 6502(b) to application for enforcement of alcohol, tobacco and firearms taxes only under Title 27!

<u>Another Misuse of the Levy Notice</u>

A huge intentional misapplication is also practiced by the IRS on the Notice of Levy form which they routinely illegally send to employers, banks or others (such as the Social Security Administration) holding monies for the account of any (alleged) "taxpayer" who has stopped withholding and stopped filing returns. First, and of utmost importance, we must remember that as we pointed out earlier in this chapter, the levy authority in I.R. Code Section 6331 is also restricted by the PARALLEL TABLE OF AUTHORITIES AND RULES to use for enforcement of taxes in Title 27-Alcohol, Tobacco and Firearms-not income tax! So, when the IRS tries to use this Code section to attach monies in banks or held by citizens' employers, they are in clear and unmistakable violation of the limited Title 27 authority only! Second, they even have the gall to print on the back of the Section 6331 Levy Notice only <u>parts</u> of Section 6331! The IRS <u>completely</u> <u>omits</u> Sub-Section 6331(<u>a</u>) which contains <u>vitally important limitations upon the application of all of the provisions in Section 6331</u>. Section 6331(<u>a</u>) states:

> **Sec. 6331. Levy and distraint.**
> **(a) Authority of Secretary.**
> If <u>any person</u> <u>liable</u> to pay any tax neglects or refuses to pay the same within 10 days after notice and demand, it shall be lawful for the Secretary to collect such tax...by levy upon all property and rights to property...belonging to such person or on which there is a lien provided in this chapter for the payment of such tax. Levy may be made upon the accrued salary or wages <u>of any officer, employee, or elected official, of the United States, the District of Columbia, or any agency or instrumentality of the United States or District of Columbia,</u> by serving a notice of levy on the employer (as defined in Section 3401(d)) of such officer, employee, or elected official...(emphasis added)

Second and foremost, it is clear from the Code section quoted above and underlined for emphasis, that the levy authority extends <u>only</u> to the salary or wages of <u>Federal employees</u>. Therefore, the <u>earnings of all citizens who do not work for the Federal government are exempt from the levy authority in this Code section</u>! There is good reason why Congress, in drafting this statute (Code section), limits the levy authority to the wages or salaries of Federal employees. In their own Legal Reference Guide for Revenue Officers on page 57 (Ed. 1/14/87) the IRS cautions its revenue officers that an appellate court in the case of <u>Freeman v. Mayer</u>, 253 F2d 295 (1968) stated in this decision that "...a levy requires that the property levied upon be brought into legal custody through <u>seizure</u>. There must be actual or constructive physical appropriation of the property levied upon. Mere intent to reduce to possession and control is insufficient...".

In keeping with the above <u>Freeman v. Mayer</u> decision, by limiting this levy authority to Federal employees' pay, the IRS avoids the problem they would have in trying to "seize" or gain physical control of the pay of non-Federal employees because the IRS, as a government agency, already <u>has control</u> of the pay of Federal employees! So no "seizure" is required to satisfy the <u>Freeman v. Mayer</u> court decision shown above. However, this limitation protects <u>ALL</u> <u>non</u>-government employees from any levy if the employer or bank holding these funds for their employee or depositor simply takes the time to read the missing section (<u>a</u>) of Code Section 6331!

Third, the wording at the beginning of Code Section 6331(a) "If <u>any person liable</u> to pay any tax..." should immediately raise the question of whether or not their employee or depositor is "<u>liable to pay</u>" any Federal tax. Even a totally uneducated employer or bank, after reading the wording "any personal liable" would logically, before complying, ask two obvious questions: "WHAT IS THE STATUTE (LAW) WHICH MAKES MY EMPLOYEE OR MY DEPOSITOR 'LIABLE' TO PAY ANY TAX.?" And also logically, the employer or bank receiving such a notice would ask: "IF I COMPLY WITH THIS REQUEST, AM I LIABLE TO MY DEPOSITOR OR MY EMPLOYEE IF I FIND LATER THAT THE LAW NEVER REQUIRED ME TO COMPLY?" Surprisingly, employers controlling payroll funds due to employees and banks who receive these unlawful levy notices usually treat them as though they were court orders, and immediately comply with their demand. Even when they ask their attorneys what they should do, amazingly, they are usually told by their own counsel to comply! Such legal advice only demonstrates how powerful the IRS has become! However, the law is all on the side of the citizen. A suit in U.S .District Court showing the inapplicability of this Code section for the reasons we have reviewed should win. Being very aware that when these questions are asked and that they would be unable to provide acceptable answers, the IRS <u>intentionally fails to include Section 6331(a)</u> so that these questions (hopefully) will not arise!

Fourth and finally, as we have repeatedly stated, over and above the reasons shown above, the levy authority is also restricted by the PARALLEL TABLE OF AUTHORITIES AND RULES to use for the enforcement of Title 27-Alcohol, Tobacco and Firearms taxes only! All of these reasons provide the citizen with powerful evidence to eliminate any unlawful use of the assessment, lien or levy authority against income tax!

Misapplication Of Code Section 6020

As we have shown in both <u>Bull v. United States</u> and <u>Brafman v. United States</u>, a signed and recorded assessment is a statutory (code section) requirement for any tax to be owed. Despite the fact, as has also been shown, that the IRS has <u>no statutory authority</u> to make any "income tax" assessment, they unlawfully attempt to create grounds for an assessment from a return. They do this by alleging that they have authority from Code Section 6201(a)(1) which we quoted earlier in this chapter even though such authority cannot constitutionally exist. In any event, even if we incorrectly assumed that such authority was created by Section 6201(a)(1), this section still clearly states that an assessment can be made only <u>from a return</u>. Acting on this fact/requirement, the IRS attempts to unlawfully use the provisions of Code Section 6020 to create a return from which they can assess an income tax despite the fact that they have no <u>authority</u> under that Code section to use its provisions for income tax!

It is clear from a reading of Code Section 6201(a)(1) that a <u>return</u> would be required under that section for the Secretary to make an assessment, even if it could be interpreted to include an assessment authority for income taxes. Let us first assume that Section 6201 authorized the IRS to make an income tax return, which is what the IRS wants us to believe. If the informed citizen does not make a return because he has learned that there is no law requiring him to do so, the IRS, despite the limitation of the assessment authority to Title 27 taxes, ignores this limitation and, acting with the <u>alleged</u> authority of I.R. Code Section 6020 (which we will quote following) prepares an unsigned "Substitute for Return" document which they pretend to be a return. They <u>falsely</u> claim that they are authorized to use this "Substitute for Return" as the basis for making the <u>statutorily-required signed assessment certificate</u> which they <u>do not make</u> because the IRS knows full well that they have no statutory authority to make any assessment for income taxes in the first place!

It has always been the IRS' position that a Form 1040 that either does not contain figures from which an alleged tax can be computed or determined is <u>not a return</u> and cannot be considered legally to be a return. Their position is also that <u>unsigned</u> Forms 1040 are also <u>not returns</u>. Therefore, these positions are inconsistent with and contradictory to their own actions when they claim they have authority to assess income taxes from unsigned, incomplete 1040 forms and/or "Account Transcripts" which do not contain figures from which a tax can be computed. Finally, they admit that these papers are mostly unsigned "Substitute(s) for Return(s)" by printing the words "Substitute for Return" on the bottom of these "Account Transcripts"! Section 6020 states as follows:

> *Sec. 6020. Returns prepared for or executed by Secretary.*
> *(b) Execution of return by Secretary.*
> *(1) Authority of Secretary to execute return.* If any person fails to make any return <u>required</u> by any internal revenue law <u>or regulation</u> made thereunder at the time prescribed therefore, or makes, willfully or otherwise, a false or fraudulent return, the Secretary shall <u>make such return</u> from his own knowledge and from such information as he can obtain through testimony or otherwise. (emphasis added)
> *(2) Status of returns.* Any return so made and subscribed by the Secretary shall be prima facie good and sufficient for all legal purposes.

Note particularly the word "<u>required</u>" in the above Code Section 6020(b)(1) which clearly makes mandatory the <u>identification</u> of a law (Code section) which <u>requires the filing of a return</u>! The IRS, however, totally ignores the "requirement" in this Code section which mandates identification of <u>some other Code section</u> that would impose a filing requirement by an alleged taxpayer who has failed to do so. They fail to identify any "requirement" statute (Code section) because they cannot-none exists! The IRS prepares, rather than a return, a piece of paper which they identify on its face as an "Account Transcript" which clearly is not a return in any sense of the word, but rather is merely a paper containing figures such as "Account Balance", "Accrued Interest", "Accrued Penalty" and similar entries. There is no possible way that the <u>alleged </u>taxpayer <u>or any court of law</u> could possibly consider that this document complies with the clear requirements of Code Section 6020(b)(1) which requires the Secretary to make a <u>return</u> as commanded by the statute. In fact, the <u>alleged</u> taxpayer can never determine where the figures shown on the Acount Transcript came from as would be the case if the Secretary (or his delegate) had actually filed a completed Form 1040 return as required by Code Section 6020(b)(1) from which the computation could easily be determined. Also, this foney Account Transcript document is always <u>unsigned</u> even though an authorized signature is clearly required by Code Section 6020(b)(2) shown above. Further, this document is even identified at the bottom that it is a

"SUBSTITUTE FOR RETURN" which is an obvious admission that the document is <u>not</u> a return as required by Code Section 6020(b)(1) because this Code Section <u>requires</u> the Secretary to "make such return"!

Sometimes, apparently before the IRS developed the ACCOUNT TRANSCRIPT as an unlawful substitute for the "return" required by IR Code Section 6020, they used a dummy, but still <u>unsigned</u>, blank Form 1040 which was improperly identified as a "return" required by IR Code Section 6020(b) by either printing or writing the words "SUBSTITTUE FOR RETURN" across the top of the 1040 form. This document also fails to satisfy the clear requirements of Code Section 6020(b)(1) and (2) because it contains no figures from which a tax allegedly due can be computed; it is <u>always unsigned</u> and is even identified on its face as a "<u>Substitute for Return</u>". Obviously, a "substitute for return" is no more a "return" than a donkey is a horse. It is this writer's opinion that the IRS' failure to file and sign even the "substitute" form as required by law is an obvious attempt by the IRS, by not signing the form and by using the word "substitute", to avoid legal responsibility of any employee who might otherwise be identified and thereby subject to severe penalties for their unlawful actions as we will see in the cases of **Bothke v. Fluor** and **Butz v. Economou** following in this chapter.

This "SUBSTITUTE FOR RETURN", whether an unsigned Form 1040 or an ACCOUNT TRANSCRIPT, is regularly used by the IRS to unlawfully create dummy <u>misnamed</u> returns for countless thousands of citizen employees who have stopped withholding and stopped filing returns. Those citizens would include self-employed persons and Social Security recipients who have not filed but whose <u>so-called</u> "income" has been reported to the IRS on W-2 forms and/or 1099 Miscellaneous Income forms from which figures the IRS has unlawfully computed an alleged tax due.

The citizen who is victimized by this unlawful use of Code Section 6020(b) has a powerful weapon available to him to force the IRS to cease and desist and even to refund any and all money, with interest, that was stolen through misapplication of Code Section 6020(b). The IRS' own Internal Revenue Manual, in Chapter 5200, describes the <u>proper</u> legal use of I.R. Code Section 6020(b), stating:

Sec. 5209.   Refusal to File I.R.C. 6020(b) Assessment Procedure 5291 Scope

(1) This procedure applies to employment, excise and partnership returns…the following returns <u>will be involved</u>: (a) Forms 940-Employer's Annual Federal Unemployment Tax Return (b) Form 941-Employer's Quarterly Federal Tax Return (c) Form 942-Employer's Quarterly Tax Return for Household Employees (d) Form 943-Employer's Annual Tax Return for Agricultural Employees (e) Form 11-B-Special Tax Return-Gaming Devices (f) Form 720-Quarterly Federal Excise Return (g) Form 2290-Federal Use Tax Return on Highway Motor Vehicles (h) Form CT-1-Employers' Annual Railroad Retirement Tax Return (i) Form 1065-U.S. Partnership Return of Income

Note that the above list <u>from the IRS' own manual</u> applies <u>only</u> to employment, some excise and partnership tax returns-<u>not to income tax!</u> The IRS knows very well that no direct tax can be applied on the earnings of U.S. citizens and that is why the use of Section 6020(b) is so limited.

I.R. Code Sections 6061 and 6065 repeat what we have already stated previously in this book-that is, that any "return", "substitute for return" and other document such as the "Account Transcript" prepared by the Secretary (or his delegate) <u>must be signed</u> (Section 6061) and <u>verified under penalties of perjury</u> (Section 6065). Remember also that Section 6020(b)(2), which we quoted earlier stated that "any return so made <u>and subscribed</u> (signed) by the Secretary shall be prima facie good and sufficient for all legal purposes." The IRS NEVER SIGNS any of these documents as required whether they are incomplete Forms 1040, Account Transcripts or any other documents that they unlawfully prepare under the alleged authority of Code Section 6020(b)!

Finally, execution of documents such as returns and any other papers related to returns are authorized by the IRS under their own "delegation orders" which must be kept on file in the district offices of each IRS office. The delegation orders for completion of all returns under Section 6020(b) are authorized for revenue officers at a level of GS9 and above only. This delegation authority is limited in every district to the same returns shown in the IRS' own revenue manual for instruction of their agents as respects the <u>same coded forms</u> as quoted above-namely, Form 940, Form 941, Form 942, Form 943, Form 11-B, Form 720, Form 2290, Form CT-1 and Form

1065. None of these forms are authorized for income tax!

Unfortunately, for Social Security recipients and for others who receive any form of payment from any agency of the Federal government, these Federal agencies, including the Social Security Administration, simply roll over and give up whatever payments they ordinarily make to their beneficiaries whenever demanded of them by the IRS. Surrender by Social Security of 15% of the retiree's check without a court order is a clear violation of the citizen/retiree's right to due process under the Fifth Amendment of the Constitution. Where the IRS gets their legal authority to access these funds from other Federal agencies is never stated. In the case of the Social Security Administration, however, the IRS alleges that under the Debt Collection Improvement Act of 1996 (Chapter 10, Sec. 31001), they are supposedly authorized to attach 15% of the retirees' Social Security monthly pension in order to satisfy the alleged tax obligation. Based upon this alleged obligation which could not exist, lacking proper compliance by the IRS with the requirements of I.R. Code Sections 6020(b)(1) and 6201 shown above, SS retirees who are living on a very limited (often their only) income are financially squeezed even further by the IRS when they take 15% of the retiree's monthly Social Security check, even though they have not complied with the clear requirements of I.R. Code Section 6020(b) as shown above. Neither the Secretary nor his delegate ever filed a return on behalf of the alleged taxpayer whose 15% of his S.S. check is simply given away illegally by Social Security to the IRS without a court order in violation of the retiree's right to due process under the Fifth Amendment and in violation of all the other law specified throughout this chapter! In doing this, the Social Security Administration becomes equally guilty with the IRS through their failure to require proof of a valid debt and to require compliance with the Social Security beneficiary's Fifth Amendment right to due process!

IRS Agents Are Personally Liable For Their Acts

There is some good news for those who have courage enough to fight these unlawful acts. In the decision in the case of **Bothke v. Fluor, 713 F2d 1405 (1983)** the U.S. Court of Appeals ruled that an IRS employee lost her sovereign immunity when she engaged in an unauthorized action and that thererby she became personally liable. In support of its ruling, the Bothke Court quoted from the United States Supreme Court decision in the case of **Butz v. Economou, 438 U.S. 478 (1978)** which stated:

> *With the IRS' broad power must come a concomitant responsibility to exercise it <u>within the confines of the law</u>. The Court has emphasized that <u>no official is above the law</u>, and that broad powers present broad opportunities for abuse.* (emphasis added)

As we have previously stated in this book, another reason why there is no Code section or regulation authorizing the assessment and/or enforcement of income tax was also shown in a Congressional hearing in the House of Representatives Sub-Committee on Administration of the Internal Revenue Laws on February 3rd, 1953. In that hearing, Mr. Dwight Avis, head of the Alcohol and Tobacco Tax Division of the IRS explained:

> *That is where this structure differs. Let me point this out now. YOUR <u>INCOME TAX IS 100% VOLUNTARY TAX</u>, and your liquor tax is 100% <u>enforced tax</u>. Now the situation is as different as day and night.* (emphasis added)

As we showed in Chapter 1, Fact #13, the United States Court of Appeals for the Second Circuit stated in the decision of **Botta v. Scanlon, 288 F2d. 504 (1961),** at **506:**

> *Moreover, even the collection of taxes should be exacted only from persons upon whom a tax liability is imposed <u>by some statute</u>.* (emphasis added)

This Court decision clearly shows that the only way anyone can <u>be made liable</u> for any Internal Revenue tax is by means of some law (statute) which imposes liability upon him or her. This fact was again emphasized in the decision of **Higley v. Commissioner, 69 F2d. 160** where the Court stated:

> *Liability for taxation must clearly appear <u>from statute</u> imposing tax.*
> (emphasis added) See also Chapter 1, Fact #14.

As examples of this **Higley v. Commissioner** Court quotation, there are various sections in the I.R. Code which impose liability for various Federal taxes. Some of these sections are "44021(a), 5005(a), 5703(a) and 1461 which, in clear, understandable words, make certain "persons" <u>liable</u>

for payment of wagering tax, distilled spirits tax, tobacco tax and '<u>income</u>' tax respectively." The word "liable' is used in each of these Code sections as we showed in detail in Chapters I and III of this book. **Section 1461 is the <u>ONLY</u> section in the I.R. Code imposing a liability on <u>anyone</u> for payment of an "<u>income</u> tax".** Section 1461 states, in part, as follows:

> **Sec. 1461. Liability for withheld tax.**
> Every person <u>required to deduct and withhold</u> any tax under this chapter is hereby <u>made liable</u> for such tax… (emphasis added)

A simple reading of the Code Section 1461 shows that the "person… made liable" by the statute is one who is "required to deduct and withhold"… under this chapter." (Chapter 3). In that chapter, the **only** "person required to deduct and withhold" is identified in Code Section 1441(a) which states in part as follows:

> **Sec. 1441. Withholding of tax on nonresident aliens.**
> **(a) General rule.**
> Except as otherwise provided in subsection (c), all persons, in whatever capacity acting…<u>having the control, receipt,</u> custody, disposal or payment of any of the <u>items of income</u> specified in subsection (b) (to the extent that any of such items constitute gross income from sources within the United States), <u>of any non-resident alien individual, or of any foreign partnership</u>, shall deduct and <u>withhold from such items</u> a tax equal to 30 percent thereof… (emphasis added)

<u>Code Section 1461 makes the person required to deduct and withhold (a withholding agent)</u> in Section 1441 "<u>liable</u>" for the 30% deduction which is required to be made under Section 1441. Otherwise stated, Section 1441 identifies the <u>withholding agent</u>, and his responsibility to deduct from foreign persons or entities <u>only</u> and Section 1461 makes such withholding agent "<u>liable</u>" for the 30% deduction required under Section 1441(a). As stated earlier, **SECTION 1461 IS THE <u>ONLY</u> SECTION IN THE I.R. CODE IMPOSING LIABILITY FOR THE PAYMENT OF AN "INCOME" TAX AND THAT SECTION APPLIES ONLY TO THOSE REQUIRED TO WITHOLD FROM "INCOME" PAID TO FOREIGNERS.** Unless one <u>is in the status of "withholding agent"</u>, he is <u>not liable</u> for payment of income tax and is <u>not</u> <u>required to file</u> an income tax return.

The IRS knows very well about the limitations of these I.R. Code provisions which require a law (statute) making a person "liable" for a tax, and they know they can't show a Code section making any citizen "liable" for a tax on their own earnings or receipts! This is why they omit Section 6331(a) when they send out their levy notices! This intentional omission on the levy notice is clearly fraud by the IRS. Fraud is defined by *Black's Law Dictionary, 5th Edition* as follows: "an intentional perversion of the truth for the purpose of inducing another in reliance upon it to part with some valuable thing belonging to him or to surrender a legal right…"

As we explained in Chapter V, the 13th Amendment of the U.S. Constitution states: "Neither slavery nor involuntary servitude…shall exist within the United States…" (emphasis added), and this prohibition against forced withholding totally prohibits any compulsory withholding by any individual-citizen employer, from their employee unless they have such permission from the employee in the form of a voluntary W-4 Employee Withholding Allowance Certificate.

And, at the same time, the Fifth Amendment to our Constitution states in part: "No person shall…be deprived of life, liberty or property, without due process of law…" (emphasis added). This wording "without due process of law" means a court hearing, and no court would ever allow withholding from a citizen without his permission because both our Constitution and our Supreme Court have ruled that the word "property" includes wages, salary, etc. So the Fifth Amendment protects all citizen-employees from any legal requirement to make their employers withhold without the employees' permission in the form of a W-4 Withholding Allowance Certificate. (See Chapter V of this book)

Therefore, no citizen-employer or any employee can be compelled by law to withhold (employer) or submit to withholding (employee). Thus, all withholding is voluntary, requiring agreement by both the employer and the employee, and the law in the I.R. Code and the regulations as we saw in Chapter V is in complete agreement that all withholding is voluntary by all employers and employees, both government and non-government.

We have previously stated that in the United States Supreme Court decision of **Gould v. Gould**, 245 U.S. 151 (1917), a case we have discussed in earlier chapters of this book, the Court stated:

In the interpretation of statutes levying taxes it is <u>the established rule not to exceed their provisions, by implication</u>, beyond the clear import of the language used, or to enlarge their operations so as to embrace matters not specifically pointed out. <u>In case of doubt they are construed most strongly against the government, and in favor of the citizen</u>. (emphasis added)

This clearly means that there can be no implied liability beyond that which is specifically stated (Code Section) in the statute. In the **Botta v. Scanlon** decision mentioned earlier, the Court also stated in a clear reference to the citizens' protection under the Fifth Amendment:

<u>**Botta v. Scanlon**, 288, F2d 504 (1961)</u>

However, a reasonable construction of the taxing statutes does not include vesting any tax official with absolute power of assessment against individuals not specified in the statutes as <u>persons liable</u> for the tax without an opportunity for <u>judicial review of this status</u> before the appellation of "<u>taxpayer</u>" is bestowed upon them and their property is seized and sold. (emphasis added)

We note that the one word <u>term</u> "taxpayer" (not the <u>two words</u> "<u>tax payer</u>") is defined in I.R. Code Section 7701(a)(14) as follows:

Sec. 7701(a)(14). Definitions.
(a) When used in this title, <u>where not otherwise distinctly expressed or manifestly incompatible with the intent thereof-</u>
(14) Taxpayer. The term "taxpßayer" means any person <u>subject to</u> any internal revenue tax. (emphasis added)

The United States Appellate Court in the decision of **Houston Street Corporation v. Commissioner of Internal Revenue**, 34 F2d. 821 (1936) held that in tax matters the words "<u>subject to</u>" mean the same as "<u>liable for</u>" (a tax) when they stated:

We see no distinction between the phrases "<u>liable for</u> such tax" and "<u>subject to</u>" a tax. (emphasis added)

130

The **Botta v. Scanlon** Court decision, quoted earlier, further stated:

> *It is equally well-settled that the revenue laws apply only to "taxpayers".* (emphasis added)

The Botta Court's use of the one word "term" "taxpayer" clearly establishes that the I.R. Code applies only to those <u>made liable</u> for a tax by law. This holding is also supported by statements in the following decision: **Long v. Rasmussen, Collector of Internal Revenue, et al, 281 F.236 (1922)** which stated:

> *The revenue laws are a code or system in regulation of tax assessment and collection. They relate to <u>taxpayers, and not to non-taxpayers. The latter are without their scope. No procedure is prescribed for non-taxpayers, and no attempt is made to annul any of their rights and remedies in due course of law.</u>* (emphasis added)

Without quoting from the following court decisions, the fact that the I.R. Code applies only to those who are in the status of "taxpayer" (those who are <u>made liable</u> for payment of tax by some provisions in the Code) is also stated by other Federal courts in the following decisions: **Stuart v. Chinese Chamber of Commerce of Phoenix, 168, F2d. 712 (1948), First National Bank of Emlenton, Pa. v. U.S., 161 F. Supp. 847 (1958)** and **Economy Plumbing v. U.S., 470 F.2d 589 (1972)**.

Consultation with attorneys and accountants and careful study of the I.R. Code (Title 26 of the United States Code) has made it clear that the **<u>only</u> section imposing a liability upon anyone for the payment of income taxes is Section 1461, which limits liability in that section to "persons <u>required</u> to deduct and withhold" and this requirement relates to "income" only as identified in Code Sections 1441 and 1442 received by <u>non-resident aliens</u> (Section 1441) or <u>foreign corporations</u> (Section 1442).**

Because of this, in respect to income tax, only those required to deduct and withhold tax from foreigners under Sections 1441 or 1442 are in the status of "taxpayer" as that <u>term</u> is used and defined in I.R. Code Section 7701(a)(14) quoted above.

There is a very simple reason why there is no law making individual citizens earning money only on their own behalf <u>liable</u> for payment of income tax. In Chapter I, we explained that the United States Constitution limits the imposition of any direct tax on citizens of the United States of America under the provisions of Article 1, Section 2, Clause 3 and Article 1, Section 9, Clause 4. Despite the IRS' propaganda efforts to convince us otherwise, the U.S. Supreme Court has repeatedly ruled that these tax restrictions are <u>still in force</u> and that the Sixteenth Amendment did not nullify or change them. For a detailed explanation of the Sixteenth Amendment and its purpose and effect, see Chapter II of this book. It is because of these constitutional prohibitions that the income tax sections of the I.R. Code are correctly written so as <u>not to apply to the personal earnings of the general citizenry of the fifty states</u>. Therefore, <u>for citizens</u>, the 1040 form is a **voluntarily-filed** form on which a non-resident alien individual or his agent who <u>does</u> have a legal liability to file may claim exemptions and deductions, under the provisions of the I.R. Code Section 874 from the 30% tax imposed by Section 871 and withheld under I.R. Code Section 1441 so that a tax refund may be obtained.

<u>Ex-IRS Commissioner Margaret Milner Richardson</u>, being apparently aware of these Constitutional limitations of the taxing authority, reportedly stated at the time of her resignation as head of the I.R.S. that she was concerned about the "continued bashing" of her agency and expressed fears that such criticism may undermine Americans' willingness to pay taxes <u>voluntarily</u>. She stated:

> *Ultimately I worry it may have some impact on our <u>self-assessment</u> system.* (emphasis added)

Thus, ex-Commissioner Richardson expressed her knowledge of the <u>voluntary</u> nature of the income tax for citizens who are not withholding agents for foreigners. Also being aware of these Constitutional taxing restrictions, and, again, to repeat what we have previously stated, Mr. Dwight Avis, a former head of the Alcohol Tax Division of the Internal Revenue Service, stated before a Congressional committee that the <u>income tax is a "100% voluntary tax"</u> in contrast to the <u>mandatory</u> alcohol, tobacco and firearms taxes which are imposed under Sub-Title E of the I.R. Code. Such taxes are enforced under the regulations published in the Federal Register for Title 27 of the U.S. Code. These Title 27 regulations apply <u>only to alcohol, tobacco and firearms taxes.</u>

Even more proof of the truth of Ms. Richardson's comments and Mr. Avis' statement that for individuals the income tax is 100% voluntary can be shown by an examination of Supreme Court rulings, the Code of Federal Regulations (CFR) and other supporting documents. The Supreme Court has shown that the IRS regulations are laws in the decision of **Caha v. U.S., 152 U.S. 211 (1894)**:

> *Regulations prescribed...by the head of departments... may thus have, in a proper sense, the force of law...*
> (emphasis added)

Saying the same thing again, the Supreme Court in the decision of **California Bankers Association v. Schultz, et al. 416 U.S. 21 (1974)**, referring to the Secretary of the Treasury, stated, as quoted at the beginning of this chapter:

> *...we think it important to note that the Act's civil and criminal penalties attach only upon violation of regulations promulgated by the Secretary; if the Secretary were to do nothing, the Act itself would impose no penalties on anyone.*
> (emphasis added)

So, the Supreme Court has said that, if there is no regulation enforcing the statute, the statute itself has no authority or force of law.

The Supreme Court made very clear, in these two decisions, the necessity for a published regulation to enforce any section of the I.R. Code which requires or authorizes any act or action by anyone-either a "taxpayer" or the Secretary or his delegate.

Summary

The I.R.S., ignoring the Constitutional prohibitions against any taxation of U.S. citizens on their earnings, attempts to enforce collection methods through illegal and fraudulent use of unauthorized lien, levy and seizure notices sent to employers, banks and any others who have control of monies due U.S. citizens. These notices have legal authority <u>only</u> for the enforcement of alcohol, tobacco and firearms taxes under Title 27 of the I.R. Code-<u>not</u> for income tax imposed by Title 26. This limited legal application is proven by a chart called the <u>Code of Federal Regulations Individual Index</u>

and Finding Aids PARALLEL TABLE OF AUTHORITIES AND RULES. This publication which is created by the FEDERAL REGISTER from the IRS regulations written by the Secretary of the Treasury, shows that the use of lien and/or levy notices by the I.R.S. for the purpose of collecting income taxes on U.S. citizens is both illegal and fraudulent. Courts have held that I.R.S. agents engaging in collection activities which exceed their statutory authority become personally liable for such action. These are usually I.R.S. revenue agents because they are those most frequently responsible for issuance of these fraudulent notices. These agents, therefore, become personally liable for their misuse on at least two counts in addition to the fact that the lien and levy authority is limited to use only in violations of the law under Title 27 of the I.R. Code relating to alcohol, tobacco and firearms taxes! First, they are guilty of the intentional omission of a vitally important portion of Code Section 6331(a) of the levy notice, and second, they have no statutory authority to send out these notices in any event! High ranking I.R.S. personnel, including a former head of the alcohol, tobacco and firearms division and even a former I.R.S. Commissioner have testified publicly that filing and payment of income taxes is voluntary for U.S. citizens.

  The IRS routinely violates the clear provisions of Section 6020(b) (1) and (2) when they create an unsigned document called an Account Transcript which neither shows figures from which the alleged tax due can be computed, nor does it satisfy the clear requirements of the Code citations requiring preparation of a return and a signature thereon by the Secretary of the Treasury or his delegate. Based only on this counterfeit document the IRS fraudulently attaches the earnings of the alleged taxpayer without having even remotely complied with the clear provisions of the law. Never, in these collection procedures, does the IRS ever provide the alleged taxpayer with a copy of any law which complies with the statutory requirement under Section 6020(b)(1) which states: "if any person fails to make any return required…". (emphasis added) They do not because they CAN NOT show the requirement statute because it DOES NOT EXIST! Citizens who have been victimized by these unlawful, fraudulent actions by the IRS, armed with the knowledge outlined in this book, and particularly this chapter, have what they need to fight back and to stop these criminal acts by their own government.

  Unfortunately, attempts to appeal to the IRS directly for these unlawful violations of law often meet with failure. This is true because the IRS' personnel to whom an administrative appeal is addressed are trained to simply ignore the truth and the facts by rejecting the citizen's facts which he has presented quoting both law and court decisions as we have stated at length in this chapter. Any administrative action for remedy is normally possible only through <u>tax court</u> and tax court is established only for "<u>taxpayers</u>", which is a legal status foreign to the citizen who knows he is <u>not a</u> "<u>taxpayer</u>". Therefore, tax court is an <u>improper forum</u> for the citizen who has learned his true <u>non-</u>payer status.

Rather, if a knowledgeable citizen who has been victimized by the IRS' unlawful tactics described in this chapter can get his representative or his senator to intervene on his behalf, the influence that such a congressperson has with the IRS could help. Although it is somewhat difficult to study and absorb in detail, the <u>truth</u> presented in this chapter cannot be denied, and help from knowledgable and experienced patriot attorneys and/or paralegals is also available.

If the citizen or his helper fails in their attempts to discipline the IRS, his only other remedy rests in the form of a lawsuit in U.S. District Court in which he, at least, should have a <u>chance</u> to have his irrefutable, jurisdictional position get a fair hearing. In U.S. District Court, however, the citizen <u>non-</u>taxpayer must be prepared to face the potential prejudice of a U.S. District Court judge whose training and propensity are normally tuned against the citizen. However, in this lowest-level court, our irrefutable facts of both law and supporting court decisions, if properly presented, can prevail, even if the citizen non-taxpayer presents his case pro se (in person) without benefit of a lawyer. Should the citizen engage the services of licensed counsel to represent him, it is strongly recommended that such counsel be well-schooled in all law and supporting court decisions we have cited in this book and particularly this chapter, because most lawyers are totally ignorant of the information contained herein. Should a usually prejudiced District Court judge rule against the citizen, despite the abundance of law on the citizen's side, an appeals court reversal is an excellent possibility. Even a very prejudiced District Court judge doesn't want to face the likelihood of a reversal on appeal because such a loss would be a black mark against his chance for an appointment to an appellate court. His awareness of a potential loss by the IRS on appeal by the citizen will go a long way towards overcoming this prejudice in the lower-level District Court which should make any appeal unnecessary.

CHAPTER VII

LIMITATIONS OF I.R. CODE FILING REQUIREMENTS AND CRIMINAL CHARGES

For many years the IRS, with the collusion of the Justice Department, has targeted leaders of the constitutional taxation movement by bringing illegal criminal charges for <u>alleged</u> violations of the provisions of I.R. Code Section 6012(a), which the IRS <u>falsely</u> claims <u>requires</u> citizens to file income tax returns and pay tax on their earnings and other receipts.

Let's examine the deceptive wording of this key Code Section 6012 which reads, in part, as follows:

> **Sec. 6012. Persons <u>required</u> to make returns of income.**
> **(a) General rule.**
> Returns with respect to income taxes under subtitle A <u>shall</u> be made by the following:
> **(1)**
> **(A)** <u>Every individual</u> having for the <u>taxable year</u> gross <u>income</u> which equals or exceeds the exemption amount, except that a return shall not be required of an <u>individual</u>…- (emphasis added)

Of utmost importance in this Code section is its <u>heading</u> which, in this writer's opinion, intentionally and deceptively uses the misleading word "required" in the heading which we have underlined for emphasis. The words "individual" and "income" and the defined term "taxable year", shown above in Section 6012(a)(1)(A), are also underlined for emphasis, and they have limited meanings as will be shown in this chapter. First, however, we must understand that <u>headings</u> in Code sections have <u>no legal effect</u> on the body of the Code section, as explained in Code Section 7806 which states in part:

> **Sec. 7806. Construction of title.**
> **(b) Arrangement and classification.**
> <u>No reference, implication, or presumption of legislative construction</u> shall be drawn or made by reason of the location or grouping of any particular section or provision or portion of this title, <u>nor shall any</u> table of contents, table of

cross references, or similar outline, analysis, or descriptive matter relating to the contents of this title be given any legal effect..... (emphasis added)

This Section, 7806(b), shows that the word "required" which we have underlined in the heading of Code Section 6012 is clearly "descriptive matter" (as shown above) which supposedly describes the body of Code Section 6012. However, Code Section 7806 states that, as part of this heading, the word "required" legally means nothing! Headings, which are shown in bold print before the body of the Code section is stated, can be, and, in this writer's opinion, are intentionally deceptive because I truly believe that the IRS wants the uninformed reader to incorrectly assume that the word "required" in the heading is legally binding on every individual as mentioned in the body of the Code section. This mistaken assumption is incorrect as Code Section 7806 quoted above clearly shows.

Understanding the correct meaning of the words "income", "shall", "individual" and the defined term "taxable year", as used in the body of I.R. Code Section 6012, is also vitally important. As was stated by an appellate court in the decision of **United States v. Ballard, 535 F2d 400 (1920)**: "the general term 'income' is not defined in the Internal Revenue Code." (emphasis added) However, monies owing to (meaning payable to) "…any non-resident alien-'individual' and any foreign partnership…" (emphasis added) are identified in I.R. Code Section 1441 as being "income". Section 1441 states as follows (note particularly the words of limitation which are underlined for emphasis):

Sec. 1441. Withholding of tax on nonresident aliens.
(a) General rule.
Except as otherwise provided in subsection (c), all persons in whatever capacity acting (including lessees or mortgagors of real or personal property, fiduciaries, employers, and all officers and employees of the United States) having the control, receipt, custody, disposal, or payment of any of items of income specified in subsection (b) to the extent that any of such items constitutes gross income from sources within the United States), of any nonresident alien individual or of any foreign partnership shall (except as otherwise provided by the Secretary under Section 874) deduct and withhold from such items a tax equal to 30 percent thereof,

except that in the case of any <u>item of income</u> specified in the second sentence of subsection (b), the tax shall be equal to 14 percent of such item. (emphasis added)

(b) Income items.

The <u>items of income</u> referred to in subsection (a) are <u>interest</u> (other than original issue discount as defined in section 1273), <u>dividends, rent, salaries, wages, premiums, annuities, compensations, remunerations, emoluments, or other fixed or determinable annual or periodical gains, profits, and income,</u> gains described in Section 631(b) or (c), amounts subject to tax_under Section 871(a)(1)(C), gains subject to tax under Section 871(a)(1)(D) and gains on transfers described in Section 1235 made on or before October 4, 1966. <u>The items of income</u> referred to in subsection (a) from which tax shall be deducted and withheld at the rate of 14 percent are amounts which are <u>received by a nonresident alien individual</u> who is <u>temporarily present in the United States as a nonimmigrant</u> under subparagraph (F), (J), (M) or (Q) of section 101(a) (15) of the Immigration and Nationality Act and which are- … (emphasis added)

I.R. Code Section 1442(a) also directs the same withholding requirement as Section 1441(a) from <u>foreign corporations</u> who may have invested in United States securities. Section 1442 states:

Sec. 1442. Withholding of tax on foreign corporations.
(a) General rule.
In the case of <u>foreign corporations</u> subject to taxation under this sub-title, there shall be deducted and withheld at the source in the same manner and on the same items of income as is provided in Section 1441 a tax equal to 30 percent thereof… (emphasis added)

These Code Sections 1441(a) and 1442(a) <u>identify monies owing</u> or payable to any <u>non-resident alien</u> "individual" <u>or in any foreign partnership</u> (Section 1441(a) or foreign corporation (Section 1442(a) ONLY as "income". Note that over a dozen "<u>items of income</u>" are identified in Sub-Section 1441(b) as being taxable <u>but only if owed to non-resident aliens, foreign partnerships or foreign corporations</u>. These sections also <u>direct</u> the deduction and withholding of the tax by "all <u>persons,</u> in whatever capacity acting..." (emphasis added) who have the "control, receipt, custody, disposal, or payment of any of the items of income specified in subsection (b)" (emphasis added), to make the deduction and withholding of the tax. These "persons" who are <u>required</u> to deduct and withhold would normally, but not exclusively, be the officers, fiduciaries or other representatives of the U.S. companies who have control of the securities which are owned by the non-resident alien-"individuals" or foreign partnerships (Section 1441(a) or foreign corporations (1442(a)). However, it is of vital importance that we understand that the tax is required to be deducted and withheld from items of <u>income</u> payable <u>ONLY to</u> any <u>non-resident alien</u>-individual <u>or any foreign partnership or foreign corporation,</u> and <u>not</u> from earnings or receipts payable to <u>citizen</u>-"individuals" of the United States who merely exercise their God-given and <u>constitutionally-protected right</u> to earn a living, do business, invest, buy and sell property, etc. Sections 1441 and 1442 are the only sections in Sub-Title A of the I.R. Code covering income tax that identifies <u>income</u>, and that identification is limited to monies payable to <u>foreign</u> individuals, partnerships or corporations! (See also Chapter III of this book.)

The IRS' 1040 income tax form, which is printed by the IRS and distributed by the millions in banks, post offices and by thousands of tax-preparer firms, accountants and lawyers, is titled "U.S. <u>INDIVIDUAL INCOME TAX RETURN</u>". This title, which deceptively uses the word "individual" <u>implies</u> that the word "individual" means <u>everybody, including citizens</u>, when this is <u>not true</u>. As is shown in the previous paragraph, the word "individual" <u>cannot</u> include a U.S. <u>citizen</u>-"individual"-only a <u>non-resident alien</u> "individual". Also, as we have shown throughout this book, U.S. citizens cannot be taxed on their own earnings or other receipts because such a tax would be an unconstitutional, unapportioned direct tax, in conflict with the Constitutional limitation against direct taxes contained in Article 1, Section 2, Clause 3 and Article 1, Section 9, Clause 4.

The meaning of the word "<u>individual</u>", like "income", is also <u>not</u> defined in the I.R. Code. However, it is also <u>identified</u> in Code Sections 861(a)(3)(A), 871(a)(1), 7701(b)(1)(B), 7701(b)(9), and Sections 1441(a) and (b) as an <u>alien</u>-"individual" <u>only</u>! A search of the I.R. Code has found <u>no other words</u> describing an "individual" as being a <u>U.S. citizen</u>-"individual". Use of the descriptive word "alien" in all of these other Code sections to describe and limit the meaning of the word "individual" provides evidence that, <u>wherever</u> the word "individual" is used elsewhere in the I.R. Code, such as in Section 1, Section 6012 and Section 7701(a)(1) without <u>any</u> descriptive adjective, the reader can logically <u>assume</u> that it is intended to refer to an <u>alien </u>"individual" because of these <u>other</u> Code Sections previously listed wherein the "individual" <u>is described </u>as an <u>alien-</u>"individual"-a citizen of a foreign country! Again, because of the constitutional prohibition against any direct tax on U.S. citizens, the word "individual" <u>must</u> be limited to mean individuals <u>other than </u>U.S. citizen-individuals.

As we pointed out at the start of Chapter VI of this book, the IRS' implementing <u>regulations</u> (not quoted here) give force of law to the I.R. Code provisions. The necessity for regulations in order to authorize or require certain actions is specified in the parent Code in Section 7805(a) which authorizes the Secretary to write regulations which are <u>in conformity with</u> the Code section which it implements. The law requires that if ever a regulation is published which <u>exceeds</u> the provisions of the Code, then the provisions of the Code <u>not</u> the regulation governs its implementation. If a parent Code Section requires no action by the Secretary, there is no implemanting regulation published.

In the case of Code Section 6012, its implementing regulation which is No. 1.6012-1 contains wording which, in this writer's opinion, clearly attempts to broaden the provisions in the Code section beyond its limited jurisdiction as we have described in the preceding paragraph. This overly-broad wording of the <u>regulation</u> is contained in the filing requirement provision which states, in part, under Section 1.6012-1(a)(1) that "an income tax return must be filed by every <u>individual</u> for each <u>taxable year</u>…if such <u>individual</u> is-(i) a <u>citizen</u> of the United States, whether residing at home or abroad, and (ii) a resident of the United States even though not a citizen thereof or (iii) an alien bona fide resident of Puerto Rico during the entire taxable year." (emphasis added) The use of the word "citizen" twice in this regulation is a clear broadening of the apparent Code Section in obvious violation of the limited application of the Code Section. Such broadening is prohibited by several Supreme Court decisions.

This implementing regulation also repeatedly uses the words "<u>taxable year</u>" as a necessity for any filing requirement. Later in this chapter, we will show clearly that only a "<u>taxpayer</u>" can have a "<u>taxable year</u>", and to be in the status of a "taxpayer", the "individual" who is referred to must be, according to Code Section 7701(a)(14): "subject to", meaning "liable for" the tax. And to be "liable for" the tax, the individual must be a "person required to deduct and withhold" under the provisions of Code Section 1461. A U.S. citizen who has earnings in the form of wages, salaries, commissions or any other receipts earned only on his own behalf <u>and who has no withholding requirement</u> cannot come within that definition of "<u>taxpayer</u>". Consequently, he could not be an "individual" who met this broadened description of "individual" as shown in this implementing regulation.

As shown in Chapter IV, pages 68 and 69 of this book, the word "shall" as used in Code Section 6012 must be interpreted as "may", having a <u>voluntary</u> meaning whenever its use creates a constitutional conflict. Consequently, for citizen's who are not withholding agents as described in Code Section 1461, but who, rather earn only wages, salaries, or other earnings only on their own behalf, any filing requirement under Code Section 6012 must be voluntary, because a mandatory interpretation of "shall" would be a violtion of the citizen's constitutional protections against direct taxation of his earning under article 1, clause 2, section 3 and article 1, section 9, clause 4 as discussed in chapter 1 and throughout this book.

Anyone, however, including U.S. citizens, resident aliens or Puerto Rican residents <u>could become "taxpayers"</u> <u>if they were "required to deduct and withhold"</u> by the provisions of I.R. Code Sections 1441 or 1442 and could, therefore, be subject to the filing requirements of Code Section 6012 and its implementing regulation.

The IRS would like to have named the 1040 form the U.S. <u>CITIZENS INDIVIDUAL INCOME TAX RETURN"</u>. It is this writer's opinion that the IRS <u>didn't</u> give the 1040 form this title because they know that any tax imposed on a U.S. <u>citizen's</u> receipts would be a direct tax and, hence, unconstitutional because of Article 1, Section 2, Clause 3 and Article 1, Section 9, Clause 4 of the U.S. Constitution which prohibit any direct tax except those apportioned by population among the state governments.

A simple reading of Code Sections 1441 and 1442 lists over a dozen "items of income" as used in the I.R. Code. These "items of income" from which certain "persons" who <u>have control</u> of the "items of income" <u>are required to deduct and withhold</u> income tax include wages, salaries, profits and gains, etc., but <u>only</u> if such "items of income" are payable to any <u>non-resident alien </u>"individual", any foreign <u>partnership</u> under Section 1441 or any foreign <u>corporation</u> under Section 1442. Section 1441 shows the <u>term</u> "individual" to mean <u>only any non-resident alien </u>"individual".

Section 1461 of the I.R. Code identifies the person "liable for" (meaning "subject to") tax as a "person" who is required (by some other Code section) to deduct and withhold any (income) tax under Chapter 3 of the I.R. Code. The "person" who is required to deduct and withhold from the "items of income" shown in Section 1441 or 1442(a) has such a requirement but only when the "items of income" are those payable to any non-resident alien "individual" or any foreign partnership under Code Section 1441 or any foreign corporation under Code Section 1442. Sections 1441 and 1442 are the only sections in Chapter 3 which contain any requirement to deduct and withhold. We have explained repeatedly in this book that Section 1461 is the only section in the Internal Revenue Code which makes any "person" (the person required to deduct and withhold) liable for income tax. Section 1461 was quoted as Fact #12 in Chapter I of this book, and we quote it again now for repeated emphasis and study because it identifies a very restricted and limited number of "persons" as being "liable for" (income) tax-namely, only those who have a statutory (Code Section) requirement to deduct and withhold from monies they control which are payable to named foreign interests.

> **Sec. 1461. Liability for withheld tax.**
> Every "person" required to deduct and withhold any tax under this chapter is hereby made liable for such tax and is hereby indemnified against the claims and demands of any person for the amount of any payments made in accordance with the provisions of this chapter. (emphasis added)

An appeals court in Botta v. Scanlon, 288 F2d 509 (1961) stated in part:

> *...moreover, even the collection of taxes should be exacted only from persons upon whom a tax liability is imposed by some statute.* (emphasis added)

The term "person" is defined in Code Section 7701(a)(1) as follows:

> **Sec. 7701. Definitions.**
> **(a)**
> When used in this title, where not otherwise distinctly expressed or manifestly incompatible with the intent thereof-
> **(1) Person.** The term "person" shall be construed to mean

and include an <u>individual</u>, a trust, estate, partnership, association, company or corporation. (emphasis added)

It is noteworthy that the definition in Section 7701(a)(1) above includes the underlined wording "where not otherwise distinctly expressed...". This is a reference to another definition of the term "person" which is distinctly expressed in I.R. Code Section 7343 relating to crimes as follows:

Sec. 7343. Definition of term "person".
The term "person" <u>as used in this chapter</u> (75) includes an officer or employee of a <u>corporation,</u> or a member or employee of a <u>partnership</u>, who as such officer, employee, or member is under a duty to perform the act in respect of which the violation occurs. (emphasis added)

These two different definitions of the term "person" are revealing in that the first, under Code Section 7701(a)(1) includes the word "individual" which is listed first in the multiple definitions of the word "person" which also includes a <u>trust, estate, partnership, association, company or corporation</u>. This might lead us to assume that the word "individual" in this definition (7701(a)(1)) could apply to an "individual" acting on his own behalf, exclusive of any relationship to the other definitions included in the Code section. However, when we consider this definition in comparison to that contained in Code Section 7343 which, as shown above, <u>restricts the meaning</u> of the term "person" <u>for purposes of any criminal penalty</u> to be limited to the "person" acting only on behalf of a corporation or a partnership, the difference is revealing. It seems to this writer that the very limited definition <u>for criminal penalty purposes</u> of the term "person" in Code Section 7343 would lead us to the reasonable conclusion that the word "individual", as used in Code Section 7701(a)(1), is <u>also</u> meant to describe only an "individual" acting on behalf of a trust, estate, partnership, association, company or corporation!

We pointed out earlier in this chapter that the meaning of the word "individual", as used in the I.R. Code, is also <u>identified</u> in Code Sections 861(a)(3)(A), 871(a)(1), 1441(a) and (b) and 7701(b)(1) as an <u>alien</u> "individual" only! Consequently, we repeat what we stated earlier-that is, that <u>wherever</u> the word "individual" is used in the I.R. Code, <u>without any descriptive adjective</u>, such as in Section 1, Section 6012 and Section 7701(a)(1), the reader can correctly assume that it is intended to refer only to an

143

alien "individual" because of these other referenced Code sections wherein the individual is described as an alien "individual" meaning a citizen of a foreign country. Such an individual, as a non-citizen, is not protected by the constitutional prohibition against any direct tax. Therefore, the word "individual" must legally be limited to mean individuals other than U.S. citizen-"individuals".

In *Sutherland's Rules of Statutory Construction*, an authoritative reference book on the interpretation of statutes, Section 66.03 states: "... the obligation to pay taxes arises only by force of legislative action...". (emphasis added Legislative action is the passage of a statute (a law). So, to "be liable" for income tax, as the Court stated in **Botta v. Scanlon**, previously quoted in this chapter, it must be stated in the I.R. Code. This appellate court decision has never been overturned by the U.S. Supreme Court, so it is still law today. And, because it clearly requires a statute (Code section) to make anyone "liable" for income tax, and further, because Section 1461 also quoted above is the only Code section making anyone "liable" for income tax, only a "person required to deduct and withhold" under Code Section 1461 (above) from "any non-resident alien individual or foreign partnership" under Code Section 1441 or from "foreign corporations" under Code Section 1442 can be liable for or subject to income tax or because of such liability be required to file an income tax return by the provisions of Code Section 6012 or its implementing regulation 1.6012-1!

Another limitation on the application of I.R. Code Section 6012 comes from use of the term "taxable year", which is underlined in Section 6012(a)(1)(A) for emphasis, in this Code section quoted earlier in this chapter. I.R. Code Section 441 defines the term "taxable year" in Sub-Section (b), in part, as follows:

> **Sec. 441. Period for computation of taxable income.**
> **(a) Computation of taxable income.**
> Taxable income shall be computed on the basis of the taxpayer's taxable year.
> **(b) Taxable year.**
> For purposes of this subtitle, the term "taxable year" means-
> (1) the taxpayer's annual accounting period, if it is a calendar year or a fiscal year;
> (3) the period for which the return is made, if a return is made for a period of less than 12 months; or...(emphasis

added)

This Code section clearly shows in both sub-sections "a" and "b" that the only person who can have "taxable income" (Section 441(a)) or have a "taxable year" (Section 441(b)(1) must be in the legal status of a "taxpayer". As we pointed out in the decision of **Botta v. Scanlon**, quoted earlier, the I.R. Code applies only to "taxpayers", meaning only those "made liable" for a tax by some statute. This fact has been clearly confirmed in many court decisions including **Long v. Rasmussen, 281, F236 (1922), Stuart v. Chinese Chamber of Commerce of Phoenix, 168 F.2d 712 (1948), First National Bank of Emlenton , Pa. v. U.S., 161 F.Supp. 847 (1958)** and **Economy Plumbing v. U.S., 470 F.2d 589 (1972)** which we showed in Chapter I.

The word "taxpayer" (one word, not two) is a legal term defined in the I.R. Code, Section 7701(a)(14) which states: "the term "taxpayer" means any person subject to any internal revenue tax. Paying a tax, such as a sales tax, a license tax or real estate tax, does not place one in the legal status of "taxpayer" as that term is used in the I.R. Code. Further, sub-section (b)(3) of Code Section 441 ties "taxable year" to the filing of a return, which is the responsibility of a "taxpayer" only-not a U.S. citizen unless he is "made liable" for payment of income tax by I.R. Code Section 1461 (above) because he is "a person required to deduct and withhold"! The words "subject to", as used in the definition of "taxpayer" shown above, are interchangeable with "liable for" as stated in the decision of **Houston Street Corp. v. Commissioner, 84F2d, 821 (1936).** The only Code section in the I.R. Code that makes anybody a "taxpayer", because they have been "made liable" for payment of income tax, is Code Section 1461, which states that the person who is "made liable for such tax" is the "person required to deduct and withhold any tax under this chapter (3)". As a reminder, the term "person" is also defined in the I.R. Code, Section 7701(a)(1) to include not only an "individual" but also a "trust, estate, partnership, association, company or corporation". Only one who is a "person required to deduct and withhold any tax under this chapter" (emphasis added) from monies payable to a non-resident alien-individual, foreign partnership or any foreign corporation can be a "taxpayer".

A description of the term "taxable year" is in Code Section 7701(b)(9)(A) which states in part:

Sec. 7701. Definitions.
(b) Definition of resident alien and nonresident alien.
(9) <u>Taxable year.</u>
(A) In general. For purposes of this title, an <u>alien individual</u> who has not established a <u>taxable year</u> for any prior period shall be treated as having a <u>taxable year</u> which is the calendar year... (emphasis added)

In this Code section, an <u>alien-individual</u> is the only individual described as having a "<u>taxable year</u>"-<u>not</u> a <u>citizen</u>-individual. The only individual shown as having a "taxable year" in I.R. Code Section 6012 must be an <u>alien</u>-individual, or a person "required to deduct and withhold" monies payable to or <u>on behalf of</u> a non-resident alien-individual, foreign partnership or foreign corporation under Code Sections 1441 or 1442.

If a citizen who is <u>not acting</u> on behalf of a taxable entity, such as a non-resident alien-individual, foreign partnership or foreign corporation is charged with failure to file under Code Section 6012, this writer would suggest that the citizen so charged should discuss with his attorney the advisability of filing a simple <u>Motion for Summary Judgment</u> in U.S. District Court showing all the limitations of Code Section 6012 explained in this chapter to destroy any attempt by the IRS through the Justice Department to <u>even begin</u> a criminal prosecution against the citizen by charging him with "failure to file" under Code Section 6012. As we previously showed in this chapter, <u>Section 7343 of the I.R. Code authorizes criminal prosecution only of persons who are acting as, or on behalf of, a corporation or a (limited) partnership.</u> Section 7343 does <u>not</u> allow criminal prosecutions against any citizens who are acting for themselves or any of the <u>other entities</u> included in the definition of "person" in Code Section 7701(a)(1). This includes, in addition to, an "individual", a "trust, estate, association or company".

It is also noteworthy that, in the past, the Justice Department, acting for the IRS, has falsely charged citizens with willful failure to file an income tax return in <u>alleged</u> violation of I.R. Code Section 7203. Code Section 7203 specifies <u>penalties,</u> but imposes <u>no requirements</u> to file any return. Therefore, use of this <u>purely penalty</u> Code section as one which <u>requires</u> filing of a return was, and still is, improper.

Both Code Sections 7701(a)(1) and 7343 identify certain "persons" as "taxpayers" if they can be held "liable for" income tax under the provisions of Section 1461 of the Code. The difference between those described in these two Code sections is that those "persons" described in Code Section 7343 who are required to deduct and withhold only from corporations or (limited) partnerships are those who can be held criminally responsible for their failure to deduct and withhold. As we have explained repeatedly in this book, CODE SECTION 1461 IS THE ONLY CODE SECTION IMPOSING LIABILITY FOR PAYMENT OF INCOME TAX, THEREBY CREATING A TAXPAYER STATUS ONLY FOR THE "PERSON REQUIRED TO DEDUCT AND WITHHOLD" UNDER I.R. CODE SECTIONS 1441 AND 1442.

For many years the Justice Department prosecutors have been able to unlawfully criminally prosecute and convict <u>citizens who do not, and never have met, the definition of a "person" as defined in Code Section 7343</u>. The Justice Department's unlawful criminal prosecutions of U.S. citizens were unlawfully accomplished in past years because of the incompetence of defense counsel who were obviously unaware of this restriction contained in Code Section 7343. Had they done their proper homework, it seems apparent to this writer that defense counsel could have filed a simple summary motion for dismissal of all charges based on the inability of their client-U.S. citizen to come within the definition of "person" as used in I.R. Code Section 7343.

Further, the <u>body</u> of Code Section 6012, which we have now learned is where the law is stated (not the heading), states that returns, "with respect to income taxes", "<u>shall</u>" be made by every individual having a certain amount of "income". The <u>body</u> of the Code section does not state that returns are "required" to be made by them. Courts have repeatedly ruled that, for citizens, "shall" means "may" when used in statutes (Code sections) in order to avoid any constitutional conflict under the Fifth Amendment's prohibition against any citizen's requirement to be a witness against himself and under the Thirteenth Amendment's prohibition against involuntary servitude. (See also Chapter IV of this book)

For example, in the decision of **Cairo & Fulton Railroad Co. v. Hecht, 95 U.S.170** the U.S. Supreme Court stated: "as against the government, the word 'shall' when used in statutes (Code sections) is to be construed as 'may', unless a contrary intention is manifest." Also, in the decision of **Gow v. Consolidate Coppermines Corp., 165 Atlantic 136**, the court stated: "if necessary to avoid unconstitutionality of a statute, 'shall' will be deemed equivalent to 'may'".

Black's Law Dictionary, Fifth Edition, defines the word "shall" in part as follows:

> But it <u>(shall) may be construed as merely permissive or directory (as equivalent to 'may')</u>, *to carry out the legislative intention and in cases where no right or benefit to any one depends on its being taken in the imperative sense, and where no public or <u>private right</u> is impaired by its interpretation in the other sense.* (emphasis added)

This *Black's Law Dictionary* explanation of the meaning of the word "shall" is clearly in keeping with the decision in **Gow v. Consolidated Coppermines Corp.,** quoted above, which shows the necessity of interpreting the meaning of the word "shall" to mean "may" wherever a mandatory interpretation of the word "shall" would create a constitutional conflict. The *Black's* definition and particularly the underlined words in the definition, shown above, supports the conclusion that <u>"shall" in Code Section 6012(a) must have a voluntary meaning for citizens,</u> all of whom are constitutionally not subject to any Federal taxation on either their own earnings or on any monies received from any source such as interest from bank accounts, other investments, rental receipts, profits or gains from business dealings, capital gains, etc. All of these monies or other receipts, of whatever nature, are not only not subject to taxation <u>for citizens</u> according to the provisions limiting direct taxes by Article 1, Section 2, Clause 3 and Article 1, Section 9, Clause 4 of the Constitution, but also any filing requirement would also conflict with both the Fifth and the Thirteenth Amendments as previously shown.

<u>Because no U.S. citizen-"individual's" (as the word "individual" is used in Code Section 6012) personal earnings or other receipts are "income", as identified in Code Section 1441, the provisions of Code Section 6012 cannot constitutionally apply to him.</u> Also, citizens cannot be required to supply information certified under penalties of perjury, which they would be doing if they filed income tax returns, because the information on the return could be used against the filer in a criminal case, and any such <u>requirement would be unconstitutional</u> because it would violate the citizen's Fifth Amendment right <u>not</u> to be required to be a witness against himself.

Finally, the Thirteenth Amendment to the Constitution, which prohibits both slavery <u>and involuntary servitude,</u> provides yet another level of protection to the citizen against any mandatory interpretation of the word "shall" as used in Code Sections 6012, 1441 and 1442. The Thirteenth Amendment states as follows:

> *Neither slavery <u>nor involuntary servitude</u>, except as a punishment for crime whereof the party shall have been duly convicted, shall exist within the United States, or any place subject to their jurisdiction.* (emphasis added)

The Thirteenth Amendment prohibition against "involuntary servitude" means that, for U.S. citizens acting on their own behalf, "shall" must have a <u>voluntary meaning</u> in its application to all Code sections. This voluntary meaning of the word "shall" for citizens acting on their own behalf, prohibits any requirement to make a return under Code Section 6012, or to deduct and withhold under Code Sections 1441 and/or 1442. It is this writer's opinion that the Thirteenth Amendment protection would <u>not apply</u> to an individual or a person who was acting <u>for or on behalf of a taxable, privileged entity</u>, such as a corporation, a (limited) partnership or an alien individual who has no protection under the Thirteenth Amendment against involuntary servitude. Under those circumstances, the word "shall" would have a <u>mandatory meaning because he would be acting in a capacity as</u> an agent on behalf of such a taxable entity, instead of as a citizen on his own behalf.

Therefore, because of the above court decisions, the Fifth and Thirteenth Amendments, and the constitutional limitations prohibiting any taxation of citizen's receipts shown above, the word "shall", as used in Code Section 6012, must be interpreted as meaning "may", which has a voluntary meaning. It is obvious, for all of these reasons, that no individual U.S. citizen, under these circumstances, can be <u>required</u> to file income tax returns, regardless of the amount of their receipts.

Use of the word "required" in the legally-meaningless <u>heading</u> of Code Section 6012, and misuse of the words "individual" and the terms "income" and "taxable year" in the <u>body</u> of Code Section 6012 and the IRS' improper interpretation of the word "shall" are all obvious misapplication of the provisions of this Code section. The IRS usually gets away with these misapplications because citizens are unaware of the correct meanings of these words and terms as they are used in Code Section 6012.

In this chapter we have not discussed the possibility of a criminal felony charge of <u>evasion</u> by the IRS under the provisions of Code Section 7201, because in order to be guilty of any such felony charge, a positive act must have been committed such as falsifying figures on a tax return. For purposes of this chapter, we are dealing with citizens who have stopped deducting and withholding, stopped filing returns and have revoked all previously-filed returns by an AFFIDAVIT OF REVOCATION OF RECISSION, which will be discussed in detail in Chapter VIII. The chance of the IRS, through the Justice Department, of ever bringing a felony charge against such a citizen is unlikely, since because all previous filed returns have been revoked, they would have <u>no valid</u> return on which to base a claim that the citizen's earnings are income, and that he is liable for (subject to) a tax on his earnings.

Because of these very important facts which prove that U.S. citizens are not "liable for" (subject to) income tax and are not required to pay income tax on their personal receipts, the question arises: "Why are people sometimes sent to jail for not filing income tax returns?" The answer is that most are convicted by their peers-fellow individual jurors who do not understand the law and have been trained since childhood to falsely believe that every American who works for a living is required by law to file and to pay income tax on his earnings and other receipts. Uninformed and incompetent defense counsel usually have not read long-standing Supreme Court decisions which support the citizen's <u>non-taxable status,</u> and jurors generally are not aware of the constitutional prohibitions against taxation of citizens that we have discussed at length in this book. In the unlikely event that a citizen who is armed with these facts would be subjected to criminal prosecution under a charge of "willful failure to file", it is this writer's opinion that this mountain of evidence would present an insurmountable burden for any prosecutor and/or even any prejudiced judge to overcome in order to get a conviction.

As we have stated previously in this book, when an individual files an income tax return, he has created a document which he signed under penalty of perjury in which he has declared that his earnings and other receipts are "income", and that he is one who is in the <u>status</u> of a "taxpayer". Under the legal doctrine of "presumption", by his own action of filing a return, he mistakenly certifies, out of ignorance, but under penalties of perjury, that his earnings are "income" and that he is liable for income tax. His voluntary action of filing a return certified under penalties of perjury is considered by the statutory law in Title, Section 1746 to be an acknowledgement that he is required to file <u>as though he were</u> a "taxpayer" and that he is, therefore, <u>subject to</u> the tax. Anyone who admits <u>incorrectly</u> by such filing under penalties of perjury to being a "taxpayer" by such act of filing is caught in the trap-like definition of the term "taxpayer" in Code Section 7701(a)(14) which is defined as "any person <u>subject to </u>any Internal Revenue tax." The AFFIDAVIT OF REVOCATION AND RECISSION, which will be discussed in Chapter VIII next in this book, is the key to the citizen's escape from the trap of the wording on the 1040 return form which is the basis for any "presumption" that anyone is liable for the tax.

In the past, before the American public had been deceived into believing they owed a tax on their earnings, America prospered and became the greatest and richest country in the world when citizens properly and lawfully <u>paid no income tax,</u> and government's revenues were raised constitutionally by tariffs on imports from foreign countries, by constitutionally-authorized taxes on certain goods and services and on alien's earnings and corporations' profits and gains which they earned from the use of government-granted <u>privileges</u> of limited liability and perpetual life.

For decades now, unfortunately, money is unlawfully and deceptively removed from U.S. citizens in the productive sector of society by the income tax system to support the non-productive sector, foreign aid, give-away's and a bloated, needless bureaucracy. When income tax is voluntarily paid by citizens on their own earnings and other receipts, it sharply reduces these receipts to be spent or invested in the marketplace causing business to decline. This leads to unemployment and depression and lowers the standard of living for all Americans. The income tax laws, when misapplied to the receipts of U.S. citizens, creates havoc in America's economy, in addition to the loss of liberty and the harassment of our people by the IRS' oppressive and unlawful collection practices.

The IRS' unlawful collection tactics employed against U.S. citizens is enforced by fear and intimidation, and is as un-American as the origin of the income tax itself. A graduated income tax was and is the second plank of Karl Marx's *Communist Manifesto*. Deceiving citizens into believing that they owe a tax which, by law, they do **not** owe, is fraud. Compounding the felony of fraud, and even worse, when individuals who do not voluntarily subject themselves to the income/excise tax by voluntarily filing returns, and then have claims of tax liability or criminal charges brought against them by the IRS, this is a blatant violation of the citizen's constitutional <u>right</u> to earn a tax-free living. If the IRS then unlawfully claims that they have levy and seizure authority for payment of income tax against U.S. citizens, as we have explained in Chapter VI, and in this chapter, such confiscation of the wages and/or other property of citizens is <u>pure theft under color of law</u> because no levy or seizure action against any citizen or his property for income tax is authorized by a code section or its implementing regualtion.

History has proven that governmental abuses of citizen's rights, if left unchecked, always leads to revolution. As we have shown, the IRS acts both knowingly and unlawfully when it initiates criminal charges against individual citizens who are <u>not liable</u> by law for income tax and who do <u>not</u> subject themselves to the income/excise tax by voluntarily filing income tax returns. The IRS' policy is also unlawful when they selectively target outspoken leaders who expose the IRS' abuses of citizen's rights. If they obtain convictions of these spokesmen through misapplication of the law, the ignorance of jurors, the incompetence of defense attorneys and the prejudice of judges, this acts to intimidate other citizens, effectively discouraging them from speaking out publicly in defense of citizens' rights. Fortunately, in recent years, knowledge of this subject has become so much more widely known that criminal violations unlawfully brought against citizens who do not owe the income tax are increasingly rare.

Thankfully, the right to trial by jury, for the specific purpose of preventing government oppression of the people, is provided in our Constitution to prevent injustice. If only one juror in a group of twelve, who has the courage to nullify an oppressive prosecution by voting "not guilty" when such criminal charges are improperly brought against citizens, this would stop any conviction and support citizen's constitutionally-protected rights. Our Constitution's guarantees of liberty are only as effective as the will of the people to enforce them. Our labor and our brain-power are our property, and the earnings we realize from utilization of these most precious of our properties is an inalienable right which is protected from taxation by our Constitution, as we have repeatedly stated in this book. Knowledge of the law gives us the power to keep and enjoy <u>all</u> the fruits of our labor, but this knowledge must be aggressively stated, both with the IRS and in our courts when required, if the citizen is to prevail.

CHAPTER VIII

AFFIDAVIT OF REVOCATION & RECISSION- AN ESSENTIAL DOCUMENT

For the U.S. citizen who has read the first seven chapters of this book and has become satisfied as to the accuracy of the facts and the law contained in this book and has therefore decided to stop volunteering to file returns and pay income taxes which they don't owe, the citizen's next step, in this writer's opinion, should be to make a public declaration of his knowledge by filing an AFFIDAVIT OF REVOCATION AND RECISSION in the public records section of the courthouse in the county of the citizen's residence. This dated, valuable document explains in depth why the citizen has stopped volunteering to file Form 1040 and to pay any further income tax which he now knows that he does not owe. A sample AFFIDAVIT OF REVOCATION AND RECISSION which is similar to those that have been used by many citizens is reprinted at the end of this chapter.

The vitally important reason for filing the AFFIDAVIT becomes clear when one reads the law as set forth in Title 28, United States Code, Section 1746 which states, in part, as follows:

> ***Sec. 1746. Unsworn Declarations Under Penalty of Perjury*** Wherever, under any law of the United States or under any rule, regulation, order, or requirement made pursuant to law, any matter is required or <u>permitted to be supported, evidenced, established, or proved by the sworn declaration, verification, certificate, statement, oath, or affidavit, in writing of the person making the same</u> (other than a deposition, or an oath of office, or an oath required to be taken before a specified official other than a notary public), <u>such matter may</u>, with like force and effect, <u>be supported, evidenced, established, or proved by the unsworn declaration, certificate, verification, or statement, in writing of such person which is subscribed by him, as true under penalty of perjury</u>, and dated, in substantially the following form...
>
> (2) <u>If executed within the United States</u>, its territories, possessions, or commonwealths: "<u>I declare (or certify,</u>

verify, or state) under penalty of perjury that the foregoing is true and correct… (emphasis added)

Because the wording in this Code section includes the phrase "under penalty of perjury…", which is the same as those used on the citizen-affiant's previously filed Forms 1040, it becomes essential that these forms be retroactively revoked and rescinded so that they can no longer be used against the citizen. The AFFIDAVIT accomplishes this purpose. Without the AFFIDAVIT, the IRS might be able to use the legal doctrine of presumption against the citizen under which doctrine, along with Section 1746 quoted above, all previously filed returns and other forms which he might have filed in the past could be used by the IRS to attest to his admission that he was in the legal status of "taxpayer" in order to establish a conclusion that he had a legal obligation to file and pay income taxes. The grounds for this legal conclusion are legally nullified by the AFFIDAVIT shown at the end of this chapter. This writer feels that it is essential that any citizen who has made the decision to stop the fraud by no longer volunteering should eliminate, by means of the AFFIDAVIT, the use of any legal documents that the IRS might use to charge him criminally because of the previously-filed returns and other documents which he declared under penalties of perjury to be true and correct.

By filing the AFFIDAVIT, all previously-filed IRS forms such as 1040's, W-4 Withholding Allowance Certificates and/or any other documents or forms, which were signed under penalties of perjury, are revoked and rescinded retroactively as though they had never been executed and filed. Without the AFFIDAVIT, Title 28, United States Code, Section 1746, quoted above, might legally support the government's claim that the citizen is "liable" for the payment of income tax because the citizen had filed the forms under penalties of perjury. Therefore, they had the same legal effect as a document which contains a notarized signature under oath. It becomes essential, therefore, that any citizen who has made the decision to stop volunteering should nullify, by means of the AFFIDAVIT, any legal grounds that the IRS might have, because of these previously filed returns and other documents to use as grounds in order to bring a "failure to file" charge against him.

It is this writer's opinion that if, at a later date, the IRS is made aware of the citizen's knowledge, as executed and dated in the AFFIDAVIT, and because they also became aware from the recorded date on the document

<u>when</u> it was filed either with a recognized public information registry or in the court house of the county of the citizen's residence, the chance of the citizen ever being prosecuted for failure to file a return, which he knows would be a <u>voluntary</u> act is greatly lessened. After a citizen has stopped withholding and stopped filing tax returns, the IRS' standard procedure is to commence unlawful civil collection proceedings against him. First, this takes the form of a series of letters advising him that they have no record of having received a tax return from him for alledged taxed obligation for monies shown on W-2 or 1099 forms they have received and asking him to file. In this writer's opinion, the citizen should consider the advisability at this time of informing the IRS of his position by sending them, by certified mail, return receipt requested, a copy of his AFFIDAVIT OF REVOCATION AND RECISSION which he had filed. By so doing, the citizen would be putting the IRS on notice of his previously-dated position as set forth in the AFFIDAVIT. The IRS would then know, by reason of their knowledge of the previously-filed AFFIDAVIT, that they (the IRS) would be subjecting themselves to a possible suit by the citizen for fraud if they succeeded in a fraudulent collection action after they already had been put on notice by the AFFIDAVIT. This writer believes that the citizen would then have legal grounds to bring a suit for fraud against the IRS for their unlawful collection actions while ignoring the evidence contained in the AFFIDAVIT. All the law in the AFFIDAVIT proving that the citizen is not liable for income tax should be introduced into evidence making it difficult for the IRS to attempt a losing rebuttal. The citizen's suit could and should demand not only that the IRS not only return all money and/or property illegally acquired but also cease and desist in their fraudulent collection action, and should also demand interest, legal fees, compensation, fines and judicial sanctions against the IRS.

    The notarized AFFIDAVIT is dated and should be filed and recorded in the public records or miscellaneous section of the court house in the county of his residence or, through a reliable public information registry organization. To such which are recommended are www.getnoticed.info and/or www.NationalRepublicRegistry.com. Giving notice to the world, including the IRS, that the affiant is <u>not in the legal status of a "taxpayer"</u> as that <u>term</u> is defined in the Internal Revenue Code, and both why and when they made the statements contained in the AFFIDAVIT. As stated in the previous paragraph, because the AFFIDAVIT is a public statement of the citizen's knowledge and belief, if necessary, it can usually be admitted into evidence before a trial jury or a grand jury.

Many years ago, before the public had ever become aware of the constitutional limitations of the government's taxing authority, there were a few unlawful criminal prosecutions of outspoken leaders in the tax fight who were charged with both the misdemeanor charge of "willful failure to file" and the felony charge of "tax evasion". Unfortunately, due to the ignorance of both the defendant's lawyers and the prejudice of trial judges, convictions were obtained on both charges in a few cases. Both these criminal charges were illegally brought against a few leaders even though they had not filed any returns for the years at issue. Only a positive act such as filing a return which contains false figures can be the subject of a criminal felony prosecution for "attempt to evade or defeat any tax". A felony evasion charge is legally impossible for someone who has not filed a return. It cannot be a felony to do nothing; i.e., not file a tax return even if it were required by law. The only possible criminal tax charge against a person who may have been required to file a return, such as a corporate officer acting for his corporation, who did not do so, would be the misdemeanor charge of willful failure to file (doing nothing). Only a person who has filed a return on which he made false entries could be legally prosecuted for the felony charge of tax evasion (attempt to evade or defeat a tax).

Because of the existence of the AFFIDAVIT which would be brought to the attention of the jury, it is unlikely that the Justice Department would attempt to bring any false criminal charge against the citizen. Even though improper, the charge would have to be a false misdemeanor charge of willful failure to file a required return under I.R. Code Section 6012. The charge would be false because at the start of Chapter VII we showed why the limited provisions of this Code Section (6012) could not require any citizen who only earned monies on his own behalf to file any income tax return. Since the citizen will have stopped filing voluntary returns and because his AFFIDAVIT will have revoked all previously-filed returns and other IRS forms, it would be illegal for the IRS to charge him under I.R. Code Section 7201 which is a felony count of "attempt to evade or defeat" any tax. Without having filed a return and having revoked all previous returns, the Justice Department would be unable to legally produce any evidence such as false figures on a previously-filed return in order to prove such a felony charge. Because the AFFIDAVIT is dated, which proves when it was filed, and because it contains a wealth of positive information explaining why the citizen claims he owes no tax and has not filed, it is this writer's opinion that there is virtually no way that the Justice Department could keep it out of evidence before a petty (trial) jury. For these same reasons, this writer doubts that the Justice Department would dare to prosecute a citizen who has filed the AFFIDAVIT for even the misdemeanor "willful failure to file" charge, the penalty for which is stated in I.R. Code Section 7203. It should go without saying that the Justice Department, when considering the possible prosecution of the citizen, would never want this information in the AFFIDAVIT to come to the attention of the jury decision-makers because it would most likely prevent any guilty verdict particularly in light of the CHEEK decision of the Supreme Court which is discussed in some detail at the end of this chapter. A copy of an AFFIDAVIT is reproduced and discussed at the end of this chapter. Most of the information contained in the AFFIDAVIT has been reviewed in some detail in this book, primarily Chapters V, VI and VII.

It is noteworthy that for every citizen-employee who is successful in stopping <u>voluntary</u> withholding by their employer, he or she will thereafter have in each paycheck whatever sum had previously been withheld for the graduated rate income tax and/or (optionally) the so-called (but <u>misnamed</u>) Social Security tax. This could be a substantial sum-possibly a twenty-five percent or even greater increase in the citizen's take-home pay. If enough people were to give themselves this immediate raise to which they are entitled, the incredible stimulus that these millions of dollars pouring into the marketplace would have on our sagging economy is hard to imagine. Certainly it would be far more valuable to our economic recovery than the printing-press inflationary billions that government has given away to select big businesses in recent years! By accomplishing this, the employee will have the use of this money to save, invest or spend, as may be desired, so the benefits will be substantial and immediate, both personally and to the recovery of our economy as the saved money is spent in the marketpalce.

Every citizen who makes a decision to stop volunteering to pay taxes which he learns he does not owe should be aware of the potential consequences of his action. We must remember that Big Brother has been so successful in deceiving the majority of the public for so long that when one decides <u>not</u> to submit to the extortion any longer, and to stop volunteering, the IRS doesn't simply roll over and admit defeat. Rather, they usually will treat the citizen thereafter as a non-filer, and, contrary to the law which this writer has set forth in this book, they will intentionally, but erroneously, contend that the citizen's wages, salaries, commissions, other earnings and receipts which he has received <u>are</u> taxable "income". The IRS will, at year's end, upon receipt of copies of Forms W-2 and/or 1099 earnings reports from the employer or payor of commissions or other receipts, send to the citizen a series of form letters at regularly- prescribed intervals in an attempt to influence the citizen to <u>volunteer</u> to report all earnings and other receipts on a Form 1040 return <u>as though</u> they were taxable monies received by a non-resident alien (see Chapter III), asking them to pay tax on these receipts.

In following these collection procedures, the IRS doesn't pretend that citizens are taxable <u>non-resident aliens</u>. Rather the IRS simply want everyone to <u>volunteer</u> to report earnings and other receipts <u>as though they were</u> taxable "income" received by a non-resident alien, despite their repeated statements in the AFFIDAVIT OF REVOCATION AND RECISSION which proves that the citizen knows better. The AFFIDAVIT explains and proves the truth in detail, including a specific reference to supporting Supreme Court decisions, constitutional limitations and I.R. Code sections which limit taxation of citizens to those who are withholding agents for taxable persons such as non-resident aliens, corporations, or other priviledged entities. In order to be consistent with the filed AFFIDAVIT, the affiant who has filed the AFFIDAVIT OF REVOCATION AND RESCISSION should support his/her filing by stopping withholding with his employer ASAP. Because most employers have been informed by their accountants and/or their lawyers that payroll withholding is manditory, depending upon the size of the employer, the employee may have to support their demand to stop withholding through several levels of management. The citizen may have to show the law in I.R. Regulation #31.3402(p)(2), previously quoted, and also as shown in Chapter V which is only one reason that clearly proves that withholding is voluntary. This regulation, which is law, as we have shown (see Chapters V and VI), proves that withholding is voluntary for <u>everyone</u>-both government and non-government <u>employers and employees</u>. We should also remember that, as we also pointed out in Chapter V, every citizen's constitutional Fifth Amendment right <u>not</u> to be deprived of their property, <u>which includes their paycheck</u> or a part thereof, without due process of law (which means a court hearing), has been violated unless their employer complies with their request. This gives them <u>even more</u> reason to support their demand.

Diplomatic education of the employer or even his accountant or lawyer in order to prove the voluntary nature os withholding may be required in order to overcome the false impressions that most employers have that withholding mandatory. In attempting to stpp withholding, remember that all the law is on your side-the Fifth Amendment, the statutory law (Code

Section 3402(p)(3)(B) and the accompanying regulation are reproduced in Chapter V of Super Scam. Note how they clearly show the voluntary nature of withholding. Adding this proof to the Fifth and Thirteenth Amendments and the W-4 Withholding Allowance (permission) Certificate itself should be sufficient to convince any intelligent employer that withholding in voluntary.

The employer should also be informed that many emplo<u>yers,</u> if they are sole-proprietor citizen/employers, <u>are themselves protected</u> against any <u>requirement</u> to withhold by the Thirteenth Amendment to the Constitution which, in addition to its prohibition against slavery, also prohibits "involuntary servitude". This Amendment states that the employer-citizen cannot be required by law to withhold from his employee's pay if he didn't wish to volunteer to act as a withholding agent, <u>even</u> if his employee requested him to do so.

An important and valuable United States Supreme Court decision was rendered on January 8, 1991 in the case of **John L. Cheek v. The United States.** **498 U.S. 192 (1991**). This decision is not discussed in the AFFIDAVIT because it has no bearing on the affiant's knowledge gained from research into the law. It is, however, a decision which is noteworthy because it is very favorable to the citizen/defendant who may be prosecuted for any criminal tax charge. This decision contains a necessary instruction to any District Court judge to instruct the jury before their deliberations to determine an innocent or guilty verdict about what is known as a "reasonable belief" by the defendant who would have been charged with a tax crime described by either Section 7201 (evasion) or 7203 (willful failure to file). Because of the **Cheek** decision, the judge is required, when requested by defense counsel, to tell the jury that they must find the defendant <u>not guilty</u> if they believe the reasons why he elected to either take or omit the actions he took were reasons that <u>he truly believed</u>, <u>regardless of whether the reasons were either reasonable or unreasonable</u>. As an example, this decision would support a not guilty verdict of a defendant who, as a corporate officer, was <u>required</u> to file on behalf of his corporation and either failed to file or entered false figures on the return. Let's say that defense counsel told the jury that his client's (defendant's) failure to file or his act of putting false figures on the return was done because "he felt that the moon was made of green cheese". Whether such a reason was reasonable or not (and in this example it would surely be unreasonable), if the jury thought that <u>the defendant truly believed</u> this ridiculous reason, their (the jury's) belief that he (the defendant) <u>truly believed</u> it would be sufficient to find him not willful and, therefore, not guilty. This decision has undoubtedly been one of the major stumbling blocks for the U.S. Department of Justice since it was handed down in 1991 and is likely the reason why the number of criminal tax trial prosecutions have fallen off so dramatically. The **<u>Cheek</u>** decision expresses an understanding by the U.S. Supreme Court that the tax code is incredibly complex and adds an additional blanket of protection for U.S. citizens against any future criminal prosecutions for alleged income tax offenses. Such an understanding should be a great comfort to any citizen/defendant who is concerned about facing trial for any alleged willful failure to file or evasion charge.

AFFIDAVIT OF REVOCATION AND RECISSION

I, _____, being duly sworn and over eighteen (18) years of age do hereby make the following statements of acts, and affirm:

1. That I recently became aware that under the provisions of the United States Code, Title 28, Section 1746, the law thereunder states that any statement such as IRS/Income-Excise Tax Form 1040 which is signed under the penalties of perjury has the same legal effect as a document which contains a <u>notarized signature under oath</u>; that the knowledge I had acquired from reading the said Section 1746 of Title 28, United States Code, led me to look up the term "presumption" in *Black's Law Dictionary* because I remembered that I had, over many years past, filed IRS Form 1040 tax returns which I had signed under penalties of perjury, thereby certifying that my earnings in the form of wages, salaries, commissions, and other receipts were income and that I owed an income tax on these earnings. All such actions were legal grounds for a <u>presumption</u> by any court that I was subject to or liable for the payment of Federal and/or state income tax. I related such action on my part to acts that I wanted to rescind and cancel retroactively; that I found the following definitions (in part) of the word "presumption" contained therein: "A <u>presumption </u>is a rule of law, statutory or judicial, by which finding a basic fact gives rise to existence of presumed fact, "<u>until presumption is rebutted</u>"- **<u>Van Wart v. Cook</u>, Okl. App. 557 P2D, 1161, 1163…**"; that I further read in said *Black's Law Dictionary* under sub-heading "<u>effect of presumption</u>" the following: "…the better rule is that once evidence tending to rebut the presumption is introduced, the presumption loses all its force"; that I understand from this definition that the rebuttal burden falls upon me to effectively state my reasons for writing and filing this AFFIDAVIT, providing detailed rebuttal information of the knowledge and beliefs that I have acquired in order to establish this, my rebuttal, and these reasons for my rebuttal are contained in statement numbers 1-30 in this AFFIDAVIT.

2. That I was unaware that a completed, signed and submitted "Form 1040" or "income tax return" and a "W-4 Employee's Withholding Allowance Certificate", the authorization document that <u>allows</u> an employer to withhold a worker's money form his pay, are <u>voluntarily</u>-executed instruments which could be used as admissible

evidence against me in criminal trials and civil proceedings to show that I had <u>voluntarily</u> waived my constitutionally-secured rights, and that I had <u>voluntarily</u> subjected myself to the income/excise tax, to the provision of the Internal Revenue Code, and to the authority of the Internal Revenue Service (hereinafter referred to as the IRS) by signing and thereby affirming under penalties of perjury, under the legal doctrine of "presumption", that I was, in effect, a "person" subject to the "income" tax thereunder.

3. That I was unaware that the signing and filing of an income tax return and other IRS forms are acts of voluntary compliance for a free, sovereign individual citizen; that I was unaware that in a court of law the completed and signed IRS documents can become prima facie evidence sufficient to sustain a legal conclusion by a judge through the legal doctrine of "presumption" and the provisions of Title 28, Section 1746 as stated in Statement #1 of this AFFIDAVIT that the signer has <u>voluntarily</u> changed his legal status from that of a free, sovereign individual citizen who is <u>not subject</u> to any Federal tax and who possesses all his God-given, constitutionally-secured <u>rights</u> when dealing with government, into a new legal status of a "<u>taxpayer</u>", being one who is <u>liable for or subject to</u> such attacks.

4. That through research I discovered that "taxpayer" is a <u>term</u> defined in the Internal Revenue Code in I.R. Code Section 7701(a)(14) as "any <u>person</u> subject to any Internal Revenue tax"; that I further found that a "person" is also a defined term in I.R. Code Section 7701(a)(1) as "an individual, trust, estate, partnership, association, company or corporation"; that the only one of these definitions of the term "person" that could possibly apply to me would be the word "individual"; that I am <u>not</u> such a "person" or "individual" who is "subject to" or "liable for" any Internal Revenue tax; that I found that an appellate court, in the decision of **Houston Street Corp. v. Commissioner, 84 F2d 821 (1936) (5ᵗʰ Circuit)** explained in their decision that the terms "subject to" and "liable for" were interchangeable terms; that, thereafter, I determined that the only "person" "made liable" for any income tax in the Internal Revenue Code is a "withholding agent" who is "made liable" <u>only</u> under I. R. Code Section 1461; that a "withholding agent" is also defined in Code Section 7701(a)(16) as "any person <u>required</u> to deduct and withhold any tax under the provisions of (Code) Sections 1441, 1442, 1443 or 1461"; that I am <u>not</u> a "person required to deduct and withhold" as those words are used in Code Sections 1441, 1442, 1443 or 1461;

because I am not a person who is, or has ever made, any payments to any foreign person, partnership or corporation; that I saw that Chapter 3 of the I.R. Code applies only to those who are handling monies being paid to foreigners; that Code Section 1461 <u>imposes liability</u> only on those handling money being paid to foreigners; that, therefore, I am <u>not</u> a person or individual "made liable for such tax"; that I am, therefore, not subject to the authority, jurisdiction and control of the Federal government under Title 26 of the U.S. Code (the Internal Revenue Code), the statutes governing Federal taxation or to the regulations of the Internal Revenue Service; that it was never my intent to impose any income tax on myself or to waive my God-given, constitutionally-secured rights in respect to the Federal income/excise tax statutes or to their administration by the IRS, thereby establishing myself as one who has privileges only, but no rights in dealings with the IRS, the same as a corporation.

5. That I read the United States Court of Appeals Second Circuit Appellate Court decision in the case of **Botta v. Scanlon, 288 F2d. 504 (1961)** which was decided March 6, 1961 and in which decision the following statements were made by the Court:

1. Moreover, even the collection of taxes should be exacted only from persons <u>upon whom a tax liability is imposed by some statute.</u>

2. It is equally well settled that the revenue laws <u>apply only</u> to taxpayers.

3. However, a reasonable construction of the taxing statutes does not include vesting any tax official with absolute power of assessment against individuals not specified in the statutes as <u>persons liable for the tax without an opportunity for judicial review</u> of this status before the appellation of "taxpayer" is bestowed
upon him.... (emphasis added)

After reading the above quotations from this **Botta v. Scanlon** decision, I became even more firmly convinced that I was not a "person required to deduct and withhold" which would make me a person "made liable for such tax" as those words were used in I.R. Code Section 1461 referred to in Statement #4 of this AFFIDAVIT.

6. That it is my understanding that the change of status resulting from signed IRS documents can be very similar to the change of status that occurs when one enlists in the military service and voluntarily takes an oath that subjects him to the authority, jurisdiction and control of the Federal government under Title 10 of the United States Code, the statutes governing the Armed Forces and to the regulations of the military service, thereby waiving his constitutional rights in relation to dealings with the military service; that I was unaware of these legal effects of signing and filing an income tax return as shown by the decision of the United States Court of appeals for the 9th Circuit in the 1974 ruling in the case of **Morse v. U.S., 494 F.2d 876, 880**, wherein the Court explained how a citizen became a "taxpayer": "Accordingly, when signed returns were filed by Mrs. Morse declaring income to her for 1944 and 1945 and making her potentially liable for the tax due on that income, she became a taxpayer within the meaning of the Internal Revenue Code." under the legal doctrine of "presumption" discussed in number 1 of this AFFIDAVIT.

7. That my attention has been directed to the fact that an official Internal Revenue Service form letter FL1264 states: "The fact that you sent us (IRS) this Form 1040 shows that you recognize your obligation to file…"; that, contrary to the conclusion stated in this IRS form letter, it has never been my intention or desire to show the Internal Revenue Service or anyone else that I recognize any such obligation and that, as a United States citizen protected by the United States Constitution, I legally do not have such an obligation.

8. That I am a natural-born, free, sovereign United States citizen, and I am endowed by my creator with numerous inalienable rights including my right to "life, liberty and the pursuit of happiness", which rights are specifically identified in the Declaration of Independence and protected by the United States Constitution; that my birthright to "pursuit of happiness" has been interpreted by both the framers of the Constitution and the U.S. Supreme Court as including my inalienable right to contract, to acquire, to deal in, to sell, rent and exchange properties of various kinds, real and personal, without requesting or exercising any privilege or franchise from government; that I have learned that these inalienable property rights also include my right to contract for the exchange of my labor-property and for other properties such as wages, salaries, property exchanges and other earnings or receipts, and that I have never

knowingly or intentionally waived any of these inalienable rights either through the legal doctrine of "presumption" or by filing IRS forms 1040, W4 or others.

9. That I understand that, if the exercise of constitutionally-protected rights were subjected to taxation, the rights could be destroyed by increasing the tax rates to unaffordable levels; therefore, courts have repeatedly ruled that government has no power to tax the exercise of the constitutional rights of any citizens, as shown by the U.S. Supreme Court in the case of **Murdock v. Pennsylvania, 319 U.S. 105 (1943)** which stated: "A state may not impose a charge for the enjoyment of a right granted by the Federal Constitution."

10. That for years past I have been incorrectly influenced by numerous and repeated public warnings by the IRS via radio, television, the printed press and other public communication media warning of the "deadline" for filing a "Form 1040 Income Tax Return" and/or other IRS forms and documents, which warnings had falsely convinced me that I had an obligation to file IRS forms 1040 and others.

11. That in addition to the aforesaid warnings, I have also been influenced by misleading and deceptive wording of IRS publications, IRS-generated news articles, the pressure of widespread rumors and misinformed public opinion and the advice and assurance of lawyers, CPA's and income tax preparers who misled me to incorrectly believe that the Sixteenth Amendment to the United States Constitution somehow authorized Congress to impose a direct tax on me, my property, my exchanges of property and/or property received as a result of exercising my constitutionally-secured right to earn a living and to contract; that I was further misled into incorrectly believing that because I now know to be false information, I had a legal duty and obligation to sign and file a "Form 1040 Income Tax Return" every year and a "Form W-4 Employees' Withholding Allowance Certificate" and/or other IRS forms and documents.

12. That I have in the past also been further influenced, misled and alarmed by rumors, misinformed public opinion and the advice and assurance of lawyers, CPA's and income tax preparers to the effect that "the IRS will get me", and that it would be a crime punishable by fine and/or imprisonment if I did not fill out, sign and file with the IRS a "Form 1040".

13. That in addition to all of the reasons already stated in the previous paragraphs of this AFFIDAVIT, I was influenced by the common and widespread practice of employers who unknowingly mislead

their employees into believing that they are also subject by law to withholding of "income taxes" from their earnings, either with or without their permission, based upon those employers' mistaken assumption that they, as employers, are required by law to withhold "income taxes" from the paychecks of their employees, all of which I now know is not true.

14. That I have also been influenced by the IRS' annual public display and indiscriminate offering of large quantities of the "Form 1040" in banks, post offices and through the U.S. mail which also reminded me of and induced me to "volunteer" by filling out, signing and sending to the IRS a "Form 1040".

15. That neither the "Form 1040" or its instruction booklet contained any reference to any law or laws which would explain just exactly who is or is not subject to or liable for the income tax, nor did it contain any notice or warning to me or to anyone that by merely sending said signed and completed "Form 1040" to the IRS I would waive my right to privacy secured by the Fourth Amendment and my right to not having to be a witness against myself secured by the Fifth Amendment to the United States Constitution, and that the completed and signed "Form 1040" would, in itself, constitute legal evidence admissible in a court of law under the law of "presumption" that I was subject to and liable for the income/excise tax, even though and regardless of the fact, that I, as a free, United States citizen-individual, am actually and legally not subject to or liable for any income/excise tax and have no legal duty or obligation whatsoever to complete and file a "Form 1040".

16. That at no time was I ever notified or informed by the IRS, by any of its agents or employees, nor by any lawyers, CPA's or tax preparers of the fact that the Sixteenth Amendment to the United States Constitution as correctly interpreted by the U.S. Supreme Court in such cases as **Brushaber v. Union Pacific R.R., 240 U.S. 1 (1916)** and **Stanton v. Baltic Mining Co., 240 U.S. 103 (1916)** identified the income tax as an indirect excise tax in accordance with, and authorized by, Article 1, Section 8, Clause 1 of the United States Constitution. I further learned that the Sixteenth Amendment did not repeal Article 1, Section 2, Clause 3 or Article 1, Section 9, Clause 4 of the Constitution which sections protect me as a citizen against any direct taxation on my salary, wages, property dealings or any other receipts.

17. That at no time was I ever notified or informed by the IRS, its agents

or employees or by any lawyer, CPA or tax preparer of the fact that the tax on income which is referenced in the Sixteenth Amendment to the Constitution has been identified by the Supreme Court as an <u>excise</u> tax upon activities involving the exercise of government-granted privileges such as doing business in the United States as a corporation or as a non-resident alien. By contrast, I have not asked government for any such privilege. To the contrary, I now know that both the Constitution and the U.S. Supreme Court protect my non-taxable right, as a U.S. citizen, to earn a living by any means or in any lawful occupation of my choice.

18. That my attention has been called to Report No. 80-19A titled *Some Constitutional Questions Regarding the Federal Income Tax Laws* published by The American Law Division of the Congressional Research Service of the Library of Congress updated January 17, 1980 and that this publication described the tax on "income" identified in the Sixteenth Amendment of the United States Constitution as an indirect excise tax; that this report stated that "The Supreme Court, in a decision written by Chief Justice White, first noted that the Sixteenth Amendment did not authorize any new type of tax, nor did it repeal or revoke the taxing limitations of Article 1, Section 2, Clause 3 or Article 1, Section 9, Clause 4 of the United States Constitution." I have learned that these sections prohibit any direct tax unless apportioned amongst the states of the union (Article 1, Section 2, Clause 3) or any capitation tax which means a tax on me or my labor (Article 1, Section 9, Clause 4). These taxing limitations can clearly be determined from decisions of the United States Supreme Court which identifies the income tax as an <u>indirect tax in the nature of an excise</u>, thus proving in my mind that the income tax is not a tax on me or my earnings as an individual citizen. Rather, I have learned that it is a tax as described by the U.S. Supreme Court **in <u>Flint v. Stone Tracy Co.</u>, 220 U.S. 107 (1911)**), wherein the court defined excise taxes as "...taxes laid upon the manufacture, sale or consumption of commodities within the country..., and upon corporate privileges.", none of which classifications apply to me; that, in fact, such a corporate-privilege tax is imposed under the I.R. Code in Section 11 which is also inapplicable to me.

19. That I was unaware of the IRS' rarely publicized statement that the "income" tax system is based upon "voluntary compliance with the law, and self-assessment of tax"; that it has never been my intention or desire to voluntarily self-assess any tax upon myself; that I always

previously mistakenly thought that my compliance was required by law.

20. That I have examined Sections 6001, 6011, 6012, 7201, 7203 and 7205 of the Internal Revenue Code (Title 26 USC), and I am convinced and satisfied that, as a United States citizen protected by the Constitution, that I am not now and never was any such "person" or individual referred to by these sections; that I noticed that, although Code Section 6012 has the misleading <u>heading</u> "persons <u>required</u> to make returns of income", I found that by reading the wording in Code Section 7806 which reads "nor shall any descriptive matter relating to the contents of this title be given any legal effect…"; that the heading in Code Section 6012 which includes the word "required" has no meaning; that, in fact, the word "shall" is used in the body of this Code section means "may" in my case, because a mandatory meaning of this word would be unconstitutional according to the U.S. Supreme Court in the decision of **Cairo and Fulton R.R. Co. v. Hecht, 95 U.S. 170 (1877),** in which decision the Court stated: "…as against the government, the word 'shall', when used in statutes, must be construed to mean 'may' unless contrary intention is manifest."; that this decision was confirmed by the decision of **Gow v. Consolidated Coppermines Corp., 165 Atlantic, 136 (1933),** wherein the Court stated: "If necessary to avoid unconstitutionality of a statute, 'shall' will be deemed equivalent to 'may', and the word 'may' obviously has a voluntary meaning." I now know that I am not either a "taxpayer" or a "person" or an "individual" "liable for" or "subject to" income taxes under Sub-Title A as those terms are defined and/or used in the Internal Revenue Code.

21. That after careful study of the Internal Revenue Code, I have never found or been shown any section of the Internal Revenue Code that imposed any requirement on me as a free, sovereign, unprivileged individual United States citizen to file a "Form 1040 Income Tax Return" or that imposed a requirement upon me to pay a tax on "income" or that would classify me as a "person liable", a "person made liable" or a "taxpayer" as the term "taxpayer" is defined in 26 USC, Section 7701(a)(14) which states: "The term 'taxpayer' means any person subject to any Internal Revenue tax."

22. That including in the study previously mentioned, my attention was called to 26 USC, Chapter 1, Sub-Chapter A, Part 1, Section 1 which is deceptively titled *TAX ON INDIVIDUALS*; that a careful

study and examination of this part of the Code showed no provision in the body of the I.R. Code which covers income tax imposing any liability or requirement on me as a U.S. citizen-individual for payment of a Federal excise tax on "income". That my study previously mentioned in this AFFIDAVIT showed me that the law is determined by the actual wording contained in the body of any Code section and <u>not by the title</u>; that the title of a statute is merely a general guide to the contents of the Code section, and the title has <u>no force or effect at law</u> as stated in I.R. Code Section 7806(b).

23. That after more study and consultations, my attention was called to Chapter 21 of the Internal Revenue Code which is deceptively titled: *Federal Insurance Contributions Act* "<u>Social Security</u>" and to Sub-Chapter A of Chapter 21 titled: *Tax on Employee*"; that Chapter 21 includes Sections 3101 in which the "<u>Social Security</u>" tax is identified as a tax on "income" and not as an *Insurance Contribution*; that it is also not a "tax on employees", nor on wages or earnings, and that there is no provision in the Code that imposes the so-called "<u>Social Security</u>" tax on employees or requires them to pay the tax; that only a <u>voluntarily</u>-signed and completed W-4 *Employees Withholding Allowance Certificate* allows (permits) an employer to withhold money from a workers' pay for the so-called "<u>Social Security</u>" flat-rate "income tax"; that no employer has any authority to withhold money from a workers' pay for the <u>mis</u>named "<u>Social Security</u>" "income" tax or the graduated "income" tax or any IRS-imposed penalty or assessment unless there is a voluntarily-signed W-4 form in force which has been <u>voluntarily</u> signed by the employee.

24. That my attention was called to I.R. Code Section 1441 titled "*Withholding of Tax on Non-Resident Aliens* which identifies "dividends, rents, salaries, wages, premiums, annuities, compensations, remunerations, emoluments or other fixed or determinable annual or periodical gains, profits and income…" as being "items of 'income'" but <u>only when received by non-resident alien individuals, foreign partnerships or corporations</u> as set forth in Sections 1441(a) or 1442(a). After reading these Code sections, I recognize that all the provisions therein were applicable only to non-resident aliens, foreign partnerships or foreign corporations or those acting for or representing those individuals, foreign partnerships or foreign corporations, but <u>not to me as a United States citizen</u>!

25. That after the study described in the preceding paragraphs, my attention was called to Section 61(a) of the Internal Revenue Code

which lists under Section 61(a)(1) "compensation for services including fees, commissions, fringe benefits and similar items"; that these items are <u>sources</u> of "income" as confirmed by former IRS Collection Summons Form 6638 (12-82) which identifies these items as <u>sources</u>, not "income", by stating that the <u>following items are "sources"</u>: "wages, salaries, tips, fees, commissions, interest, rents, royalties, alimony, state or local tax refunds, pensions, business income, gains from dealings in property and any other compensation for services (including receipt of property other than money)"; that <u>sources are not "income"</u>, but sources can be and or become "income" <u>if they are entered as "income"</u> on a signed "Form 1040" because <u>the signer affirms under penalty of perjury that the items entered in the "income" section of the "Form 1040" are "income"</u> to <u>the signer</u>, or if I were a non-resident alien as stated in paragraph 26 following.

26. That after further study it appears clear to me that the only way that property received by <u>me</u> as a free, sovereign, unprivileged, individual citizen in the form of wages, salaries, commissions, tips, interest, dividends, rents, royalties, pensions could be, or could have been, legally considered to be taxable as "income" would be if I were a non-resident alien individual as stated in I.R. Code Section 1441, Sections (a) and (b), which status I deny; or if I voluntarily completed and signed a *Form 1040 Income Tax Return*, thereby affirming under penalties of perjury that information on the "Form 1040" was true and correct and that any amounts listed on the "Form 1040" in the "income" block are "income", thereby acknowledging, under oath, that I am or was subject to the tax and had a duty to file *Form 1040 Income Tax Retu*rns and/or other IRS forms, documents and schedules, none of which instruments I have ever signed with the understanding that they are voluntarily signed, but rather that I thought such acts were legally required.

27. That with reliance upon the previously-numbered statements in this AFFIDAVIT and the aforementioned U.S. Supreme Court rulings and upon my constitutionally-protected rights, and particularly those rights enumerated in the Fourth, Fifth, Ninth, Tenth and Thirteenth Amendments to the Constitution, and my right to lawfully contract, to work and to lawfully acquire, buy, sell and possess property without interference by government, I am convinced and satisfied that I, as a U.S. citizen, am not now, nor was I ever subject to, liable for, or required to pay any income/excise tax on any of my

earnings or other receipts; that I am not now and never was in the legal status of "taxpayer" as that term is defined and used in the Internal Revenue Code, and that I have never had any legal duty or obligation whatsoever to file any "Form 1040", make any "income tax return", sign and file with any employer or the IRS any W-4 *Employees' Withholding Allowance Certificate* or other Internal Revenue forms, submit documents or schedules, pay any income tax, keep any records or supply any information to the IRS.

28. That the Internal Revenue Service (IRS), by deceptive and misleading words and statements in the Internal Revenue Code, as well as IRS publications and IRS-generated news articles, has committed constructive fraud by misleading and deceiving me and the general public into believing that I was required to file *Form 1040 Income Tax returns, Form W-4 Employees' Withholding Allowance Certificates* and other IRS forms, documents and schedules and also to keep records, supply information and to pay income taxes, when I now know that, as a free, sovereign, individual U.S. citizen I do not have, nor have I ever had, any requirement to file any such forms.

29. That further I do hereby declare that I am not, and never was, in the legal status of a "taxpayer" as the term "taxpayer" is defined and used in Section 7701(a)(14) of the Internal Revenue Code, as a "person required to deduct and withhold any tax" or a person "made liable for such tax" as these phrases are used in the I.R. Code Section 1461, which my study and research shows is the <u>only section of the Internal Revenue Code that makes anyone liable for payment of income tax</u>; that I am and have always been a "non-taxpayer"; that courts have recognized and acknowledged that individuals can be <u>non</u>-taxpayers as stated by several court in **Long v. Rasmussen, 281 F. 236 (1922), Economy Plumbing & Heating., U.,S. 470 F2d. 585-589 (1972)** and affirmed in **Delima v. Bidwell, 182 U.S. 176, 179** and **Berth v. United States, 132 F. Supp. 894 (1955)**.

30. That by reason of the aforementioned facts, I do hereby exercise my right as a free, sovereign U.S. citizen, upheld by various court decisions, to revoke, rescind, cancel and to render null and void both currently and retroactively to the time of signing, based upon the constructive fraud perpetrated upon me by the U.S. Congress and the Internal Revenue Service, all *Form 1040 Income Tax Returns*, all *Form W-4 Employees' Withholding Allowance Certificates*, all other IRS forms, schedules and documents ever signed and/or submitted by me and all my signatures on any of the aforementioned items;

that this revocation and rescission is based upon my rights in respect to constructive fraud as established in, but not limited to, the cases of **Tyler v. Secretary of State**, 183A2d, 101 (1962), **Economy Plumbing and Heating v. U.S.**, 470 F.2d 585 at 589 (1972) and also **El Paso Natural Gas Co. v. Kysar Insurance Co.**, 605 Pacific 2d, 240 (1979) which stated: "Constructive fraud as well as actual fraud may be the basis of cancellation of an instrument."

I now affix my signature to these affirmations.

_____
                Affirmant   (SEAL)

Subscribed and sworn to before me, a Notary Public, of the State of _____, County of _____ _____, this _____ day of _____, 2_____.

_____   _____
              Notary Public   Commission Expires

CHAPTER IX

FREQUENTLY ASKED QUESTIONS AND ANSWERS

Q#1. I've heard that there is no law that requires U. S. citizens to file a tax return or pay a tax on their earnings. Is this true?

A. Yes! <u>There is no such law</u>. For <u>individual</u> U.S. citizens, their monies in the form of receipts from compensation for services, rents, royalties, commissions, dividends, interest, investment profits, business profits, capital gains, etc. they have received for themselves is not taxable under our Constitution. Such a tax would be an unapportioned <u>direct</u> tax, and any such direct tax that is not apportioned (divided) among and billed to the governments of the states of the union, according to the population of each state, is prohibited by both Article 1, Section 2, Clause 3 and Article 1, Section 9, Clause 4 of the U.S. Constitution (see Chapters I and II). The top management people in the Internal Revenue Service, along with many lawyers, accountants and other tax professionals and most Federal judges know that this is true. For these reasons, there cannot constitutionally be any law imposing income tax on U.S. citizen's earnings or other receipts!

However, the IRS intentionally promotes false information that the Sixteenth Amendment to the Constitution authorized a direct tax on the earnings and other receipts of U.S. citizens. This propaganda has become so widely accepted today, over the many years since passage of the Amendment in 1913, that a majority of the American public has been successfully deceived by the IRS into erroneously believing that they actually owe a tax on their earnings and other receipts. This book, and particularly Chapter II which is an in depth history of the Sixteenth Amendment, proves the truth about the limited taxing authority created by the Sixteenth Amendment.

Common sense tells us that, if the Sixteenth Amendment had changed the Constitution to authorize an income tax on U.S. citizen's receipts, there would be a law shown by a Code section in the Internal Revenue Code which plainly stated that all U.S. citizens would be subject to an income tax on their own wages, salaries and other receipts. No such law (Code section) exists because it would be in violation of the Constitutional prohibitions against any unapportioned direct tax which we have discussed repeatedly in great detail in this book. These constitutional prohibitions <u>were not repealed</u>

by the Sixteenth Amendment, and they are still in full force and effect today, protecting all U.S. citizens from any direct taxation on their earnings or other receipts. As is shown throughout this book, and particularly in the analysis of key Code Sections 1, 6012, 1441, 1461 and 7343, all requirements for filing returns, paying income tax or for violations subject to criminal penalties are limited to those enjoying taxable government-granted privileges such as corporations and non-resident aliens or those representing such parties, either as responsible officers of corporations or as those having control of monies owing and payable to non-resident aliens or other Federally taxable entities.

Q#2. I have heard that the term "income" as used in both the Sixteenth Amendment and the I.R. Code doesn't mean what we have always thought it meant in common usage-that is, that "income" does not include a citizen's wages, salaries, commissions or other receipts. Can you explain?

A. To answer this question, we must go back to the taxing provisions in Article 1, Section 8 of the Constitution which were discussed in some depth in Chapter I of this book. Only two classes of taxation are authorized in the Constitution by Article1, Section 8. These are, first: "Taxes"; and second: "Duties, Imposts, and Excises". The Supreme Court has always identified "Taxes" as being in the "direct" class, and the words "Duties, Imposts and Excises" as being in the "indirect" class.

In the decision of Brushaber v. Union Pacific Railroad Co., 240 U.S. 1 (1916) the Supreme Court explained that "excises" fell into the category of indirect taxation when they explained that all United States Federal taxes fall into one or another of these two distinct classes of taxation. The Brushaber court emphasized this point in some detail when they quoted from a previous Supreme Court ruling which stated:

> *In the matter of taxation, the Constitution recognizes two great classes of <u>direct and indirect</u> taxes, and lays down two rules by which their imposition must be governed, namely, the rule of <u>apportionment</u> as to direct taxes, and the rule of <u>uniformity</u> as to duties, imposts and <u>excises</u>.* (emphasis added)

In the decision of **Stanton v. Baltic Mining Co., et al., 240**

U.S. 103 (1916), the Supreme Court very specifically stated soon after ratification of the Sixteenth Amendment that:

> *The provisions of the Sixteenth Amendment conferred <u>no new power of taxation</u>, but simply prohibited the previous complete and plenary power of <u>income</u> taxation <u>possessed by Congress from the beginning</u> from being taken out of the category of <u>indirect</u> taxation to which it inherently belonged... that such a tax is not a tax upon property as such because of its ownership, but a <u>true excise</u> levied on the results of the business of caring on mining operations.* (emphasis added)

So the Supreme Court in the **Stanton** decision described "<u>income</u> taxation" as in the "<u>indirect</u>" class and said, further, that such "indirect" taxation was an "excise". Therefore, we must determine the meaning of the <u>term</u> "excise". And, to do so, again, we turn to the Supreme Court, which stated in **Flint v. Stone Tracy, 220 U.S. 107 (1911)** that:

> **<u>Excises</u> are taxes laid upon the manufacture or sale of commodities within the country, upon licenses to pursue certain occupations, and upon <u>corporate privileges</u>.** (emphasis and parenthasis added)

These Supreme Court decisions tell us in the **Brushaber** and **Stanton** decisions that the "income" tax is an <u>indirect</u> tax that was authorized in the Constitution from its origin. Second, the **Flint** Supreme Court tells us that an "excise" is also a tax on the activity of doing business <u>as a corporation</u> when they stated in their decision that:

> *The requirement to pay such taxes (excises) involves the exercise of the <u>privilege</u> and if business is not done in the (corporate) manner described, no tax is payable.* (emphasis added)

Therefore, the **Flint** decision stated that <u>excises</u> are taxes imposed on the exercise of government-granted privilege such as doing business as a corporation.

In Chapter I, we cited several Supreme Court decisions which stated that a citizen's right to earn a living was an "<u>inalienable</u>" right and, therefore, <u>non-taxable</u> as stated in the Declaration of Independence and protected by our Constitution from <u>any</u> taxation by government. For these reasons, the word "income" <u>cannot</u> be construed to mean wages, salaries or other receipts received by U.S. citizens on their own behalf!

The I.R. Code itself supports this conclusion, as is pointed out in detail in Chapter III of this book. In that chapter, we pointed out that the word "income" is <u>identified</u> in I.R. Code Sections 1441(a) and (b) as monies in the many forms listed in Section 1441(b) as "income", but <u>only</u> when received by non-resident aliens, foreign partnerships or foreign corporations. U.S. citizens have <u>always</u> been protected against any taxation on their person, property, or, more importantly, their <u>labor-property</u> because such a tax would be direct in the constitutional sense and forbidden by Article 1, Section 2, Clause 3 and Article 1, Section 9, Clause 4 of the Constitution. (See Chapter I of this book.)

Q#3. Wherever I work, they tell me they <u>have to</u> take taxes out of my pay and make me sign a Form W-4 authorizing the deduction. How do I deal with this problem?

A. By law, as we showed in detail in Chapter V, <u>all</u> withholding is voluntary, for both government and non-government employers and employees. I.R. Code, Section 3402(p)(3)(A) and (B) for all employees and its implementing Regulation #31.3402(p)(2) as emphasis for government employees clearly state that withholding is voluntary. Because employers have been <u>mis</u>informed (intentionally in this writer's opinion) by the IRS, and possibly by ignorance of their own attorneys or accountants, to believe that withholding is <u>required</u> by law, it becomes necessary to convince them of the truth about the law. This is best done by simply showing them the law (Code Section 34302(p)(3)(A) and (B)) and for government employees who want to stop withholding Regulation Number 31.3402(p)(1) and (2) as quoted in Chapter V of this book. The law is all on the citizen's side. As we pointed out in Chapter VII in this book, in addition to the Code section and the regulation shown above, an employee's Fifth Amendment right not to be deprived of life or liberty or property (his pay is his property) without due process of law, meaning a court hearing, under the Fifth Amendment to the Constitution, is also violated if any employer denies any employee's right to receive his full paycheck.

In this writer's opinion, if <u>any</u> employ<u>er</u> were to consult with his lawyer or accountant, the employer should be aware that almost all lawyers are predisposed by years of erroneous training to believe the IRS lie that withholding is required by law. Because of this, many, and possibly even most lawyers, not having done their own research on this question, will be inclined to tell their client that withholding is mandatory. This will require the employer to show his attorney the indisputable evidence in Code Section 3402(p)(3)(B) for non-government employees and for government employees regulation 31.3402(p)(2) that withholding is voluntary. We quoted this Code Section and the regulation in Chapter V of this book for the reader's reference.

Most lawyers may very well have denied the voluntary nature of withholding out of ignorance because of their years of dependence on the IRS' misinformation rather than their own research. Such a mistake would be extremely embarrassing to the lawyer because it would show his negligence in not having done his homework (researching the law) on behalf of his client. I.R. Code Section 3402(p)(1) and its implementing Regulation 31.3402(p)(2), referenced above, and quoted in Chapter V have repeated references to the voluntary nature of withholding and to the necessity for the employer to secure permission in the form of a signed W-4 Withholding Allowance Certificate to start withholding in order to not be in conflict with the employee's right to due process under the Fifth Amendment to the Constitution. This Fifth Amendment, as is also explained in Chapter V, makes all withholding voluntary by its provision alone. If the employer's tax lawyer or accountant were doing their job as they should, they would have learned the truth and advised their employer/client in advance about the voluntary nature of all withholding so that all their employer's employees would have the information necessary to make an informed choice about withholding before they ever start their employment!

Q#4. The IRS' tax Form 1040 includes a space for you to enter wages, salaries and commissions as "income". If they are not taxable to citizens, why do they ask you to enter them as "income" on the 1040 form?

A. Because the IRS wants citizens to volunteer to state their earnings and other receipts as income. There is no Code section (no law) in the tax code covering income tax stating that a U.S. citizen's wages, salaries, commissions and/or other receipts are income. By suggesting on the 1040 form that citizens should list their wages, salaries and commissions as though they were "income" on the 1040 form, it is this writer's opinion that the IRS is guilty of constructive fraud. I believe this because, as is proven throughout this book, and particularly in Chapter I, both the Constitution and many Supreme Court decisions deny the taxability of any U.S. citizen's earnings or other receipts. Therefore, at a minimum, this IRS Form 1040 <u>should</u> (but doesn't) explain that wages, salaries, commissions or other receipts should be listed in this box <u>only</u> when received by non-resident aliens-but <u>not</u> by U.S. citizens (see Chapters I, III and VII).

Q#5. Didn't the Sixteenth Amendment authorize the government to tax our salaries, wages and other receipts?

A. No. That's a common misunderstanding. Wages, salaries and other receipts of U.S. citizens have <u>never</u> been constitutionally taxable in our nation's history. After ratification of the Sixteenth Amendment in 1913, its provisions came under scrutiny by the U.S. Supreme Court in the decision of **Brushaber v. Union Pacific R.R., 240 U.S. 1 (1916)** in which the Court ruled that the tax authorized by the amendment was an <u>indirect</u> <u>tax</u> in the nature of an <u>excise</u>. Just a month after the **Brushaber** decision, the U.S. Supreme Court, in direct reference to the **Brushaber** decision, reaffirmed this finding in the decision of **Stanton v. Baltic Mining, 240 U.S. 103 (1916),** stating again that the Sixteenth Amendment authorized an <u>excise tax</u> on income and that the amendment created <u>no new power</u> of taxation. The **Stanton** court was stating in this decision that Congress always had the power in the original Constitution to impose excise taxes on income. No <u>statement</u> was made by the court in either the **Stanton** or the **Brushaber** decisions that a <u>citizen's</u> constitutional right to earn a living or to make money in other legal way was taxable by reason of the passage of the Sixteenth Amendment. In 1909, President Taft's speech to Congress disclosed that his <u>only purpose</u> in proposing the Amendment was to override the effect of a prior Supreme Court decision in the 1895 case of **Pollock v. Farmers Loan & Trust Co., 157 U.S. 420**, in which decision the Supreme Court held that to tax gains derived from property was the same as taxing the property itself, and, therefore, unconstitutional because such taxation would not satisfy the requirement of apportionment in Article 1, Section 2, Clause 3 of the Constitution. President Taft wanted to break up the corporate trusts that had been created to form monopolies to stifle competition. To do this, he wanted the Sixteenth Amendment to overrule the **Pollock** decision which would authorize Congress to tax the <u>profits earned</u> in the <u>exercise of the corporate privilege</u> <u>only</u>!

The two provisions in our Constitution which have always prohibited any direct tax on U.S. citizens-Article 1, Section 2, Clause 3 and Article 1, Section 9, Clause 4 <u>were not repealed by the Sixteenth Amendment</u> and are still in full force today protecting our citizenry from any direct tax on their earnings or other receipts. (See Chapters I and II).

Q#6. Are profits or gains made by citizens from purchase and sale of properties such as dealings in real estate, stocks, bonds, commodities or other properties or from interest or dividends subject to income tax?

A. Not if the profit or gain is earned by a U.S. citizen on his own behalf. These types of profits or gains are still non-taxable to the U.S. citizen who earns them by reason of the exercise of his right as a citizen to do business, invest, buy and sell property or engage in other lawful activities. Most of our nation's millionaires, in fact, have made their money as a result of their investment or business expertise which the law treats in the same manner as wages, salaries or commissions. The court cases covering taxable profit or gain are almost exclusively related to privileged <u>corporation</u> profit or gain- not profit or gain realized or earned by citizens through the exercise of their own intelligence. President Taft in his 1909 speech to Congress proposed: "…an amendment to the tariff bill imposing <u>upon all corporations…an excise tax</u> measured by 2% on the net income of such corporations. "…this is an <u>excise tax upon the privilege of doing business as an artificial entity</u>…". (emphasis added) In support of this taxing proposal, the President further noted in his speech: "The decision of the Supreme Court in the case of **Spreckels Sugar Refining Co. against McClain** (192 U.S. 397) seems clearly to establish the principle that such a tax as this (his proposal) is an <u>excise tax upon privilege</u> and not a direct tax on property and is within the federal power without apportionment according to population." (emphasis added) Clearly, the President was proposing an <u>excise tax on corporate profit or gain</u> which had been previously sustained in the **Spreckels** case as he specifically noted. However, in order to prevent any possible Supreme Court objection to such a tax on the corporate privilege, he simultaneously proposed what became the Sixteenth Amendment and in passing <u>both</u> the 1913 Tariff Act <u>and</u> the Sixteenth Amendment, Congress gave him exactly what he asked for. The President felt that a constitutional Amendment was necessary to accompany his tariff bill proposal because he was concerned that the Supreme Court might overturn his proposed excise tax as being direct and, therefore, one requiring apportionment because of the 1895 decision in **Pollock v. Farmers Loan & Trust Co**. All of this history preceding enactment of the Sixteenth Amendment shows that President Taft, who later served as Chief Justice of the Supreme Court, knew very well that the Constitution provided no authority to tax, wages, salaries, profits or gains earned by citizens.

Q#7. I've heard people say that those who stop filing tax returns wind up in jail. What chances do I have in avoiding incarceration?

A. Unless you are a leader in the constitutional tax movement, your chances of facing a criminal prosecution are insignificant. The IRS understandably doesn't want the truth broadcast by anyone, and they primarily limit their criminal prosecutions to leaders in the movement who are educating the public about the scam. They seldom prosecute those who have learned the truth, stopped voluntary withholding and stopped filing all IRS forms. Unlawful administrative civil procedures by the IRS, however, in order to collect money for income taxes not owed on citizen's wages, salaries or other earnings are commonplace, and should be expected. These unlawful procedures are discussed in detail in Chapter VI. However, a citizen, by preparing and recording an AFFIDAVIT OF REVOCATION AND RECISSION, in the court house of the county of their residence or, alternately one of the information public registries, has virtually insulated himself against any criminal prosecution. The Justice Department would never be able to prevent the AFFIDAVIT from being submitted into evidence in a jury trial, and they know that the information contained therein would almost guarantee a not guilty verdict in any criminal trial (see Chapter VIII). In addition to the AFFIDAVIT, the favorable Supreme Court decision in **U.S. v. Cheek**, which is discussed in detail in Chapter VIII, provides even more protection against any criminal prosecution for all U.S. citizens.

Q#8. What are the Code sections that the IRS and the Justice Department would use if they were to prosecute a citizen who has stopped filing tax returns and paying taxes on his own receipts?

A. First of all, as we explained in Question #7 above, the chances of a citizen facing a criminal prosecution are very unlikely-probably insignificant. This is true because the IRS understandably doesn't want to have the truth broadcast in a public trial. This would be the case for any citizen who had only earned money or other receipts on his own behalf and not as a fiduciary or other custodial representative of a non-resident alien, a corporation or other taxable entity. His position against any prosecution would be much stronger still if he had filed an AFFIDAVIT OF REVOCATION AND RECISSION which is discussed in great detail in Chapter VIII of this book.

If, for some reason, the IRS, through the Justice Department, had decided to prosecute a citizen for willful failure to file, the alleged filing requirement they would have to prove is contained in I.R. Code Section 6012 which states as follows:

> **Sec. 6012. Persons required to make returns of income.**
> **(a) General Rule.**
> Returns with respect to income taxes under subtitle A shall be made by the following:
> **(1)**
> **(A)** Every individual having for the taxable year gross income which equals or exceeds the exemption amount, except that a return shall not be required of an individual... (emphasis added)

A detailed, lengthy discussion of the many reasons why Code Section 6012 cannot prove any "requirement" to file any income tax return by a citizen who merely earns monies through his own efforts in the form of wages, salaries, commissions or other receipts is contained in Chapter VII of this book, and a careful study of this chapter is this writer's best answer to this question.

Years ago, the IRS falsely charged citizens criminally with failure to file income tax returns in alleged violation of I.R. Code Section 7203. This section specifies only penalties, but imposes no requirement to file any return. Therefore, use of this purely penalty Code section as one which requires filing of a return was, and, if used today, still is improper. In recent years, failure to file charges are so infrequent that this writer is not familiar with the Code section that the Justice Department would use today to make a failure to file charge. I am only aware that they mistakenly used Code Section 7203 in years past. Should that Code section be used today for alleging a failure to file, this improper use would, in this writer's opinion, be the proper subject for a Summary Motion to Dismiss for Failure to State Any Requirement. This writer would recommend that the citizen consult with his attorney about the advisability of such a motion.

The other possible criminal Code section which the Justice Department could use against the citizen is Code Section 7201 which is a felony charge of evasion. The possibility of such a charge ever being brought against a citizen is even more remote-particularly if the citizen had filed the AFFIDAVIT OF REVOCATION AND RECISSION as discussed in Chapter VIII of this book. Having revoked all previous returns and other IRS forms, the Justice Department would have no evidence predicated upon which any evasion charge could ever be substantiated. Again, as is the case with Section 7203, Code Section 7201 is a penalty statute only and imposes no requirement. Like Code Section 7203, it cannot stand alone as a requirement to do anything. Consequently, it, too, would lend itself to a similar Summary Motion for Dismissal for the same reasons as stated above.

Q#9. I see frequent advertisements on TV by income tax guru's promising that they can settle old tax obligations to the IRS for small fractions of what is allegedly owed. Some of their clients testify in these TV ads that, with the help of these firms, they settle with the IRS for as little as 10-20% of the IRS' claims. How can these firms do this?

A. From the frequency of these TV ads, it seems logical that these claims by the tax guru firms are probably true. The IRS has a well-known tax settlement program which they call OFFER IN COMPROMISE. The name itself tells its intent! This writer's opinion is that, because the IRS knows very well that their claims of taxes owed by citizens on their own receipts are false to start with, they are anxious to settle for whatever amount they can get without detailed argument. This avoids any possible legal controversy that might be raised by these tax guru firms on behalf of their clients. The IRS would be naturally concerned that such exposure might lead to a broader public understanding that the citizen non-taxpayer never owed any income tax in the first place!

Q#10. I've heard that Section No. 1 of the I.R. Code which has the heading TAX ON INDIVIDUALS imposes an income tax on everybody and makes everybody liable, including me. Is this true?

A. Again, this is a common misunderstanding. Chapter III of this book has a detailed analysis of the many provisions of this Code section which proves that Section 1 of the Code cannot apply to U.S. citizen-"individuals", but rather, only to non-resident alien- "individuals" or to those custodians or withholding agents who have a statutory responsibility (under Code Sections 1441 or 1442) for deducting and withholding monies payable to such non-resident alien individuals, foreign partnerships or foreign corporations. Code Section 1461 makes such <u>individuals</u> (regardless of citizenship) who <u>are required to deduct and withhold</u> "liable for" income tax but <u>only</u> (as stated in Section 1461) <u>if</u> they are among those who have this withholding requirement under Code Sections 1441 or 1442.

Q#11. When we state the fact that U.S. citizens are not subject to the income tax on their earnings or other receipts, the IRS always tells us that the courts have ruled against us on this issue. How do we respond to this?

A. As this book shows, particularly in Chapters I and II, and in the I.R. Code as well, the truth is that the highest court in the land, the U.S. Supreme Court and many appellate and district courts as well are totally in agreement with <u>our position</u>. Throughout this book, and in particular Chapter I, we have quoted several U.S. Supreme Court, and even a number of appellate court decisions which confirm the non-taxability of the earnings or other receipts of U.S. citizens. The IRS' erroneous statement that the courts have ruled against us is based on a comparatively few, relatively recent decisions from the lower level district or appellate courts which have misread the decision in the landmark Supreme Court case of **Brushaber v. Union Pacific Railroad Co., 240 U.S. 1 (1916).** These comparatively few lower court <u>misreadings</u> of the **Brushaber** decision were rendered, in this writer's opinion, in order to falsely support the IRS' erroneous position that the Sixteenth Amendment authorized taxation on the earnings or receipts of U.S. citizens despite the constitutional prohibitions against any such taxation contained in Article 1, Section 2, Clause 3 and Article 1, Section 9, Clause 4. We must remember that, over the past sixty years or more, a <u>huge tax preparation industry</u> has grown up, supporting many thousands of people, including many influential lawyers, accountants and others, all dedicated to the erroneous proposition that the law authorizes an income tax on the earnings or other receipts of U.S. citizens. The vested monetary interest that these hordes of people have in maintaining this myth is politically difficult to overcome. The goal of my book is to prove and spread the truth so widely that it will create a public outrage sufficient to turn the tide in the interest of American citizens who are constitutionally entitled to keep 100% of the fruits of their labor, regardless if that labor is physical or mental!

Q#12. If I stop withholding and stop filing returns, can the IRS <u>legally</u> impose an income tax on my earnings or other receipts?

A. The U.S. Supreme Court, in the case of **Bull v. United States**, 295 U.S. 247 (1935) requires an assessment for any money to be owed for income or any other taxes imposed by the I.R. Code. This assessment authority and REQUIREMENT is stated in I.R. Code Section 6201. An implementing regulation is necessary to give force of law to a Code section. An official volume of the I.R. Code regulations titled CFR INDEX AND FINDING AIDS which is published by IRS itself (see chapter 6) contains a cross-reference chart which shows the implementing regulations that give force of law to the various Code sections. This chart is called the CFR PARALLEL TABLE OF AUTHORITIES AND RULES. The chart shows that the regulation for enforcement of the provisions of the Code Section 6201 is implemented only in Title 27 relating to alcohol, tobacco and fire arms, and not to income taxes which are implemented only in Title 26! Otherwise stated, this means that, as stated in the PARALLEL TABLE OF AUTHORITIES AND RULES, there is no assessment authority for income tax-only for those taxes levied under Title 27 relating to alcohol, tobacco and firearms!

In addition to the fact, as explained above, that the IRS has no authority to assess income taxes, even if such authority did exist, the only published regulation for Code Section 6201 is shown as #301.6201-1 which, under sub-sections (1) and (2), limits the authority to taxes shown on a return (sub-section 1) and to unpaid taxes paid by stamp (sub-section 2). Obviously, neither of those conditions requiring assessment could apply to a citizen who had not filed a return for the year in question.

For all of the above reasons, the answer to this question for those citizens who have stopped both withholding and filing returns is clearly "NO"! A more detailed explanation of the above summary in answer to this question is contained in Chapter VI of this book.

Q#13. What is the key to understanding the verbal trickery and deception in the I.R. Code?

A. The I.R. Code uses many words as terms which have one meaning in common usage and another, always different meaning, when used in the I.R. Code. Unless the reader is careful to examine and understand the definitions of these key words used as terms in many Code sections, he can easily be left with a misunderstanding of the Code section's true legal meaning. Some words which are used as terms in the Code have both expanded and limited meanings. The term "person" which is defined in Code Section 7701(a)(1), for instance, has many different definitions including "individual, a trust, estate, partnership, association, company or corporation". However, in Code Section 7343, the same term "person" has a limited and restricted definition for use in Chapter 75 dealing with tax crimes only as: "an officer or employee of a corporation or a member or employee of a partnership, who as such officer, employee, or member is under a duty to perform the act in respect of which the violation occurs." The reader must be careful to note these varying definitions of <u>terms</u> as used in the I.R. Code which have different, sometimes expanded and sometimes limited, meanings in different Code sections.

The term "income" is used as a <u>term</u> in the I.R. Code according to the decision in **U.S. v. Ballard, 535 F2d. 400 (1976)** in which the court stated: "The general <u>term</u> 'income' is <u>not defined</u> in the Internal Revenue Code." "Income" is a term that has a <u>limited meaning</u> in the I.R. Code because its meaning is specifically <u>identified</u> as <u>only</u> monies payable to non-resident aliens, foreign partnerships or foreign corporations in Code Sections 1441 or 1442! A U.S. citizen's wages, salaries, commissions or other earnings or receipts are <u>not identified anywhere in the I.R. Code as being "income"</u>.

A flagrant example of these varying definitions is evident when one examines the <u>fourteen</u> different definitions of the <u>term</u> "United States" which are used in different sections of the Code. These varying definitions are required, as is pointed out in Chapters IV and V of this book, in order to prevent the unconstitutionality of the particular Code section to which the term "United States" applies.

Some of the other words which are used as "terms" in the Code have meanings different from those in common usage are discussed in detail throughout this book, but particularly in Chapters IV and V. These include (but are not limited to) "state", "states", "includes and including", "trade or business", "wages", "employer", "employee and employment".

The reader must be very careful to identify the defined legal meanings of words used as <u>terms</u> in different sections in order to understand their various limited or expanded legal meanings. Failure to do so causes the common misunderstanding and confusion which is so prevalent when reading the Code without such study.

Q#14. If all or most of our nation's citizens stopped volunteering to file tax returns and pay income tax on their earnings or other receipts, how would the nation function without this money?

A. Before the enactment of the Sixteenth Amendment to the Constitution in 1913, the United Stated functioned not only very well, but also comparatively debt-free by comparison to the almost 100 years which have passed since enactment of the Amendment at the time this book was written. Despite our government's long-term success in deceiving the American public into believing they owe an income tax on their earnings, which is forbidden by the Constitution, our nation's debt has steadily increased to several trillions of dollars! Therefore, a strong case can be made from the fact of this ever-increasing public debt over the past 97 years that this system has been <u>counter</u>-productive, despite the fact that the public has been <u>voluntarily</u> paying income tax during this same period. As we pointed out in Chapters I and II of this book, the Constitution, under Article 1, Section 2, Clause 3 and Article 1, Section 9, Clause 4 prohibits any income tax on U.S. citizens or on their earnings or other receipts.

Our nation's history, going all the way back to 1787, when our Constitution was written, proves that we got along very well financially before our citizenry was deceived by the IRS after enactment of the Sixteenth Amendment in 1913. The indirect taxes authorized in the Constitution in the form of duties, imposts and excises have almost always been adequate to finance the functions of government. Whenever an emergency arose because of war or other concerns, the direct taxes which are also authorized in the Constitution to be levied on the states of the union by the apportionment requirement (see Chapter I) contained in the Constitution were raised to meet the problem. In our nation's history, this was done five times-the last having been enacted in 1861 to help pay for the Civil War. As we pointed out in the epilogue to this book, if our nation's citizens were to all stop filing tax forms and paying a tax they do not owe, not only would our nation continue to prosper, but, in fact, the current economic dilemma from which we suffer as this is written, would be relieved in large measure through the billions of dollars saved by individual citizens. This money would then be spent and/or invested in the marketplace acting as <u>the most effective, NON-INFLATIONARY</u> remedy for our current economic woes that the nation has ever seen. Contrast this to the HYPER-INFLATIONARY billions in new "stimulus" or "bailout" billions the current administration has created right off the printing press with the aid of the unconstitutional

Federal Reserve bank!

In addition, most of the 100,000+ employees now employed by the IRS would be released into private employment, providing an additional saving of a substantial portion of their one billion dollar plus budget. This would provide another huge impetus to the recovery of our economy.

EPILOGUE

Unfortunately, to our nation's everlasting shame, for many years our Constitution has not been taught in our public schools. As a result, at least two generations of Americans have grown up mostly ignorant of its mandates and restrictions. At the same time, the Internal Revenue Service, taking advantage of this ignorance, in their own self-interest beginning as far back as 1913, when the sixteenth amendment was enacted has successfully imposed on the public an unconstitutional authority to directly tax the earnings of our citizens. We have shown in this book why such taxation is forbidden as a direct assault on one of the most precious and "inalienable" fundamental rights to earn a living which are protected by our Constitution and even referenced as such in the Declaration of Independence.

In Chapter I, we pointed out the many Supreme Court decisions that restated that precious liberty of our right to earn a living tax-free. Freedom from taxation was the battle cry of our founding fathers. Common sense tells us that if government had the authority to tax our right to earn a living they could easily <u>totally enslave us merely by increasing the rate to 100%!</u> The founding fathers knew this, and, therefore, forbade it in 1787 when the Constitution was written. Unfortunately, constitutional encroachments on our liberties by our government are nothing new in our nation's history. Greed is a positive motivator and a taxing opportunity was created by the somewhat nebulous wording in the Sixteenth Amendment which enabled an intentional misapplication of the amendment's true meaning. As we explained in Chapter II, President Taft's intent in proposing the Amendment was to limit its authority to tax, <u>as an excise only</u>, profits earned through exercise of the government-created privilege of incorporation. In truth, it is somewhat understandable that Congress took advantage of the wording in the Amendment that may have led at least some members of Congress, both then and today, to honestly, but incorrectly, believe that the Amendment authorized an income tax on the earnings of U.S. citizens. However, this book, and particularly Chapter II, both <u>explains and proves</u> that the Sixteenth Amendment simply identified the so-called "income" tax as an indirect tax in the nature of an excise which had been authorized by the Constitution from its beginning, and that the Amendment should never be incorrectly interpreted, as some district and appellate courts have done, to allow any tax on the earnings or other receipts of American citizens.

This writer is convinced that at least the top-level people in the

IRS are aware of their agency's unlawful activity in attempting to force an unconstitutional taxing authority on American citizens. Given this knowledge, the IRS' persistence in such activity is criminal, and should be prosecuted and corrected. The U.S. Department of Justice, to their everlasting shame, has demonstrated that they are not only unwilling to act on behalf of our citizens, but, in fact, have unforgivably (because they know better) joined in conspiracy with the IRS in their efforts to force this unlawful jurisdiction and authority on a gullible public. Adding insult to injury, several of our Federal appellate courts have, in several court decisions, joined with the IRS and the Justice Department in their prejudice against the truth by ruling <u>in favor of the misapplication</u> of the Sixteenth Amendment to unlawfully allow taxation of U.S. citizens earnings and other receipts. Unfortunately, these decisions were not appealed to the U.S. Supreme Court where a remedy, if the case were properly presented, could have reversed the bad law that was decided at the lower level. Most of these bad-law circuit court cases had been brought by so-called "pro se" (meaning "for self" or no attorney) litigants who, even though they may have raised the proper, correct argument that their earnings were not taxable because of the Sixteenth Amendment, could not afford the high cost of appealing to the U.S. Supreme Court. This meant that the bad law, made at the appellate level has remained to be used against Constitutionists who might choose to challenge the continuing misapplication of the income tax to the earnings of U.S. citizens.

However, our citizens should thank God that our U.S. Supreme Court, in the landmark decision of **<u>Brushaber v. Union Pacific Railroad Co.</u>** and several other supporting decisions listed in Chapters I and II of this book, properly identified the "income" tax as being an indirect excise tax on government-granted privilege measured by profit or gain. A few, lower level Federal courts-both district and appellate-are the culprits, and these lower-level courts should be corrected by the Supreme Court which, as is shown in Chapters I and II of this book, has properly identified limitations of the tax authorized by the amendment.

This lower level court error is a product of decades of false propaganda by the IRS leading to misunderstanding by the public and even some of the judiciary itself. This makes correction through judicial remedy difficult. The doctrines of "separation of powers" and "judicial independence" protect the judiciary from Congressional intervention in their decisions, so they are, at best, only minimally responsive when a citizen seeks help through his or her Congressional representative. Federal judges are lifetime appointees, and can be dismissed only if they do not exercise "good behavior". Unfortunately, correcting district and appellate court judges who have ruled incorrectly by approving the IRS' improper misapplication of the income tax against the earnings of U.S. citizens is a difficult task. Judicial accountability on this issue very difficult, unless or until it is either self-imposed by appellate court embarrassment over their own error. But that remedy can be forced by an adequate public out cry. I have writen this book to gain wide spread knowledge of this fraud sufficient to generate a public demand that our Supremem Court, on their own initiative, issue a corrective edict that those few erring must follow hereafter.

As this book is written, several giant financial corporations such as Fannie Mae, Freddie Mac, AIG and others, through incompetent management, have fallen on the verge of bankruptcy. Suggesting that their failure would impact our country in unacceptable ways, Congress authorized in late 2008 a 750 billion dollar "bailout" of these companies, and, on the heels of this huge, inflationary, new-money bailout, an even greater so-called "stimulus' of almost 800 billion more new printing press dollars, allegedly to help the auto companies and many others, has passed Congress. What we hear in the news on TV and in the press is that these billions will be <u>borrowed</u>-mostly from China. In fact, however, it is this writer's opinion that the Chinese purchase of our nwly-issued bonds, was only a fraction of the bonds sold.

Most of the bonds created in order to borrow the money were actually purchased by the Federal Reserve Bank-a <u>privately-owned</u> bank which was authorized and created by Congress in 1913 under the provisions of the Federal Reserve Act. Known, and referred to today as "The Fed", this private (non-government) bank was unconstitutionally given the power to create money (issue currency) in order to solve the alleged monetary crisis that existed in our country at that time. Although it has never been effectively challenged in a court of law, it is this writer's opinion that the Federal Reserve Act is unconstitutional because it gave to the Fed a new power to create money which power has always been reserved to Congress by the provisions in Article 1, Section 8, Clause 5 of our Constitution which is still in full force and effect today. In this writer's view, a constitutional amendment authorizing the Fed to issue the nation's currency supply was required and should have been passed. Such an amendment and still is, constitutionally required in order to make the Federal Reserve Act constitutional.

Knowledge of the foregoing brief history of the Federal Reserve Bank's origin should be helpful for the reader's understanding of how and why this new power erodes the purchasing power of our dollar through the creation of billions of dollars in <u>new money</u> by a private (non-government) bank.

Here's what actually happens when billions of dollars of new money are put into circulation by the Fed in order to allegedly solve the current economic crisis: Our government creates billions of dollars in face value of bonds, most of which are purchased by the Fed, by giving the U.S. government credit on the books of the Fed in the amount of the face value of the newly-created bonds. The U.S. government then spends this money by issuing checks against this newly-created account with the Fed. When these checks are cashed by the payees for currency, the currency supply of the banks which cash the checks is reduced. This reduction in the bank's currency supply is remedied by getting new currency from the Fed through cashing of these government checks with the Fed. Since this also reduces the Fed's currency supply, they (the Fed), using their money-creation power in the Federal Reserve Act, replaces this currency loss by ordering newly-printed currency from the U.S. government's Bureau of Printing and Engraving. The Fed's costs of purchasing the newly-printed currency is only the cost of the printing which is about three cents per bill- whether it is a $1.00 bill or any other denomination up to and including a $100.00 bill-the cost is the same. But the (so-called) Federal Reserve, a private bank, charges the U.S. government interest on the bonds they buy! When currency is needed by the Fed, using their money-creating power, they have it printed for almost nothing and collect billions in interest from our government on the bonds they purchase!

Those in Congress and our administration who have sponsored and created their humongous new debt don't tell us that their "bailouts" and stimuli will be the most inflationary giveaway actions that have ever occurred! When government bureaucrats create over 1500 billion dollars of new money, this is inflation of the money supply with a capital "I". And it has been suggested by many knowledgeable financial gurus that these billions in new money are just the beginning-that as our depression deepens, many more billions will be created as more businesses demand what they perceive as their fair share of government "bailout" or "stimulus" money. As these billions find their way into our money supply, the massive inflation it causes will, in turn, further greatly erode the purchasing power of the dollar, causing huge increases in the cost of EVERYTHING!

If all Americans were able to safely keep 100% of what they earn and to which they are constitutionally entitled, they would spend most of these new-found billions in the marketplace and our economy would expand immediately from the huge increase in business generated by such spending. This remedy would be both positive and NON-INFLATIONARY because it would not increase the nation's money supply! This writer believes that the elimination of the unlawfully, misapplied income tax to U.S. citizens on their earnings and other receipts would cause a great increase in economic activity and would go a long way toward reducing our government's multi-trillion dollar debt which reduces the standard of living of all Americans.

This author has written SUPER SCAM to prove that the Sixteenth Amendment to our Constitution and the I.R. Code both limit application of the income tax authorized by the Amendment to an indirect tax in the nature of an excise on government-granted privileges including incorporation and on the privilege granted by government to specified, non-citizen, foreign entities to do business in the U.S. The author hopes, by this knowledge, to instill a public hue and cry for justice similar to that which motivated the founding fathers and, thereby, force obedience by our government to both the Constitution and the statutory law on this vital issue.

When asked about remedies for Congressional and judicial misconduct, President Thomas Jefferson replied: "Bind them down by the chains of the Constitution." It's long past time that we, the people, revive the Constitution and demand that our public servants, in both Congress and the judiciary, obey its mandates. Remember the old adage: "The squeaky wheel gets the grease." In order to force our government, through the IRS, to obey both the Constitution and the I.R. Code we must also insist that our judiciary enforce IRS' obedience to its limited taxing authority!

Finally, our nations Founding Fathers, as devout Christians were well aware of the Scriptural mandates in the Holy Bible against government taxation of God's people. One of the most direct is in Matthew 17:25 and 26, Wherein the Lord Jesus appointedly answered the apostle Peter's question by declaring that His children (meaning His people) should be "free" of any king's form of tribute or taxation.

In keeping with God's command with this Scripture our Founding Fathers built into our Constitution two prohibitions against any such taxation. These are embodied in Article 1, Section 2, Clause 3, and Article 1, Section 9 and Clause 4 as discussed in detail throughout this book. So, these Scriptural admonitions are further support for the Constitutional and statutory provisions detailed herein. In this Christian writers's view, if God says it, I believe it, and that's the end of it.